Master ASL!

LEVEL ONE

By

Jason E. Zinza

Sign Illustrations by:
Xiaohong Fang
James Sbarra
Linda C. Tom
Svetlana Zinovieva

Non-sign art by:
James Sbarra

Sign Media, Inc.
4020 Blackburn Lane
Burtonsville, MD 20866-1167
www.signmedia.com

ISBN 1-881133-20-6

How to order:
Copies may be ordered from Sign Media, Inc., 4020 Blackburn Lane, Burtonsville, MD 20866-1167. For credit card orders, place your order online at www.signmedia.com or phone 1-800-475-4756.

For my parents, because they gave me this language,
and for my students, who wish to learn it.

TABLE OF CONTENTS

ACKNOWLEDGMENTS

The cover of **Master ASL! Level One** features only my name, but behind it stretch the names of students, teachers, reviewers, professors, editors, artists, illustrators, sign models and more — simply too many to list individually, but incomplete if just one is overlooked. In the limited space below I thank those people who are my foundation, my unflagging advocates, and my tireless partners in the pursuit of excellence. Foremost, I am grateful to Dr. Marilyn Severson, Dr. Luke Reinsma, Dr. Kathryn Bartholomew, Dr. John West, and Dr. Susan Van Zanten Gallagher of Seattle Pacific University for being outstanding servant scholar role models. I emulate each in my teaching and passion for the learning process, which leads me to acknowledge the many students I have taught at the high school, community college, and university levels; truly, my students are my teachers. I appreciate beyond words their patience and insight as they provided feedback on my ideas, materials, and teaching methods. As with any textbook, this work belongs to them. Fortunately for them, **Master ASL!** took a different path and relies on the insight into language learning and teaching inspired by Dr. Penelope Eckert and Dr. Eve Clark of Stanford University. Additionally, a heartfelt thank you goes to Dr. Samuel Mbongo of the University of California at Berkeley, for sparking the inquiry that led me here: "Tell me about your culture."

Special gratitude goes to those who encouraged me throughout this long project: Dana Vollmar, Aundrea Love, Stephanie Pintello, Glenna Ashton, Alysse Rasmussen, my Mission Springs family who constantly rallied support and delivered much-needed pats on the back, all my proud coda brothers and sisters, and my colleagues at the Center for American Sign Language Literacy at Gallaudet University. Without them, **Master ASL!** simply would not be.

The Level One sign models were poised and articulate from start to finish, even after long days spent under bright lights. Krystle Berrigan, Rita Corey, Chris Corrigan, Maher Eshgi, and Kami Padden have each placed their own stamp on the overall character of **Master ASL!**, and I am grateful for it. Similarly, the artists and illustrators whose works fill these pages elevate ASL instruction and the field of sign illustrations to a new level of excellence.

This project could not have been possible without the dedication of my editor, Barbara Olmert, and my Producer/Director, Verden Ness, at Sign Media, Inc. A note to aspiring writers and curriculum developers: You want to work with Barbara and Verden. While they may have privately rued the fateful day we sat and discussed my ideas, I cannot think of anybody who has been more enthusiastic, supportive, and excited about **Master ASL!** In closing, I am keenly aware that I wrote this book; it is Barbara that brought it to fruition. I am lucky to have worked so closely with such an outstanding woman.

And lastly, I owe everything to my community, my culture, my people of the eye.

STUDENT INTRODUCTION

Welcome to **Master ASL! Level One**. This textbook introduces you to American Sign Language (ASL), the language used by the majority of Deaf Americans, and to the culture of the Deaf World. The Master ASL series was developed in response to the tide of interest in American Sign Language among people of all ages and is designed to provide a thorough foundation for using ASL as a second language with your Deaf neighbors, children, coworkers, and friends.

In the not-so-distant past, few hearing individuals aside from children of Deaf adults and those who worked closely with the Deaf knew ASL. Signing in public drew stares, quizzical looks and often, mocking or teasing by people amused by the sight of individuals talking with their hands. In this environment the Deaf community came together and formed a close, tight-knit culture where ASL flourished and being Deaf was not considered a handicap but simply a way of life. Today, the Deaf community forms one of many minority cultural groups in the United States and Canada, and interest in learning ASL has surged, bringing with it greater opportunities for mutual benefit. Using ASL in public is now a common, and proud, experience for both Deaf and hearing people.

While attitudes are changing, more work remains to be done. Though ASL and Deaf individuals are seen on TV, in movies, the theater, restaurants, stores and crowded classrooms, many people view deafness as an obstacle or a pitiable handicap. Deaf individuals are routinely denied employment because companies are uncertain how Deaf employees can communicate with their hearing colleagues, applicants for driver's licenses are asked "Can Deaf people drive?" and the many contributions the Deaf have made to the larger hearing society are generally unknown and overlooked. As quickly as an ASL class is offered, it is filled with students who often think ASL is an easy language — and other language teachers, administrators, and counselors reflect this misunderstanding as well.

Do not be misled by these gross misunderstandings and myths surrounding American Sign Language: ASL is not easier to learn than spoken languages. ASL is a unique, visual language that does not simply match a sign to an English word. Instead, ASL has its own grammar, structure, and specific features that pose a challenge to learn, like other spoken languages. Indeed, students of ASL must develop a pleasing visual accent, exactly like learning a satisfactory accent in spoken languages! The best way to learn any language is by direct, frequent contact with the people who use the language on a daily basis. Take a chance and initiate signed conversations with Deaf people!

The following pages provide you with an introduction to several important aspects of American Sign Language that will assist your experience with **Master ASL! Level One**. Take a few minutes to read these pages and refer to the DVD that accompanies this text. You will use both the text and DVD as a study guide to help you learn American Sign Language.

Good luck!

Jason E. Zinza
www.masterasl.com

BECOMING ACQUAINTED: MASTER ASL! LEVEL ONE

Master ASL! Level One includes a student textbook, student companion, and a DVD.

Textbook

In the textbook you will find extensive lessons on:

Language & Structure
- *ASL Up Close*, highlighting important functions of ASL grammar
- *Eyes On ASL*, presenting the basic rules of signing in ASL
- *Accent Steps*, tips and advice to help hearing students improve their ASL skills
- *Expression Corner*, exposing students to ASL idioms, phrases, and expressions

Culture
- *Deaf Culture Notes*, featuring relevant aspects of Deaf culture
- *ASL Focus*, a two page section examining an important issue in the Deaf World
- *Did You Know?* sections presenting information about the Deaf World
- *Deaf Culture Minute*, explaining cultural tidbits
- *I Want to Know*, answering common questions about ASL

Comparison & Reflection
- Exposure to Deaf art
- Poetry and other writings by Deaf authors
- Journal opportunities to analyze and reflect on aspects of ASL, Deaf culture, and the Deaf experience

Student Companion: Fingerspelling, Numbers, and Glossing

The student companion includes:
- ASL Fingerspelling, including 200 exercises to develop fingerspelling skills
- ASL Numbers, with more than 150 exercises provided to develop ASL numerical skills
- Glossing instruction and exercises to assist students to become familiar with the notation system used by many people within the fields of ASL and Deaf studies
- A glossary for linguistic, social, and cultural terms addressed in **Master ASL!**

DVD

DVD segments are highlighted in the textbook with the DVD icon. The DVD component contains:

- Select dialogues from each unit
- Narratives that incorporate the language and cultural skills featured in each unit
- Shorter narratives on a variety of topics relevant to each unit
- Language and structure lessons with examples on each feature of ASL grammar covered in the text
- Examples of ASL literature, including ABC and classifier stories, handshape rhymes, and number stories

THINGS TO KNOW

Important Terms

Explanations of all terms in bold are found in the glossary section of the **Student Companion: Fingerspelling, Numbers, and Glossing**.

Eye Contact

The most important background knowledge to have before learning American Sign Language is to understand the role of eye contact. In Deaf culture, not maintaining eye contact during a conversation is considered rude. Develop or improve the habit of looking people in the eye as you sign to others and as you watch others sign to you. Your eyes are like your ears! Breaking eye contact signals that you aren't paying attention, are day-dreaming, or don't wish to participate in the conversation. Keep in mind that maintaining eye contact does not mean to stare!

You may be surprised how quickly your ASL teacher notices that you don't have eye contact. Since Deaf people generally rely on their eyes far more than hearing people, broken eye contact is easily spotted.

The Sign Space

An important concept to understand is the ASL **sign space**. This refers to the area in which most signs are made in normal conversation. Signing outside the sign space is uncomfortable on your hands, wrists, and shoulders. Generally, most signs are centered to the right or left of your middle torso.

The ASL Sign Space

Which Hand Do I Use?

Sign with the hand that feels most comfortable and natural for you, which tends to be the hand with which you write. The hand you use most often to sign with is called the **dominant hand**, and the other is called the **non-dominant hand**. Switching the dominant and non-dominant hands in conversation is a common error that should be avoided. If you are left handed and your teacher is right handed, you do not need to match or produce mirror-image signs. Allow your eyes and brain to tell your hands what to do.

Dominant Left Hand

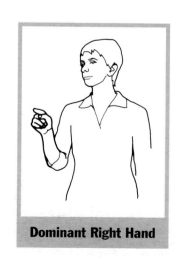

Dominant Right Hand

Facial Expressions

What happens when you speak in a monotone voice, devoid of inflection or expression? Usually people tune out or become bored and disinterested in the conversation. The same results happen when you sign without using **facial expressions**. Auditory information, such as tone of voice, emotion, and intent must be made visual in American Sign Language. Throughout **Master ASL! Level One** you will learn the essential facial expressions and when to use them, a challenge for many students. Facial expressions not only convey emotion and meaning, but ASL grammar as well.

Do not become frustrated if you feel you're trying hard with facial expressions and your teacher wants more. The point of facial expressions is to clearly convey grammar and meaning, and sometimes what hearing people think is "good enough" falls short of what ASL requires. Note that you do not match each sign with a specific facial expression. Instead, match your face to the overall meaning of what you're signing. If you're unsure about something, make a puzzled expression while signing *I'm confused*. Some facial expressions are used more often than others in ASL, especially the two Question Faces. The Question-Maker must be used when asking a general question such as *Are you learning ASL?* and the WH-Face for questions using the signs *who, what, when, where, why,* and *which*.

To help you develop your facial expressions, **Master ASL!** incorporates exercises designed to improve your confidence and skill. Practice the expressions as a way to loosen up your facial features to reflect the intended emotion, and don't feel intimidated or embarrassed: You do not look as silly as you may think! For inspiration and practice, watch any of the well-known Deaf storytellers and emulate their animated facial expressions.

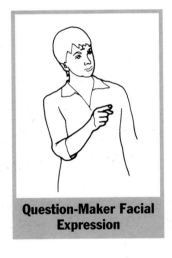

Question-Maker Facial Expression

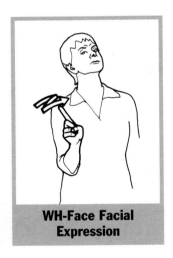

WH-Face Facial Expression

Precision is Important

Signing clearly is the same as speaking clearly. Sloppy, uncertain signing is exactly like mumbling. Sloppy signing also causes careless errors that drastically affect meaning. In the famous example below, one handshape has three different meanings based on the location where the sign is made.

Summer

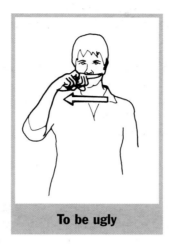
To be ugly

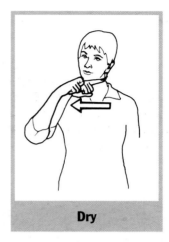
Dry

Making the right sign in the wrong place or vice versa affects meaning. "Close enough" or sloppy signing interferes with comprehension. As a beginning signer, it is natural to make mistakes as you develop dexterity with your hands and fingers, but be sure to practice often to gain confidence and improve your skills.

Part of signing precisely is understanding that ASL makes visual sense. If you talk about someone and point to him or her during the conversation, and then that person leaves, you still point to the area where he or she was located before. Likewise, if you're talking about going *there*, but point in the opposite direction, you communicate something entirely different! How does the illustration below emphasize visual sense?

ASL is Not English

American Sign Language is not English. This key concept is essential in learning ASL. You must learn to think in ASL rather than using ASL signs matched to English words. If you "mouth" words or talk silently in English while signing, then you are not using American Sign Language. You can sign in ASL and "speak" English at the same time as easily as you can speak Spanish in English word order. It simply doesn't work. Signing and talking at the same time is not ASL, period. Some Deaf people do sign and mouth English words at the same time, but only when they choose to sign in English word order. Deaf people do this most often when signing with hearing people who are not fluent in ASL. Surprise Deaf people and gain their respect by using ASL properly! You will learn of other types of signing, but only ASL is a real language. Other forms are called Signing Exact English (SEE) and Pidgin Sign English (PSE). If you don't use ASL syntax (the way signs are ordered into sentences) and facial expressions, then you're not signing in ASL.

The best way to learn ASL or any foreign language is to keep an open mind and respect the differences between each language.

Fingerspelling

Fingerspelling is an important part of ASL, but it is not a substitute for signs you should learn. Fingerspelling is used for specific purposes so avoid the temptation of fingerspelling words or sentences. Try to communicate in other ways before using fingerspelling apart from the particular instances when fingerspelling is required. Learning to fingerspell is challenging for most ASL students, but remember it is a step by step process. The illustration below details the **Fingerspelling Space**, the location your hand is held while fingerspelling.

Fingerspelling Space

Refer to your **Student Companion: Fingerspelling, Numbers, and Glossing** to begin your study of fingerspelling.

The Five Parameters of ASL

Each ASL sign can be broken down and analyzed into five separate features called **parameters**. For a single sign to be correct, each of the five parameters must be used correctly. Below are explanations of these parameters with examples to help you understand the concept.

1. Handshape

The handshape difference between *me* and *mine* is simple to identify, yet ASL students often confuse the two. Common handshape errors include the differences between: 1/D, D/F, E/O.

Sample sentence: I am Rita/My Rita.

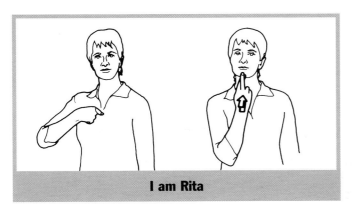

I am Rita

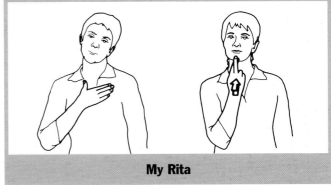

My Rita

2. Palm Orientation

Palm orientation errors are easy to make if you are unsure whether a sign faces up, down, left, or right. Signing while nervous or without practice causes many palm orientation errors. Often, these mistakes are "big" and obvious.

Sample sentence: The table is over there.

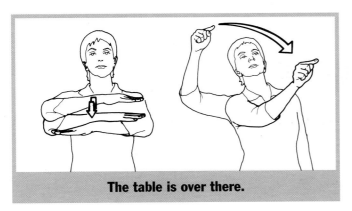

The table is over there.

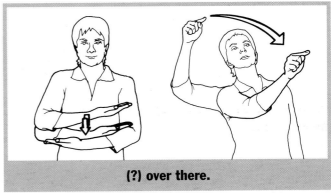

(?) over there.

3. Location

Avoid making location errors by remembering most signs are made in front of your body in a comfortable location. If your arms feel awkward, it's a clue the sign's location may be wrong. Keep in mind that some signs are directional and originate away from the body but end close, or begin close to the body and terminate away, as in the sign *to drive to.*

Sample sentence: I'll see you tomorrow.

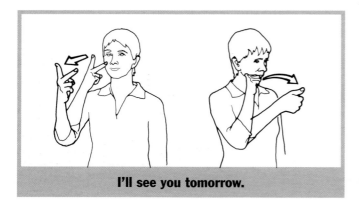

I'll see you tomorrow.

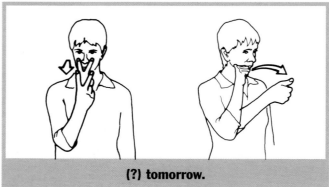

(?) tomorrow.

4. Movement

Movement affects meaning, as seen in these examples. Practicing and paying attention to ASL vocabulary is key to knowing the movement needs of particular signs. If your hands and arms feel awkward or constricted, check the sign's movement parameter for a possible error.

Sample sentence: I'm happy/I'm enjoy.

I'm happy.

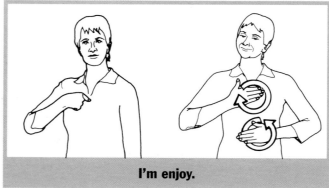

I'm enjoy.

5. Non-manual signals / facial expressions

Specific **non-manual signals** (NMS) alter the meaning of a sign. Facial expressions, head nods / shakes, eyebrows, nose, eyes, and lips each carry meaning that can be attached to a sign.

Sample sentence: I'm late/I haven't.

I'm late.

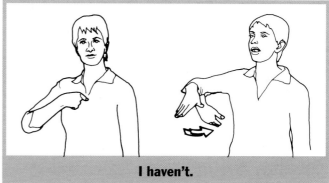
I haven't.

Illustrating American Sign Language

Illustrating a visual, three-dimensional language like ASL poses several challenges. A primary challenge is showing the movement parameter of each sign. Illustrating movement relies on the use of arrows to show different types of movements and changes.

1. Types of movement
   a. Arc
   b. Straight line
   c. Circle
   d. Alternating in-and-out
   e. Twist of the wrist
   f. Finger flick

2. Changes in movement
   a. Location changes — one or both hands move/s from one location to another
   b. Direction changes — one or both hands change/s direction
   c. Handshape changes — one or both hands change/s handshape in mid-sign

Each arrow shows the beginning and ending location of any movement, with the arrowhead indicating the final resting position of the handshape. Familiarize yourself with the following explanations of how movement is illustrated in **Master ASL! Level One**.

1. *Single movement in one direction.* One or both hands may move in the direction shown by the arrow.

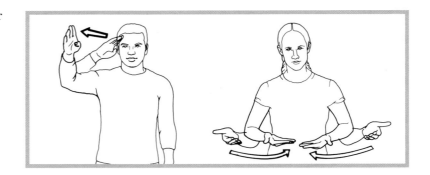

2. *Plural movement in one direction.* Some signs include several small changes in location and type of movement before reaching its final location.

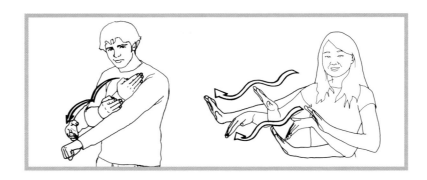

3. *Single movement, with change in direction and/or handshape change.* Direction changes may include handshape changes. If a handshape changes while moving, the new handshape continues to the sign's final location.

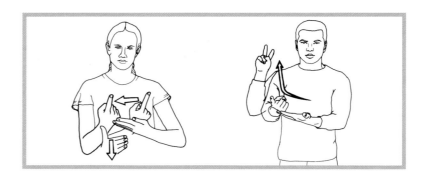

4. *Double movement.* Many signs have a double back-and-forth or tapping movement. This movement may be up-down, side-to-side, or in-out. Generally, the movement or tapping occurs twice and does not move very far. This arrow is also used with head shakes and nods.

5. *Multiple movement.* This arrow indicates a continuous, repeated back-and-forth or up-down movement.

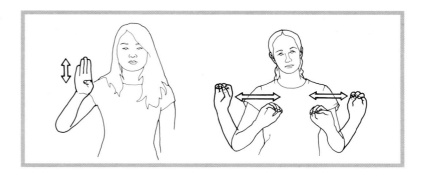

6. *Wiggle movement.* Wiggle your fingers back and forth in a repetitive motion. The wiggle marks may also be located near the head to suggest a very slight back-and-forth motion.

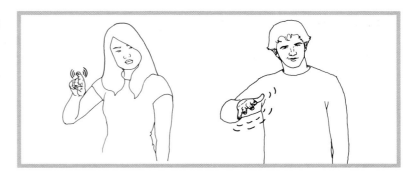

7. *Circular movement.* One or both hands move in a repeated horizontal or vertical circular movement. Some signs with a circular movement may be outward- or inward-directed, and other signs will have both hands moving in opposite circular directions simultaneously.

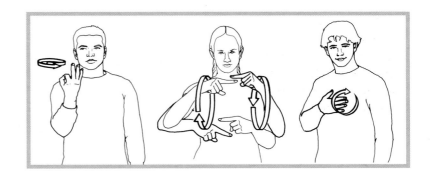

8. *Circular movement with direction.* One or both hands may move forward or backward in a circular movement.

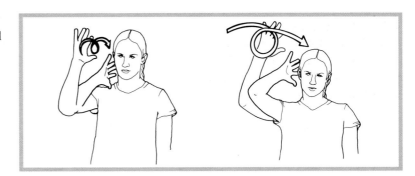

9. *Twist movement.* Twist your wrist once. Generally only one hand will make a twist movement.

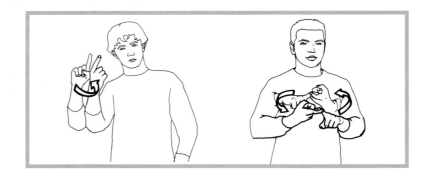

10. *Strike marks.* Strike marks emphasize contact is made between two parts of the body as part of a sign.

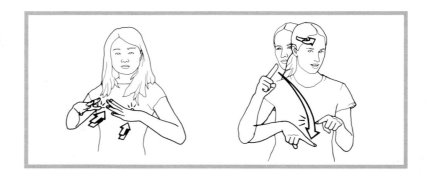

11. *Fingerspelling.* Fingerspelling is not like using a keyboard to type individual letters one after the other away from your body. Hold your hand still in the Fingerspelling space (see page xviii) and form each letter "on top" of each other. In some cases you will need to move your hand slightly while fingerspelling. <u>Do not fingerspell letters moving across your torso.</u> Fingerspelling has been illustrated in **Master ASL!** from left to right to make it easier to use and understand. The first sample illustration shows how fingerspelling is actually done and the second shows how fingerspelled words are printed in **Master ASL!**

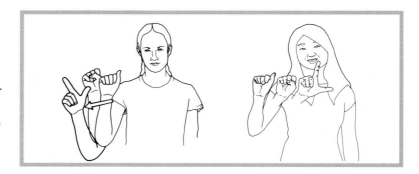

UNIT ONE

Welcome!

Unit One Objectives

- To learn proper greetings and farewells in ASL
- To introduce yourself and others
- To learn basic ASL sentence structure
- To ask and answer questions
- To learn how to interact appropriately with Deaf people
- To learn the role of facial expressions and non-manual signals

Unit One Vocabulary

Key Phrases

Meet the Characters

Four characters highlighting the variety of backgrounds within the Deaf community are profiled throughout **Master ASL! Level One.** They will present useful vocabulary, highlight aspects of Deaf culture, and share their accomplishments and interests. You will realize that the lives of Deaf people are very much like your own.

SEAN

Sean lives in Boston, Massachusetts, and is the only Deaf person in his family. Originally from Texas where he attended the Texas School for the Deaf, he now attends a public school and uses sign language interpreters in his classes.

MARC

Marc, his brother, and a younger sister are Deaf; his mother is hard of hearing, and his father is hearing. He plays football at a school for the Deaf, is a member of the speech and debate team and is involved in student government. He plans on attending Gallaudet University, the world's only university for Deaf students.

KRIS

Kris is a university student studying government and law whose siblings, parents, and grandparents are all Deaf. An avid athlete, she loves to snowboard, ski, and play tennis. When she isn't studying, she can be found spending time with her family and is especially fond of story-telling competitions.

KELLY

Kelly, like Sean, is the only Deaf person in her family, though she considers herself lucky because her parents and older brother all learned American Sign Language. Kelly enjoys drama, photography, and spending time on her creative writing. She wants to teach Deaf children after college. A pet peeve? When hearing people say, "I'll tell you later" or "It's not important."

In her role as an ASL teacher, Rita presents information that focuses on ASL grammar and Deaf culture, gives tips on how to improve your signing, and answers common questions students have about ASL. For example, a frequent questions is: "What is the difference between *deaf* and *Deaf*?" When deaf is not capitalized, it describes one's hearing status. When capitalized, Deaf describes those individuals who are proud to be deaf and consider themselves members of the Deaf culture. They use American Sign Language as their preferred means of communication.

RITA

Greetings

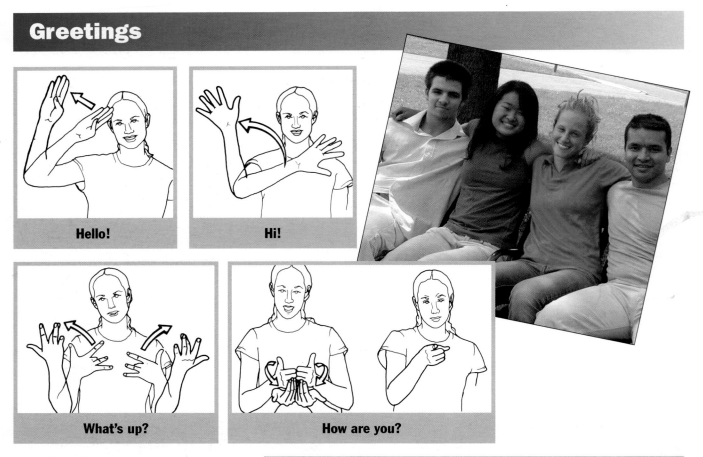

Hello!

Hi!

What's up?

How are you?

When signing to a friend, sign *Hi!*, but with adults or people you don't know well, use the more formal *Hello*. Whether you want to be formal or casual, accompanying the sign with a smile means a lot to both Deaf and hearing people! *What's up?* is an informal way to ask *How are you?* in both American Sign Language and English. You can also sign *What's up?* one-handed, but both signs must include raising your chin.

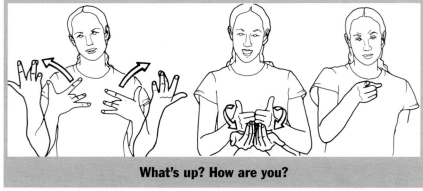

What's up? How are you?

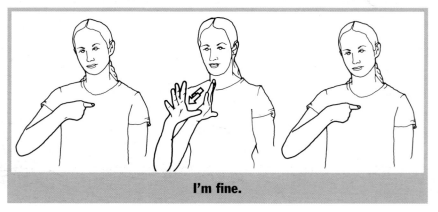

I'm fine.

Classroom Exercise

1   *Hello!* Exchange greetings with a classmate and ask how he or she is doing.

2   *How are you?* Ask a partner to tell you how another classmate is doing.

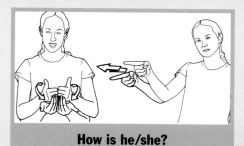

How is he/she?

He/she is happy.

3   *Greetings.* Look at the list of people in italics. Would you use *What's up?* or *How are you?* to greet them?

1. *an acquaintance*	**4.** *your partner*	**7.** *buddy*	**10.** *school administrator*
2. *parents*	**5.** *your ASL teacher*	**8.** *younger brother*	
3. *an ASL student*	**6.** *grandmother*	**9.** *teacher*	

Vocabulary   How are you? & What's up?

To be busy

Confused

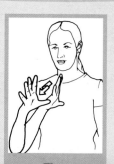

Fine

To be good, well

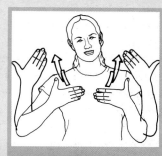

To be happy

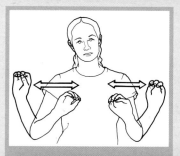

Nothing, not much

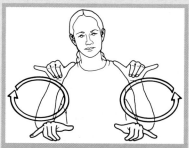

Same old, the usual

Sleepy

So-so

To be tired

ASL Up Close

Conjugating Verbs: *To Be*

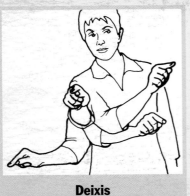

Deixis

I am, me

You are

He, she, it is

Pointing is a logical feature of a signed, non-spoken language. It is not considered rude or impolite. If a person or object is not visible, point to an empty space and continue signing. Using the index finger to point is called **deixis**.

We are, us

You are (plural)

They are

Classroom Exercise B

How is everybody? Sign each sentence in ASL following the example. Use deixis as needed.

I'm not too bad

1. *They are busy.*
2. *She is happy.*
3. *I am confused.*
4. *We are happy.*

5. *She's good.*
6. *I'm sleepy.*
7. *It's so-so.*
8. *He's fine.*

FYI Don't forget to point back to the person.

66 American Sign Language is of great value to the deaf, but could also be of great benefit to the hearing as well.... It is superior to spoken language in its beauty and emotional expressiveness. It brings kindred souls into a much more close and conscious communion than mere speech can possibly do. 99 —*Thomas H. Gallaudet, 1848*

Vocabulary   **More Greetings**

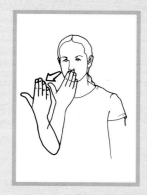 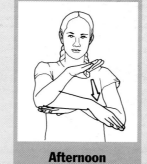  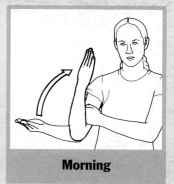

| **Afternoon** | **Evening, night** | **Morning** |

Classroom Exercise **C**

1   *Greetings.* Greet your classmates and ask how they are doing.

2   *Dialogue.* Work with a partner to sign a dialogue using vocabulary you've learned.

3   *What time of day is it?* Is it afternoon, evening, or morning in each illustration?

Eyes on ASL #1

DVD

Maintain eye contact when signing to others or when others sign to you.

Maintaining eye contact does not mean staring. If you must look away, make the *hold on* sign first.

Eye contact

Hold on

Look at me

Which sign means *focus* or *pay attention*, and which means *no eye contact*? How do you know?

Classroom Exercise D

1. *Using Eyes on ASL.* Work with a partner to sign a dialogue that includes signs learned in Eyes on ASL #1.

2. *Eye contact.* What similarity do you see in the signs *eye contact*, *look at me*, and *no eye contact?* What do you think it means?

3. *Hold on.* Practice using the *hold on* sign with your teacher or a classmate. What is a polite way of signing *hold on*? What about a rude or impolite way?

Homework Exercise 1

What's for homework?

A. Teach a friend or family member how to greet you in American Sign Language.

B. Practice fingerspelling your first and last name until you become comfortable spelling quickly and clearly. Watch the DVD for examples of fingerspelling.

Fingerspelling Names
DVD

I Want to Know . . .

Why do I have to point twice?

Pointing back to yourself or the person you're talking about shows completion of a train of thought. This allows somebody else to begin signing without interrupting you. Using deixis at the end of a sentence is called a **closing signal**. Closing signals are especially important when asking questions using the Question-Maker (page 15) or the WH-Face (page 42). Remember to use a closing signal when:

- Making a statement or comment about yourself or somebody else.

- Asking a question.

Question-Maker (page 15) or the WH-Face (page 42)

Eyes on ASL #2

Always use a closing signal to complete a signed sentence.

ASL sentences lacking closing signals are incomplete.

Names

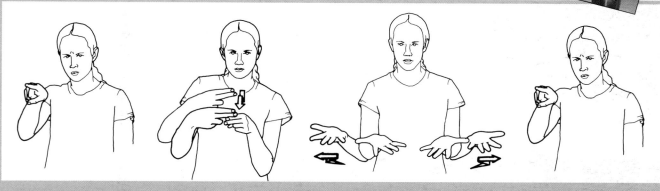
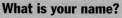

What is your name?

My name is Kelly Boyd.

Classroom Exercise E

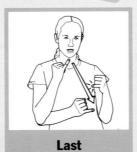

Name   **Last**

1. Introduce yourself to your classmates, finger-spelling your complete name carefully.

2. Practice signing each sentence in ASL.

1. *She is Nina Patel.*
2. *My name is Cheryl.*
3. *He's Tyler Brophy.*
4. *I'm Niki, he's Aaron.*
5. *He's Luis Cortez.*
6. *My name is __?__.*
7. *She is Erin.*
8. *His name is Jeff.*
9. *Her name is Lisa.*
10. *Her name is __?__.*

Eyes on ASL #3

There is no such thing as a one-word answer or reply in American Sign Language.

When responding to a question or statement, one-word replies are incomplete.

Deaf Culture Minute

Introductions in the Deaf community tend to include both first and last names. Often, new acquaintances know relatives or have friends in common. Many Deaf people have stories about meeting a friend of a friend in other cities, states, and even countries! How is this similar or different from your own community?

Classroom Exercise F

1. *What are their names?* Provide each person's name in a complete ASL sentence, following the example.

2. *What is your name?* Ask classmates for their names. Fingerspell it back to make sure you're right.

3. *First & last.* Practice fingerspelling the first and last names of your classmates. Pause slightly between the first and last name.

Introductions

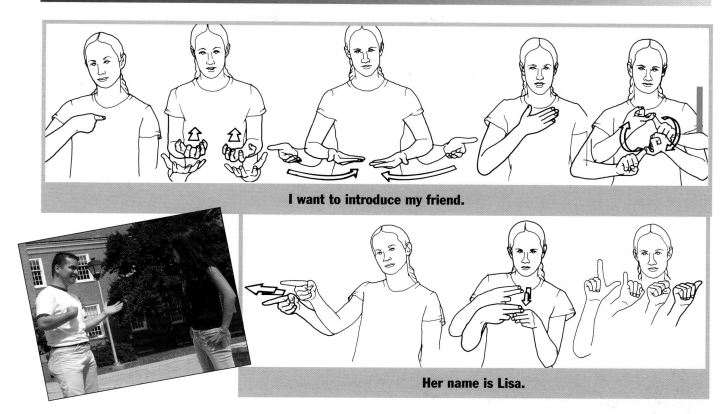

I want to introduce my friend.

Her name is Lisa.

Introductions in the Deaf community vary depending on whether one is hearing or Deaf. If you are Deaf, background information like where one goes or went to school is exchanged. If you are hearing, then you will be introduced as a hearing person who knows or is learning American Sign Language. This exchange of information allows everybody to understand where he or she is coming from and reduces cultural misunderstandings. It is culturally appropriate to shake hands when meeting new people or greeting friends. Like many hearing people, Deaf friends often hug each other when saying hello and good-bye.

Classroom Exercise G

 1 *Classroom introductions.* Introduce two classmates to each other.

2 *Introductions.* Sign the following dialogues in pairs or groups of three as needed. Use deixis to sign "this."

Dialogue 1

Student A. *Hi! How are you?*
Student B. *I'm fine. How are you?*
Student A. *I'm good. I'm Eric Morse. I'm Deaf.*
Student B. *Hi, my name is Chris Sarn. I'm hearing.*

Dialogue 2

Student A. *What's up? How are you?*
Student B. *I'm busy. How are you?*
Student A. *Same old. I want you to meet my friend Cara.*
Student B. *Hi, Cara. How are you?*
Student C. *I'm fine. Nice to meet you.*

Vocabulary — Introductions

Deaf	**Friend**	**Hard of hearing**	**Hearing**
To introduce	**To meet**	**My**	**Nice**

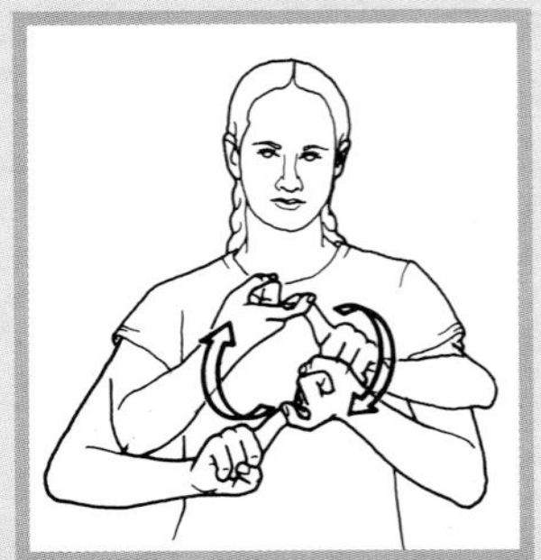

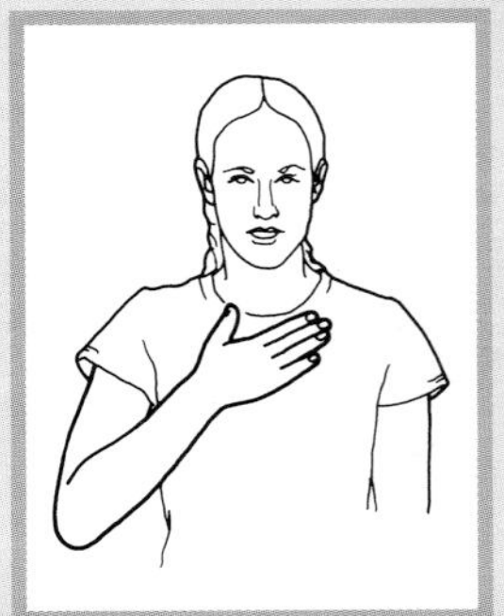

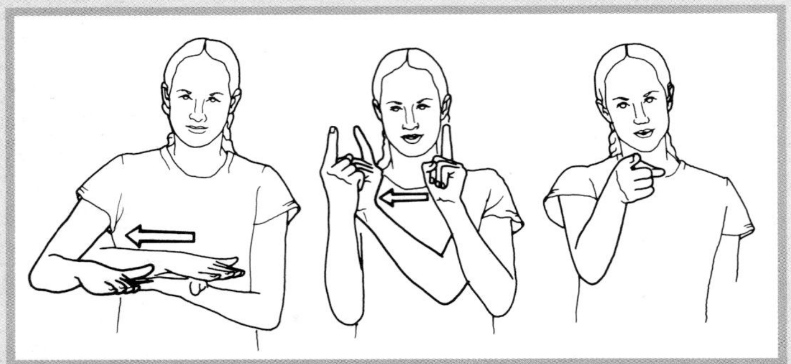

Nice to meet you

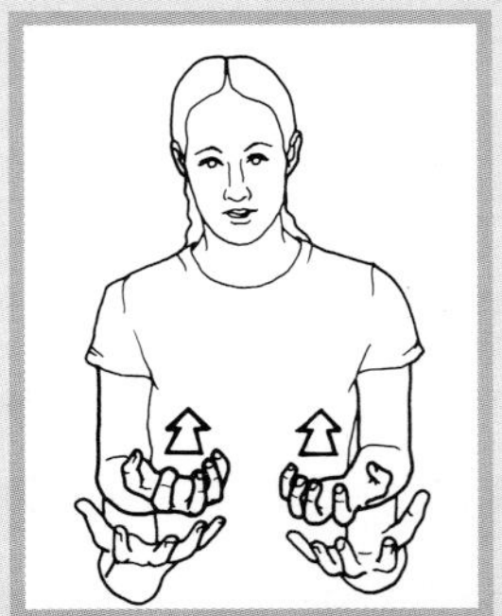

To want

Accent Steps

When fingerspelling your complete name, you don't need to sign *last name* between the first and last name. Just pause briefly and continue on!

FYI Use deixis instead of the sign *my* when signing "My name is..."

Classroom Exercise

DVD

Introducing a Friend

Dialogue. Practice signing the dialogue with a classmate. Answer the comprehension questions when done.

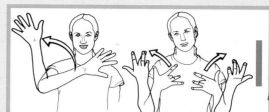

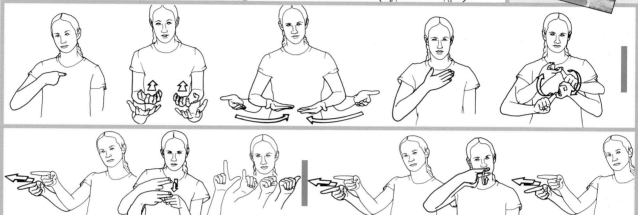

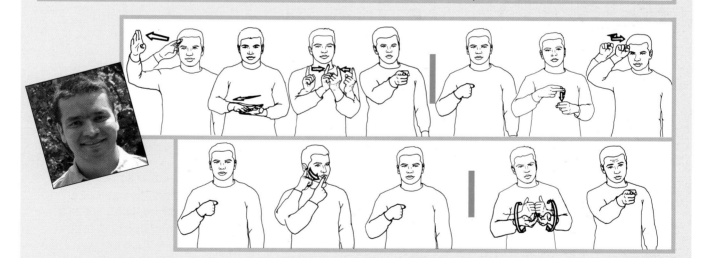

1 *Comprehension.* Answer each question in ASL.

1. *Who is Deaf? Who is hearing?*
2. *Is Lisa a friend of Kris or Sean?*
3. *Who introduced Lisa?*

2 Sign the dialogue with a different partner.

FYI   These blue segments show the completion of a thought or concept, like punctuation markers. When signing classroom or homework exercises, take a slight pause each time you see the blue marker.

Deaf Culture NOTE

DVD

Interacting with Deaf People

As a student of American Sign Language, learn how to interact with the Deaf community by becoming familiar with Deaf cultural behaviors that differ from the way you are used to doing things as a hearing person. One cultural behavior you've already learned is that it is considered rude to break eye contact when signing with Deaf people, which for most hearing people is often difficult. Think of how often you turn your head in the direction of sound and you can realize it will be a challenge to break this habit!

GETTING ATTENTION

Getting the attention of a Deaf person is different from the way you interact with hearing people. Many hearing people tend to work harder than necessary to gain a Deaf individual's attention by wildly swinging their hands in the air, stomping on the floor, or flashing overhead lights in a strobe-like pattern. None of this is necessary! Gently tapping the Deaf person's shoulder or slightly waving a hand in his or her direction until you are noticed is the most effective and considerate way to get attention.

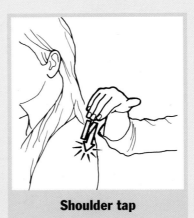

Shoulder tap

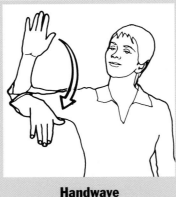

Handwave

Turn off voice

VOICES

Using your voice to talk to another hearing individual instead of signing when a Deaf person is near is considered rude. Develop the habit of always signing when you know a Deaf person is in the same room with you. This way, everybody has equal access to what is being communicated. If you must speak to a hearing person who doesn't know ASL, then tell your Deaf friend or teacher that first, before speaking. You may be surprised to learn that most Deaf people know when hearing people are talking, even if someone is whispering. How so? Remember, Deaf people rely on their vision far more than hearing people do! Your teacher may remind you to *turn off voice* if you're being rude in class.

Classroom Exercise 1

1   *Questions.* Use the Question-Maker with the vocabulary on the right to make a complete sentence.

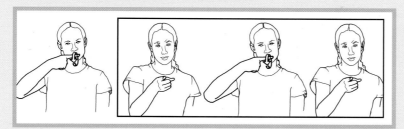

2   *Responses.* Use the signs *yes* or *no* in response to the same questions in Part 1. An example is provided.

FYI Slowly shake your head during sentences beginning with *no*.

ASL Up Close

DVD

The Question-Maker

Question-Maker

Raising your eyebrows forms the **Question-Maker**, an expression that shows you are asking a question. Keep the eyebrows raised until you've completed signing the question. In the example, notice the only difference between a question and a comment is the facial expression. The signs themselves remain the same.

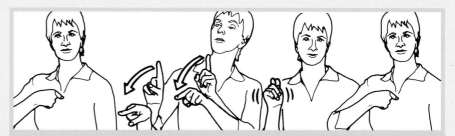
I'm going to the bathroom.

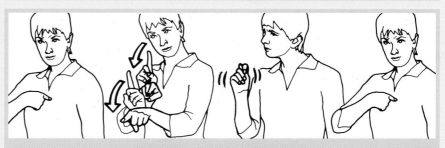
Am I going to the bathroom?

Classroom Exercise

1. *Community.* You are about to attend your first Deaf event. Practice how you would introduce yourself and explain you are learning ASL.

2. *Language differences.* Practice signing each sentence. When done, translate them into written English. What differences do you see between ASL and English?

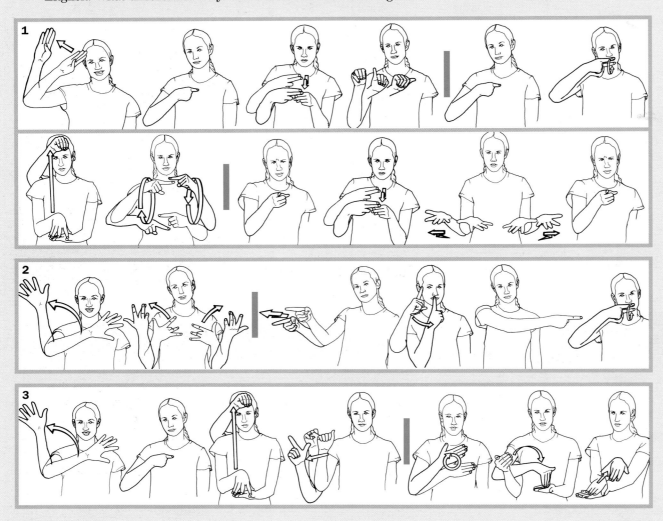

Accent Steps

Do you "talk" silently while signing? Some hearing people do this out of habit, and others think it helps Deaf people lipread. Only about 30% of the English language can be lipread. Deaf people lipread English, not American Sign Language, so don't mix the two. Sometimes a Deaf person will "talk" silently to help hearing people understand what is being signed, but don't with those who understand ASL. You will learn the role the lips have as part of the non-manual signals used in ASL. In the meantime, don't pronounce the English translation on your lips while signing!

Vocabulary — Making Conversation

American Sign Language

Bathroom

To go to

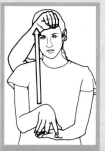
To learn

No

Please

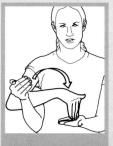
Again, repeat

To sign, sign language

Slow, to slow down

Thank you

Yes

Classroom Exercise K

1 *Making conversation.* Complete the sentence using appropriate vocabulary, and sign it to a classmate. Repeat when done.

1. *Hello, my name is _____. I'm learning _____.*
2. *What is _____ name? Are you Deaf?*
3. *Please _____ slowly.*
4. *I want to meet _____. What is your name?*
5. *I'm hearing. Are you?*

2 *More conversation.* Fill in the blanks with appropriate vocabulary and sign it to a classmate. Repeat when done.

1. *Hi, what's up? Nice _____ you.*
2. *Are you _____?*
3. *_____ hearing. _____ learning ASL.*
4. *Please _____ again.*
5. *I _____ learn sign language.*

3 *Dialogue.* Create a dialogue with a partner using vocabulary you've learned.

Accent Steps

When you use deixis, look towards the area you're pointing to. This is called **eye gaze** and helps "hold" that location for the person or thing you're signing about.

Classroom Exercise

1   *Asking questions.* Use the Question-Maker to ask a partner several questions. Be sure to respond in a complete sentence, including a closing signal. When done, switch roles and repeat the exercise.

Are you learning how to sign?

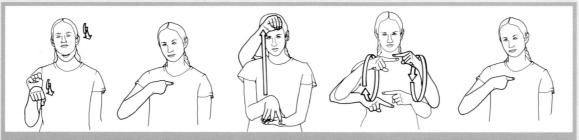

Yes, I'm learning how to sign. / Yes, I'm learning sign language.

1. *Are you learning sign language?*
2. *Are you hearing?*
3. *Do you want to learn ASL?*
4. *Do you want to meet my friend?*
5. *Good morning. How are you?*

> **FYI**   A widespread pet peeve in the Deaf community is someone who says *death* instead of *Deaf*, especially when they ask "*Are you death?*"

2   *Correcting information.* Work with a partner and ask him or her each question. Your partner will respond according to the information in bold. Switch roles and repeat.

1. *Is he/she paying attention?* **(Yes, he/she is paying attention.)**
2. *Are you sick?* **(No, I'm fine.)**
3. *Do they want to learn ASL?* **(Yes, they want to learn sign language.)**
4. *Are you sleepy?* **(Yes, I am sleepy.)**
5. *Are you Deaf?* **(No, I am hearing.)**

3   *Dialogue.* Work with a partner to make a dialogue about a hearing ASL student meeting a Deaf person.

Homework Exercise 2

A   Write a dialogue between two or more characters in which everybody is introduced. Use deixis, eye gaze, and the ASL vocabulary you've learned so far. Prepare to sign the dialogue with a partner.

B   Prepare to introduce yourself formally to your classmates in American Sign Language. Practice greeting signs and fingerspelling your name clearly.

C   Write assignments A or B in ASL gloss.

Signing Good-bye

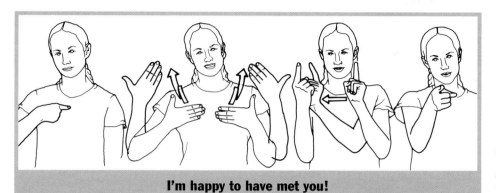

I'm happy to have met you!

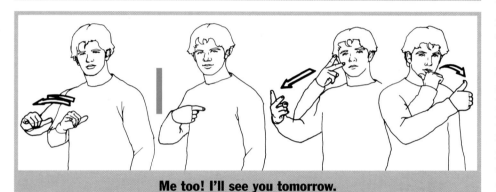

Me too! I'll see you tomorrow.

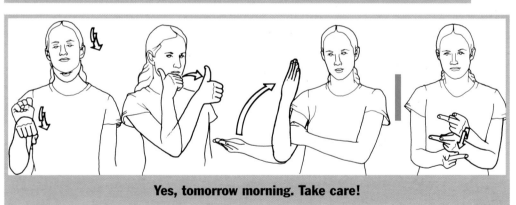

Yes, tomorrow morning. Take care!

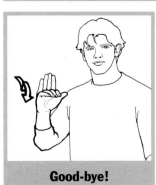

Good-bye!

The sign *good-bye* is a well-known way to say farewell. Signing *take care* is an informal way to say good-bye. Often, good-byes are never complete until plans are made for the next time friends will see each other again. Shaking hands and hugging is common. It is considered impolite and rude to leave a group of Deaf friends without saying good-bye to each person, which means farewells can take a long time!

Is this similar to how hearing people leave groups of friends?

Good-bye. Watch Marc and Kris sign farewell on your student DVD.

Accent Steps

Don't add the separate sign for *you* when signing *see you later* or *see you tomorrow*.

Classroom Exercise M

1 *Farewells.* Practice signing good-bye with your classmates. When will you see them again?

2 *Dialogue.* Create a dialogue with a partner that includes greetings, introductions, and farewells.

3 *Conversation.* Complete each sentence with signs from the vocabulary section below.

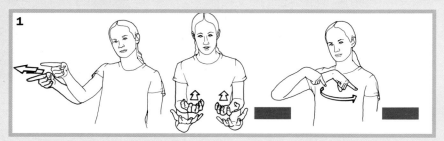

Vocabulary   Farewells

Good-bye

Later

Me too, same here

To see, to see you

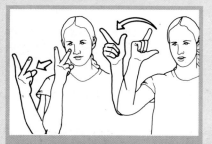

See you later

See you tomorrow

Take care

Tomorrow

Classroom Exercise

Grammar review. Can you spot the errors in each sentence? Identify the error and sign the corrected sentence.

1 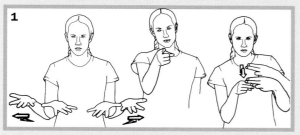   **2**

3

4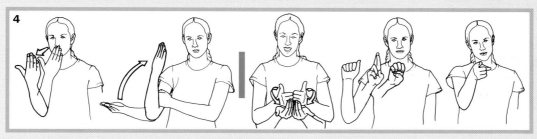

5

Homework Exercise 3

A   Practice signing three different ways of saying farewell with a friend. Practice the farewells until you sign them clearly.

B   Create 5 incorrect ASL sentences, similar to those seen in Classroom Exercise N. Explain why each sentence is wrong and how to correct them.

Focus: How do people learn

The majority of Deaf people are raised in families where deafness is not common. Approximately 10 percent of Deaf people have Deaf parents and grow up in families where American Sign Language is used daily. When these two populations came together at schools for the deaf, those who did not know sign language, learned from the Deaf children with Deaf parents. Often, the use of sign language was forbidden at schools for the deaf but the desire for a natural, visual language could not be suppressed. Many Deaf people can share stories of only being allowed to sign when class was not in session. Hearing people who learned ASL tended to be children of deaf adults or individuals who worked with the deaf.

Suppressing the learning and use of sign language has taken many forms across the centuries.

Courtesy: Signum Verlag

In the 1960s, ASL gained recognition as a unique language different from English. In the 1970s, schools for the Deaf began using ASL to teach their students and sign language classes for hearing people mushroomed across the United States. By the 1980s, the Deaf community was considered a cultural minority rather than a group of disabled persons, an important change based largely on the successful Deaf President Now movement at Gallaudet University, the world's only university for the Deaf. At the same time, Deaf accomplishments in the arts, film, and television brought wider exposure to the Deaf community. By the 1990s, American Sign Language became the fastest growing language offered as a second or foreign language, a trend that continues today.

The best way to learn any language, including ASL, is to immerse yourself in the community where the language is used. Make Deaf friends and attend Deaf sporting, theatrical, and social events when invited. You will quickly realize there is a different "Deaf World" to learn about and participate in, provided you make the effort to sign. As a student learning ASL, it is up to you to learn the language and culture of the Deaf community. You can do this by being open-minded, practicing, and taking an interest in the Deaf community.

The Deaf President Now movement is considered the breakthrough event that focused the world on the abilities, language, culture, and community of the Deaf.

Courtesy: Gallaudet University

American Sign Language?

As a student studying American Sign Language, the following principles will help prepare you to learn this challenging visual language. The most fundamental and essential point is to recognize and accept that American Sign Language is **not** English. ASL has its own grammar, structure, and nuances that are designed for the eye, not for the ear, unlike spoken languages. Remember that ASL makes visual sense and was developed to serve the language needs of a community of people who do not hear. Other considerations to keep in mind:

■ One word in English can have many separate signs in ASL, depending on the concept. For example, the word "get" and "got" in the following sentences each uses a different sign.

Can you figure out which sign matches each sentence?

1. *Please get the book . . .*
2. *Please get him . . .*
3. *I don't get it . . .*
4. *I get tired . . .*
5. *I got home . . .*
6. *I've got it . . .*

To understand

To have

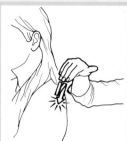

Shoulder tap

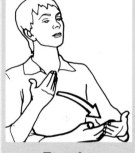

To arrive

To get something

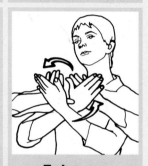

To become

■ Though it's a challenge, try not to translate word for word or sign by sign. Try to visualize the concept instead. Likewise, don't worry about not knowing specific signs for the particular English phrase you have in mind; try to communicate your concept by pointing, miming, and using other signs you know rather than fingerspelling the unknown term.

■ Don't fall into the habit of "talking silently" or whispering while you sign. You will learn how ASL uses the lips as part of its grammar. Some students rely on lipreading rather than signing skills, a sure way to become frustrated since most of the English language cannot be lipread! Using ASL signs while talking or "mouthing" English is not ASL.

■ As a beginning signer, you will naturally want to keep your eyes on the hands of the person who is signing. With exposure and practice you will learn to watch the signer's hands, face, and eyes nearly simultaneously. ASL is not only comprised of signs but also includes specific mouth movements and head shakes and nods. Eye contact informs the signer that you're paying attention!

Practice ASL and make Deaf friends and acquaintances in your community. Before long you'll be given the compliment, "You sign like a Deaf person!"

I Want to Know . . .

Where are all the "little" words like *is, to,* and *are?*

This question is often asked by beginning American Sign Language students. It is part of a much bigger question: Is ASL like English, except that it's signed instead of spoken? The answer is no, not at all. Just as Japanese, Spanish, and Latin are not English, neither is ASL. All languages have different ways of putting words together into correct sentences. If you translate an English sentence word for word into any other language, or use ASL signs in English word order, the results don't make sense. The **grammar** and **syntax** (the order in which words are put together) of ASL is different from English. ASL does not need separate "little" words because these words are *already included in each sign*.

Thank you

For example, look at the sign *thank you*. Even though English requires two words to make sense (the **verb** "to thank" and the **object** "you"), ASL uses one sign that incorporates both the verb and the object. How so? Where does the *thank you* sign point toward? The object, or you. Still unsure? What would happen if you added the sign *you* to *thank you*? It would "look funny" and make as much sense in ASL as saying "thank you you" does in English! Take a look at the ASL sentence below. Its English translation is "My name is Kelly." The sentence can be broken down and analyzed sign by sign:

Deixis conveys the verb "to be" whether it's a person or thing: I am, you are, it is, we are, they are.

I am

Named

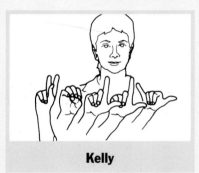

Kelly

Because ASL is a "real" and separate language different from English, it is important that you learn how to use the language properly. This means respecting the language for how it is structured, instead of wondering why it isn't like your own spoken language!

Classroom Exercise

1 *Little words I.* Sign each phrase or sentence in ASL.

1. *She is happy.*
2. *My name is _____.*
3. *He wants to learn ASL.*
4. *They are busy.*
5. *_____ is named _____.*
6. *We are _____.*

2 *Little words II.* Work with a partner to develop several sentences of your own similar to those in Part I.

ASL Up Close

Facial Expressions & Non-Manual Signals

One noticeable difference between American Sign Language and English is the use of facial expressions and non-manual signals. **Non-manual signals** (abbreviated NMS) are the various parts to a sign that are not signed on the hands. For example, ASL **adverbs** are made by the eyes and eyebrows, and ASL **adjectives** use the mouth, tongue, and lips. One important group of NMS are **facial expressions**, which convey your tone of "voice" while you sign. Your facial expressions should match the meaning and content of what you're signing so if you're signing *I am happy*, then look happy!

Why doesn't the example make sense? How can you make the sentence clearer?

Changing a facial expression modifies the *meaning* of the sign, even if the sign itself doesn't change. Think of facial expressions as occupying positions on a scale, like the one shown below. Unlike English which uses separate words to describe related meanings, ASL uses related facial expressions with the **base meaning** of a sign.

| No meaning | Not scared at all | Scared | Very scared | Terrified |

Classroom Exercise P

1. *Facial expressions.* Using one sign you know, how many different meanings can you make by changing facial expressions?

2. *Comparisons.* Use the correct sign with various facial expressions to show the difference between each meaning.

1. *I'm not afraid . . . . . afraid . . . . . terrified.*
2. *I'm not busy . . . . . busy . . . . . overwhelmed.*
3. *I'm not bored . . . . . bored . . . . . incredibly bored.*
4. *I'm not sick . . . . . sick . . . . . deathly ill.*
5. *I'm not stressed . . . . . stressed . . . . . stressed out.*
6. *I'm not sad . . . . . sad . . . . . terribly sad.*
7. *I'm not tired . . . . . tired . . . . . exhausted.*
8. *I'm not excited . . . . . excited . . . . . enthusiastic.*
9. *I'm not angry . . . . . angry . . . . furious.*
10. *I'm not happy . . . . happy . . . . joyous.*

Classroom Exercise Q

Eyebrows and more! As you make each facial expression, think about the meaning behind the face. When would you use it?

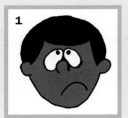   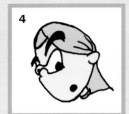 

   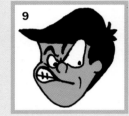 

Vocabulary — Signing with Facial Expressions

Blank face

To be bored

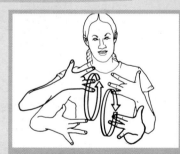
To be excited

Facial expressions

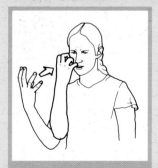
To be mad, angry

To be sad

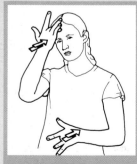
To be sick

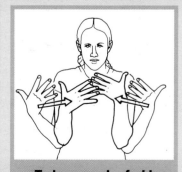
To be scared, afraid

Classroom Exercise

1 *Using non-manuals.* What can you say about each illustration? An example is provided.

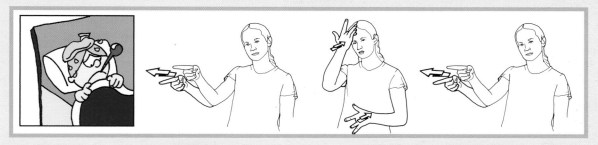

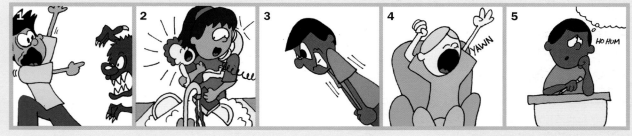

2 *Matching.* Pair the vocabulary word with the NMS or facial expression that best matches.

1. *Blank face*	3. *Sick*	5. *Happy*	7. *Tired*	9. *Good*
2. *Sad*	4. *Afraid*	6. *Bored*	8. *Confused*	10. *Busy*

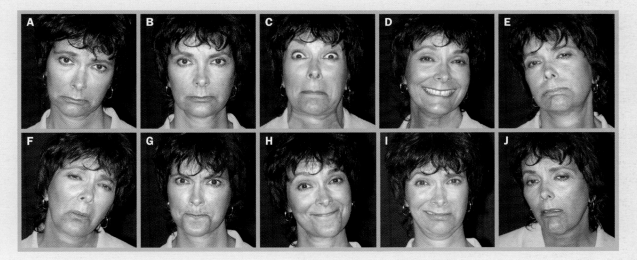

Accent Steps

It is normal to feel awkward or uncomfortable making facial expressions at first, but with practice you will become more confident and skilled. Without them you can't sign questions, show interest, or carry on a satisfying conversation. Think of learning facial expressions as a fun challenge!

Using Non-Manual Signals

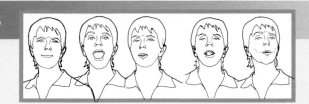

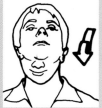  

Head shake   **Head nod**

You have already begun using two important non-manual signals when you sign *yes* or *no*. These signs must be paired with two NMS called the **head nod** and the **head shake**. Use these non-manual signals when using *yes* or *no* or when you affirm or negate sentences. Gently nod or shake your head while signing your sentence instead of wildly exaggerating your head movement! Look at the examples to see how these NMS are used in ASL sentences.

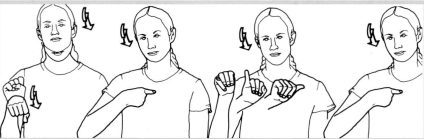

Yes, I am Mia.

No, I'm not Deaf

Homework Exercise 4

A   Most people use some sort of facial expression in every language. What are three facial expressions you tend to use most often? When do you use these expressions? Prepare to show the facial expressions to your classmates.

B   How many different meanings can you create by changing facial expressions with the signs *bored*, *fine*, *sad*, *sick*, *afraid*, and *excited*? Make a list of the meanings you develop and practice each facial expression.

Classroom Exercise S

NMS. Use the correct NMS while signing each sentence.

1. *I'm not Deaf. I'm hearing.*
2. *Yes, I'm learning how to sign.*
3. *I didn't go to the bathroom.*
4. *They aren't sick.*
5. *We're not busy.*

Accent Steps

You don't need a separate sign for *don't* or *not*. Just use the head shake while signing the sentence.

Classroom Exercise

1   *Q & A.* Sign each sentence to a partner, who will respond using the information in bold. When done, switch roles and repeat the exercise.

1. *Can I go to the bathroom?* **(No, you can't.)**
2. *Do you understand the homework?* **(Yes, I understand the homework.)**
3. *I'm not Marie. I'm Pat.* **(I didn't understand. Please sign it again.)**
4. *I don't understand. Do you?* **(No, I don't understand.)**
5. *We don't know his/her name.* **(I know his/her name. He/she is _____.)**

2   *Dialogue.* Work with a partner to sign the dialogue in ASL.

Alan	*Hi! My name is Alan. What's your name?*
Holly	*My name is Holly. Nice to meet you!*
Alan	*Are you Deaf?*
Holly	*No, I'm hearing. I'm learning ASL. Do you know how to sign?*
Alan	*Yes, I can sign.*
Holly	*Are you Deaf?*
Alan	*No, I'm not Deaf. I'm hearing. I sign okay. I want to sign well.*
Holly	*Me too! I want to understand ASL.*
Alan	*Do you want to meet me tomorrow morning?*
Holly	*Yeah! I'll see you tomorrow!*
Alan	*Good-bye!*

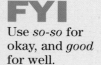

FYI

Use *so-so* for okay, and *good* for well.

Vocabulary   Using NMS

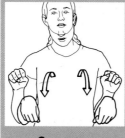

Can, may

Can't, may not

Don't know

Don't like

Don't understand

I'm not, not me

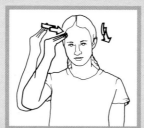

To know

To like

To understand

Classroom Exercise

1. *Using NMS.* Sign the phrase or sentence using the correct NMS.

   1. *I'm not absent.*
   2. *Not today.*
   3. *The homework isn't due.*

   4. *I don't mind.*
   5. *We don't understand.*
   6. *They don't like the movie.*

2. *More Q & A.* Sign each sentence to a partner, who will respond using the information in bold. When done, switch roles and repeat the exercise.

   1. *Do you want to go to a movie? (**Yes, tomorrow night.**)*
      *Do you like scary movies? (**So-so.**)*
      *My favorite movie is _____. Do you like it? (** ? **)*

   2. *My friend is absent today. Do you know what's for homework? (**Yes, practice ASL.**)*
      *Is the homework due tomorrow? (**Yes, the homework is due tomorrow.**)*
      *Thank you! (**You're welcome.**)*

Eyes on ASL #4

When signing *yes*, nod your head; when signing *no*, shake your head. DVD

Combining a sign and head shake negates the meaning from positive to negative.

FYI *Practice* also means *exercise*, as in "Exercise U."

Vocabulary — Conversation

To be absent

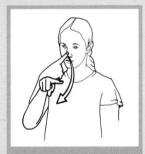

I don't mind

Due, to owe

Favorite

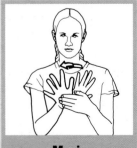

Movie

To practice

School

Today, now

Classroom Exercise

Asking & Answering Questions. Your partner will ask you a question. Respond in a complete ASL sentence. Switch roles and repeat when done.

1

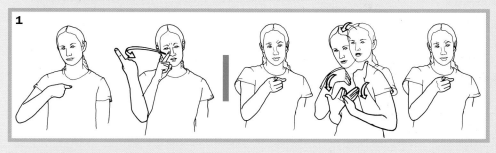

2

3

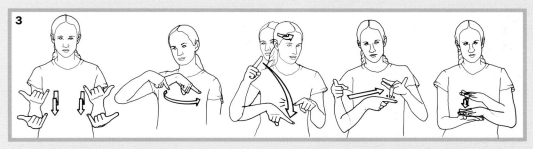

4

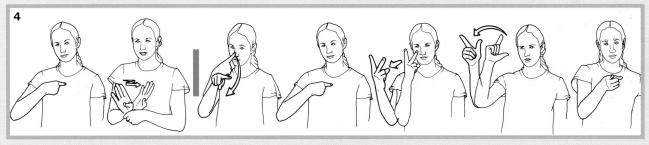

5

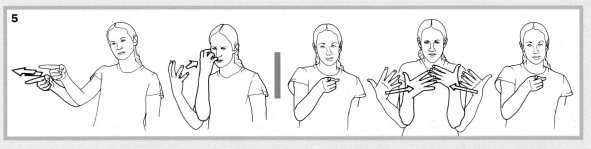

Classroom Exercise

1   *Contrasts.* A partner will sign the first sentence to you. Use the information in parentheses to sign a complete sentence in response.

   1. *They don't know my name. (**Yes, they do.**)*
   2. *He isn't paying attention. (**No, he isn't. He doesn't have eye contact.**)*
   3. *Are you sick? (**No, I'm not.**)*
   4. *I like learning ASL. (**Me too.**)*
   5. *We're very busy today! (**Yes, a lot of practice!**)*

2   *Dialogue.* Work with a partner and create a dialogue using at least three of the following prompts.

   1. *Exchange greetings and names*
   2. *Ask if one is Deaf, hearing, or hard-of-hearing*
   3. *Ask if one knows, or is learning, ASL*
   4. *Ask where one goes to school*
   5. *Ask a signer to slow down and repeat something*
   6. *Say good-bye and state when you will meet again*

> **FYI** Use a facial expression to sign "a lot of." What kind of face would show this meaning?

Deaf Culture Minute

The best way to learn any language is to socialize with the people who use it. Go out and meet Deaf people in your local community. As you make friends and practice, you'll see your signing skills improve quickly!

Accent Steps

If you use the Question-Maker with *I don't mind,* then it becomes a question: *Do you mind?*

Homework Exercise   5

A   Practice signing each sentence in ASL.

   1. *I'm not Deaf, I'm hearing. Are you Deaf?*
   2. *Sara is not absent today.*
   3. *I don't understand you. Do you mind repeating?*
   4. *He's very sick. He can't go to school today.*
   5. *We didn't like the movie. We couldn't understand it!*

B   Write five sentences in English using vocabulary you've learned so far that includes facial expressions and non-manual signals. Be ready to turn in the sentences.

C   Write Classroom Exercise V in ASL gloss using your **Student Companion** for help.

Journal Activities

1. What do you think being Deaf is like? What sorts of experiences do you think a Deaf individual would have? In what ways do you imagine being Deaf is different from your own life? How is it similar?

2. Write a reflection on the poem "Listen to Me." What is the author's point? What messages does she convey in the poem? What issues, concerns and frustrations does she allude to? What successes?

Listen to Me

I may not hear you,
But I can listen,
Listen to your hands,
Your face and your eyes.
All I ask of you
Is that you do the same.
Listen to the words
That I want to tell.
Look past hearing aids
And see the real me.
Look at what I can be
Not what I cannot.

Heather Whitestone showed you
That I can be beautiful.
Marlee Matlin showed you
That I can be in movies.
Thomas Edison showed you
That I can make history.
Ludwig van Beethoven showed you
That I can make music.
Sir John Warcup Cornforth showed you
That I can win the Nobel Prize.
Konstantin Tsiolkovsky showed you
That I can send rockets to the moon.
Helen Keller showed you
That I can overcome anything.

Now, let me show you
That I can be a friend.
I have things to tell you.
Listen to me.

— Tawnysha Lynch

3. What experience/s, if any, have you had with Deaf individuals? Describe the encounter/s, how you realized he or she was Deaf, and any thoughts or feelings you recall about the experience.

http://Search   Search the web for more information:

- Marlee Matlin
- Thomas Edison
- Sir John Warcup Cornforth

- Heather Whitestone
- Ludwig van Beethoven

- Helen Keller
- Konstantin Tsiolkovsky

Unit 1 Review

A   Explain how each function of ASL grammar is used in ASL, providing an example in a complete sentence.

    1. Eye contact   **3.** Closing signals
    2. One-word replies   **4.** Non-manual signals

B   Introduce a hearing friend to a new Deaf friend of yours. Include the following:

    1. Attention-getting   **3.** Exchanging names   **5.** Who's learning ASL
    2. Greetings   **4.** Whether Deaf or hearing   **6.** Farewells

C   Identify and correct any errors in the following sentences. Explain to a partner or friend why the errors are wrong and how to fix them. Explain how each function of ASL grammar is used in ASL, providing an example in a complete sentence.

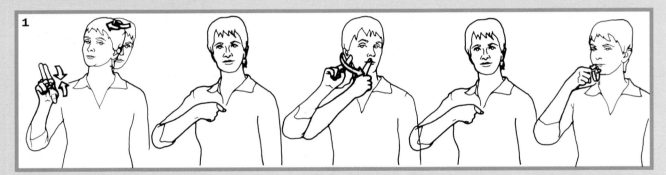

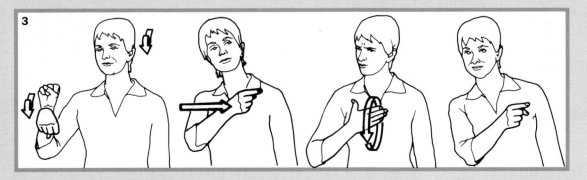

Unit 1 Review

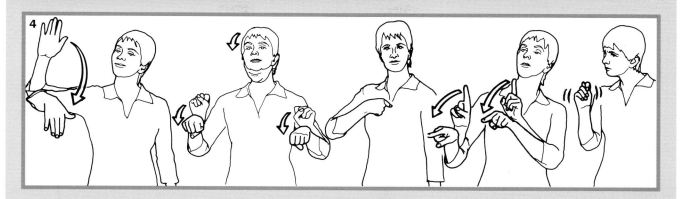

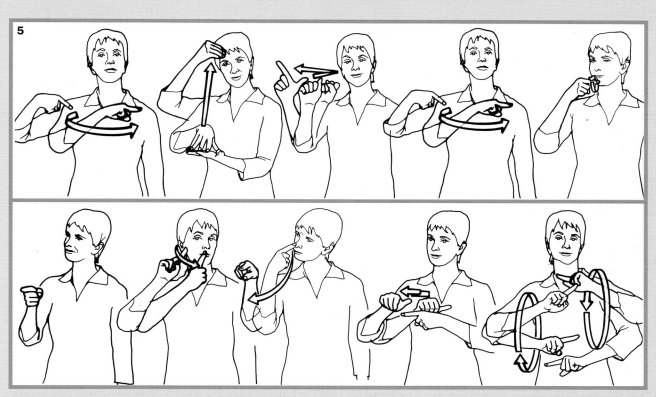

D You will meet a potential Deaf friend for the first time. Prepare to introduce yourself and say a little about who you are and what you like. Include topics like your favorite movie title, that you're an ASL student, and how you are doing. Be ready to ask a few questions of your own, so you can get to know him or her better!

Getting Started

Unit Two Objectives

- To ask for help and clarification in ASL
- To engage in basic conversation on a variety of topics
- To understand the cultural view of deafness
- To improve familiarity with ASL grammar and structure
- To learn and apply WH-signs and facial expressions
- To understand iconic and non-iconic signs

Unit Two Vocabulary

Key Phrases

My Advice

DVD

Hi. I'm Marc. How are you? Having fun learning ASL? Practice is important to get better. If you don't practice, you'll only get worse! Grab opportunities to chat in ASL with Deaf people, but here's a warning: If you're in a restaurant and see Deaf people and want to practice, think again!

My Advice Watch Marc sign in full motion on your student DVD.

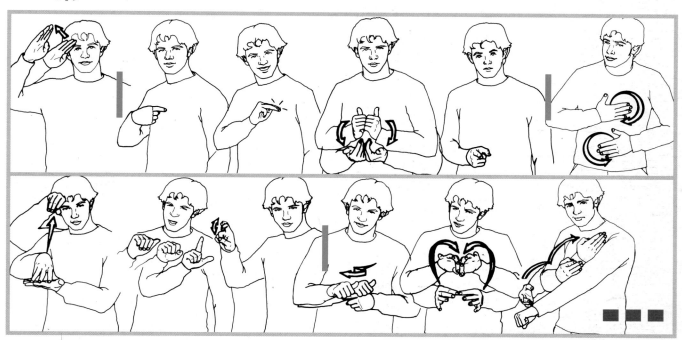

Vocabulary   My Advice

Other new vocabulary seen in the narrative is presented throughout Unit 2.

To grab

Literally meaning *grab*, use the sign when taking about sudden opportunities.

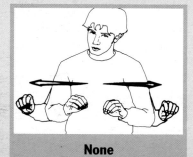

None

Related to *nothing, none* is more emphatic.

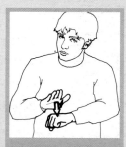

Warning

Use this sign to say *watch out.*

Did you know?

ASL students are often eager to practice ASL with Deaf people, who are generally willing to say hello to students. However, there is a time and place for ASL tutorials so be respectful and use common sense. A frequent experience is an ASL student approaching a couple dining in a restaurant and starting a conversation out of the blue!

Asking For Help

The meanings of some signs in ASL change depending on the way the signs are moved. For example, the sign *help* can mean *I help you* or *You help me* if the movement is towards the signer or someone else. This feature of ASL is called **directionality**. You need to memorize which ASL signs are directional to use them correctly. Here's a hint: If you want to sign something being done to, for, or with you, then the sign tends to be directional.

I Have a Question Watch Marc and Kris on your student DVD.

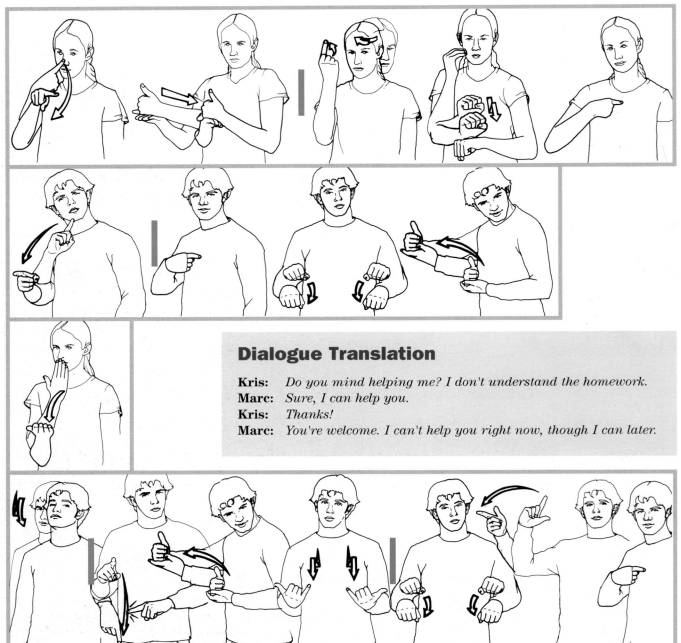

Dialogue Translation

Kris: *Do you mind helping me? I don't understand the homework.*
Marc: *Sure, I can help you.*
Kris: *Thanks!*
Marc: *You're welcome. I can't help you right now, though I can later.*

Classroom Exercise

1   *Help & Directionality.* Use the correct form of *help* in each sentence.

    1.   *Please help me.*   **3.**   *He/she can help you.*   **5.**   *Help them.*

    2.   *I can help you.*   **4.**   *Help us.*   **6.**   *You help _?_*

2   *Using directionality.* The signs *give to*, *help*, and *move* are directional. How should the signs be altered in each sentence? An example is provided.

    1.   *Help me move the table.*
    2.   *Please give her the book.*
    3.   *Can you give me a pencil?*
    4.   *We don't want help.*
    5.   *I need to give you my pen.*
    6.   *Move the desk over there.*
    7.   *She is helping me move tomorrow.*
    8.   *Give me my book.*
    9.   *Give _?_ my _?_*
    10.   *Help _?_*

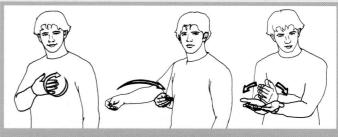

Please give me the book.

FYI   You don't need to add *me* when using directionality. It's already included in the sign!

Vocabulary   Directionality

Book

Desk, table

To give to

To help (general)

Help me

I help you

To move

To need

Pen, pencil

Sure

ASL Up Close

WH-Face

The WH-Face

Knowing how to ask for help is important in any language. In ASL, two key phrases are *mean what* and *explain again*. Both phrases use a specific non-manual signal called the WH-Face that closely resembles the Question-Maker (see page 15). You have used the WH-Face to ask *What is your name?* Use the WH-Face instead of the Question-Maker when you are uncertain, unclear, or asking a question using the signs *who, what, where, when, why* (see page 64). Use culturally-appropriate techniques to interrupt or gain attention, or raise your hand in class. Make sure you have eye contact before asking for clarification. The examples below show how the WH-Face is used to ask for help.

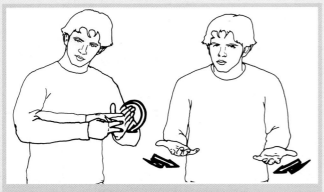

What does it mean?

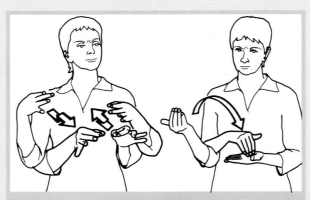

Explain it again.

Classroom Exercise B

1 *The WH-Face.* Practice the phrases with a partner. How is the WH-Face made?

  1. *What does it mean?*   **3.** *What's your name?*
  2. *Explain it again.*   **4.** *I don't understand*

2 *Faces.* Decide whether the Question-Maker or the WH-Face best matches the sentence, and sign it to a partner. When done, switch roles and repeat the exercise.

  1. *Is his name Todd?*   **4.** *No, I don't understand.*
  2. *What's your name?*   **5.** *Do you mind helping me?*
  3. *Do you understand?*   **6.** *What does it mean? Can you explain it again?*

3 *Asking questions.* Work with a partner and create four sentences using the WH-Face and Question-Maker. What differences do the faces show?

Classroom Exercise C

1 *I don't understand.* Sign the dialogue between Marc and Kris. When done, respond to the comprehension questions.

DVD

Deaf Culture Minute

What is the ASL sign for *You're welcome*? You can sign *thank you* back to the person who thanked you, or nod your head and smile. Nodding is more casual and should be used with friends and family. Seem strange? It's different than English, but not so strange. Many languages say *you're welcome* this way.

Classroom Exercise **C** (continued)

2 *Comprehension.* Work with a partner to sign and answer the comprehension questions.

   1. *What sign didn't Kris understand?*
   2. *What does it mean?*
   3. *Did Marc explain the meaning to Kris?*
   4. *How did each person say thank you?*

3 *Dialogue.* Create a dialogue with a partner in which an ASL student asks someone to explain what a sign means. Use complete ASL sentences and non-manual signals.

4 *Asking for help.* Work with a partner to sign each sentence in ASL before signing the complete dialogue.

Student A *Excuse me. Can you help me?*
Student B *Sure! Are you unclear about something?*
Student A *Yes, I'm unclear. I don't understand the sign "confused."*
Student B *The sign "confused" means you don't understand clear.*
Student A *I understand. I need to practice!*
Student B *I can help you practice. Do you want to practice today?*
Student A *I'm not sure I can. Can I meet you tomorrow?*
Student B *Sure!*
Student A *Good. I'll see you tomorrow. Good-bye!*
Student B *Take care!*

> **Accent Steps**
>
> Use the sign *unclear* for phrases like *I don't really understand, I don't get it,* or *Is something not clear?*

Vocabulary — Helpful Signs

To be clear

Excuse me

To explain

To mean

Not, don't, doesn't

To be unclear

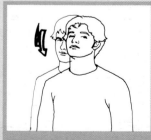
You're welcome

> **FYI** Don't add *me* to the sign *excuse me*. Doing so is redundant.

I Want to Know . . .

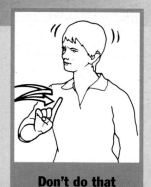

Don't do that

Isn't ASL just gestures or making "pictures" in the air?

Some people believe ASL is a simple language of gestures like *don't do that*. Using some gestures does not make ASL any less of a language than English, which also uses gestures. Can you think of gestures or signs that ASL and English have in common? Some signs resemble the meaning behind the sign (like *book*). These are called **iconic signs**, but most signs are not iconic. How many iconic signs do you know compared to non-iconic signs?

How are the signs *door* and *lights* iconic? Can you think of the sign for *window* using the same handshape as *door*?

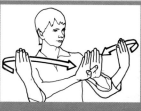

To close (door)

To open (door)

To turn on (lights)

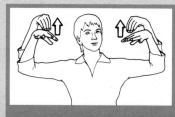

To turn off (lights)

The signs below are related to each other. Are they iconic? Why or why not?

Person (standing)

To get up, stand up

To jump

To sit down

Homework Exercise ◀ 1

A How would you use each expression in a sentence? Explain what meaning you think the expressions convey, and practice signing a complete ASL sentence for each.

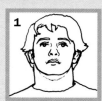

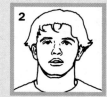

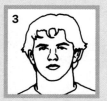

B Practice signing three sentences using the WH-Face. Make sure your eyebrows are noticeable!

Classroom Exercise D

1 *Asking questions.* Ask a partner the following questions in ASL. When done, switch roles and repeat the exercise. Remember to answer questions in a complete sentence, following the example.

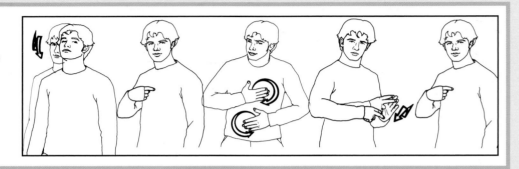

Do you like to read?

1. *Are you learning ASL?*
2. *Do you understand me?*
3. *Do you mind opening the door?*
4. *I'm tired. Are you?*

5. *Do you want to study tomorrow?*
6. *Are you sitting down?*
7. *Are you going to a party tonight?*
8. *What's for homework?*

2 *What are they doing?* Explain in a complete ASL sentence what you see in the illustration. An example is provided.

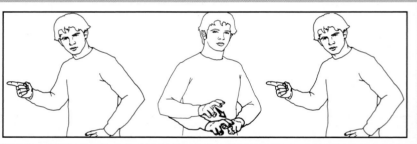

Classroom Exercise E

Yes or no? Your partner will respond affirmatively or negatively to the question asked based on the illustration. When done, switch roles and repeat the exercise.

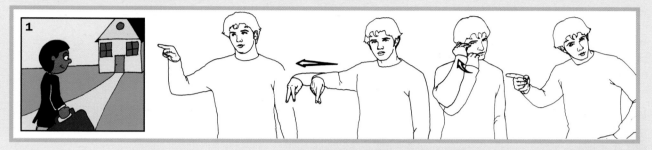

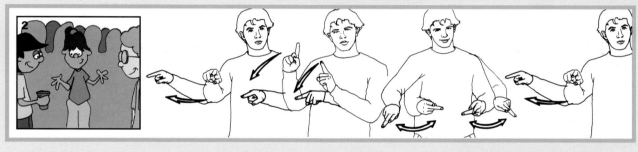

Is the book open?

Are they walking?

Is she reading?

Vocabulary — Activities

Home

I walk

Party

To read

To sleep

To walk to

Deaf Culture NOTE

Labels and identity

Minority groups are often labeled by the larger, surrounding community who are uninterested in how the group identifies itself. This is especially true with individuals considered disabled or handicapped. The Deaf community has been labeled "deaf-and-dumb" and "deaf-mute" in addition to handicapped, disabled, or abnormal. Over the years the Deaf community has worked to educate hearing people about the negative connotations of many labels, preferring that a positive view of deafness and Deaf culture be respected.

International symbol of deafness

~~Deaf and dumb~~

~~Deaf mute~~

Hearing impaired

Hard of hearing

Deaf

Deaf culture

You may have seen the term **hearing impaired** on TV or other media referring to deafness. Many people in the Deaf community prefer to sign *deaf* instead of *hearing-impaired* due to the negative connotations of "impaired" and "broken." Strangely, hearing people consider this term more polite than saying "Deaf." Deaf people are proud to be Deaf, and prefer to be called Deaf!

Hard-of-hearing refers to those individuals who have some degree of deafness and can use a spoken language, though hearing and speech skills vary from person to person. Many hard-of-hearing people consider themselves to be culturally Deaf, meaning they fully participate in the Deaf community.

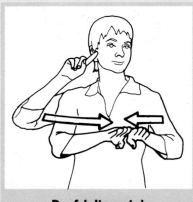

Deaf (alternate)

Deaf people form a cultural and linguistic minority whose language and experiences are unique. When a group of people who share a language and come together to offer mutual support in pursuit of common goals and interests, a **community** is formed. Over time, a culture develops from this community. **Deaf culture** is the shared experience of deaf people that has its own values, social norms (ways of doing things), a unique history, and a rich tradition of storytelling and poetry passed from generation to generation. The common bond in Deaf culture is the experience of being deaf and the use of American Sign Language.

The sign on the left is an older sign for *deaf*, still seen occasionally by older signers or in formal situations. Analyze the sign closely: Do you understand why it means *deaf*?

Accent Steps

Non-manual signals (NMS) like the head shake and eyebrows must be clear and obvious for the meaning to be understood. Make sure your NMS are visible on your face.

Classroom Exercise

1 *What are they doing?* Based on the illustrations, explain what each person is doing in a complete ASL sentence. An example is provided.

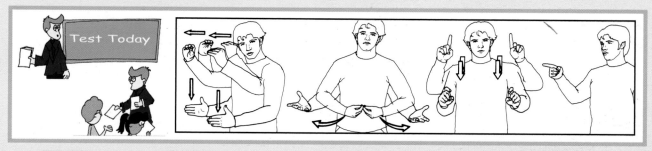

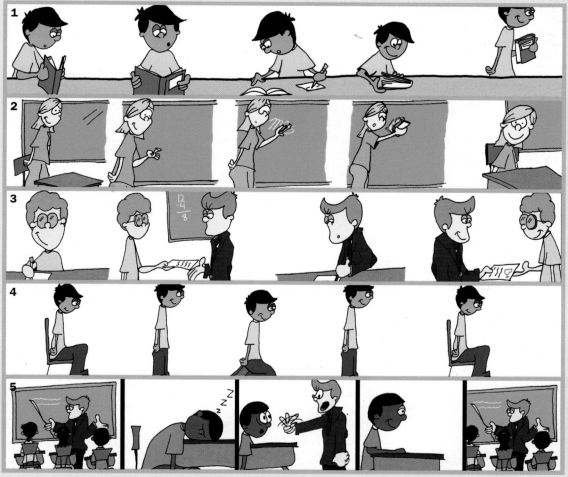

2 *Giving requests.* Ask a partner to do three specific tasks using vocabulary you've learned so far. Some ideas are provided for you. When done, switch roles and repeat the exercise.

1. *write your name on the board, then erase it*

2. *open or close the door*

3. *stand up or sit down*

4. *move your desk*

Vocabulary — In the Classroom

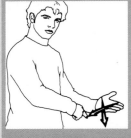

To correct, to grade

To erase (a board)

To erase (on paper)

Why do you think?

. . . there are two different signs for *erase?*

To hand out

Paper

To spot, to see

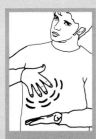

To study

Student

Teacher

Test, exam

To write

To be wrong, error

Accent Steps

Have you noticed differences between signs in **Master ASL!** and those your teacher uses? Maybe a Deaf person has taught you some signs that closely resemble the signs you've learned in this book but aren't the same. As you meet Deaf people you will encounter slight differences between signs, called **variations**. There are certain signs that vary from region to region, with some differences more well-known than others. In many ways, these sign variations resemble regional differences in spoken languages: Do you say *soda, pop,* or *cola*? The answer depends on where you live and your own preference. The same variation between signs is seen in ASL. Be sure to use the sign variation preferred by your local Deaf community unless you want to sign with an accent!

Two variants on the sign *test*

Classroom Exercise G

The highs and lows of eyebrows. Practice each facial expression, paying attention to the eyebrows and mouth.

Classroom Exercise H

Conversations with the teacher. Sign each sentence to a partner, who will respond with the information in bold. Switch roles and repeat when done.

1. *Do you want a test today?* (**No, we want the test tomorrow.**)
2. *Do you know the ASL teacher's name?* (**Yes, it's _____.**)
3. *Are you an ASL student?* (**Yes, I am learning ASL.**)
4. *I'm not an ASL student.* (**No, you are the ASL teacher.**)

Homework Exercise 2

A What is your ASL teacher's name? Practice introducing him or her to a friend of yours. Is your teacher Deaf or hearing? What can you say about your teacher?

B Change the meaning of each sentence below from the affirmative to the negative using *no* and *not*.

C Write a translation of each of the following sentences into ASL gloss.

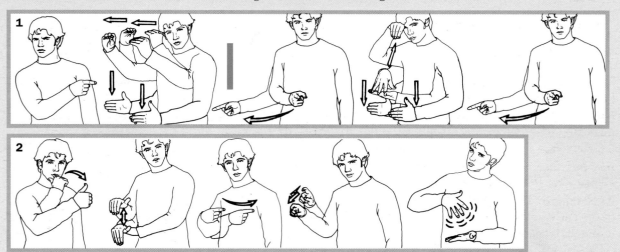

Focus: What is deafness?

What does the word "deaf" mean to you? Is the definition as simple as "someone who can't hear"? Read the American Heritage Dictionary's definition of "deaf" and compare it to your own. What differences do you see?

---

deaf

adj. **deaf·er, deaf·est**

Partially or completely lacking in the sense of hearing.

Deaf or relating to the Deaf or their culture.

Unwilling or refusing to listen; heedless: was deaf to our objections.

n. (used with a pl. verb)

Deaf people considered as a group. Used with the.

Deaf The community of deaf people who use American Sign Language as a primary means of communication. Used with the.

deaf ly *adv.*

deaf ness *n.*

Usage Note: The rise of the Deaf Pride movement in the 1980s has introduced a distinction between *deaf* and *Deaf*, with the capitalized form used specifically in referring to deaf persons belonging to the community also known as *Deaf culture* that has formed around the use of American Sign Language as the preferred means of communication. The issue of capitalization is different with *deaf* than it is for a term such as black. In the case of black, the decision whether or not to capitalize is essentially a matter of personal or political preference, while with deaf the capitalized and uncapitalized forms differ in meaning as well as style. Only persons who are self-identified as belonging to Deaf culture are appropriately referred to as *Deaf*.

The American Heritage® Dictionary of the English Language, Fourth Edition
Copyright © 2000 by Houghton Mifflin Company. Published by Houghton Mifflin Company.
All rights reserved.

As you can see, the American Heritage Dictionary has two major definitions for the word *deaf*. One refers to the sense of hearing, and the other focuses on a group of people and their culture. The first perspective is called the **pathological** or **medical model**, meaning the focus of attention is on the "broken" ear that affects how much one does or does not hear. The emphasis of the medical definition of deafness is to cure those who are deaf and make them "normal." Deafness may be caused by illness, heredity, damage from exposure to loud noise, or age, and may occur from damage in the inner, middle, and outer areas of the ear. Look at the diagram for a closer look at the various parts of the ear.

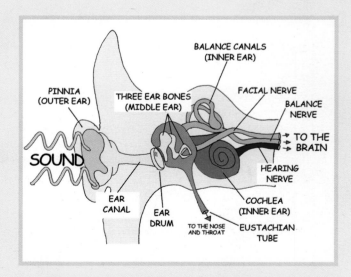

What is Deaf Culture?

The second perspective of the word *deaf* is a cultural point of view in which deafness is considered to influence a unique way of life. In this **cultural model**, deafness is not considered to be an overwhelming handicap or disability but instead is part of one's identity. Because deafness in this context is an accepted — and positive — way of life for a large group of people, Deaf is capitalized to distinguish those persons who are deaf and use American Sign Language from the medical model. In other words, deaf individuals who use American Sign Language, identify themselves as part of the deaf community, and are proud to be deaf are Deaf!

While many Deaf people use hearing aids or other technological equipment to improve their hearing or perception of sound, most Deaf individuals do not feel the need to be fixed or cured. Many Deaf people are proud to be deaf and of their achievements and successes despite not hearing. The Deaf culture has responded to and adapted to the needs of the "hearing world," a world that respects the Deaf community more than ever.

Road Signs (1996), Ann Silver.
Reproduced by permission of artist

Now that you understand the difference between Deaf and deaf, it is important to understand the meaning of **culture**. As defined by the American Heritage Dictionary, culture refers to the beliefs, behavior patterns, social organizations, and products of a particular group of people. While Deaf culture is comprised of people from all races, ethnicities, and backgrounds, the common and unifying trait is deafness and the use of American Sign Language. From this bond and the needs for mutual support, developed a community sharing goals, ideals and expectations, a rich body of literature and the arts, and a way of living that celebrates deafness as a fulfilling way of life. This way of life is called **Deaf culture**.

culture

n., v.

The totality of socially transmitted behavior patterns, arts, beliefs, institutions, and all other products of human work and thought. These patterns, traits, and products considered as the expression of a particular period, class, community, or population: *Edwardian culture; Japanese culture; the culture of poverty*. These patterns, traits, and products considered with respect to a particular category, such as a field, subject, or mode of expression: *religious culture in the Middle Ages; musical culture; oral culture.*

The predominating attitudes and behavior that characterize the functioning of a group or organization. n 1: a particular civilization at a particular stage 2: the tastes in art and manners that are favored by a social group 3: all the knowledge and values shared by a society.

Often, hearing people wonder whether the Deaf community has a "real" culture of its own. As you begin your study of ASL, you may be surprised by the depth and breadth of this culture, often called the **Deaf World**. Look at the painting by the noted Deaf artist Ann Silver. Her artwork is highly regarded for depicting the Deaf perspective, highlighting the visually-based culture that is often at odds with the hearing world. The Deaf perspective offers a different way of looking at things considered "normal" by hearing people. Are you ready and willing to look at the hearing and Deaf worlds differently?

ASL Up Close

The Signed Question Mark

Each of the signs below shares more than just the same basic handshape: A question is being asked or in the case of *test*, several questions. In many ways, this handshape is a signed question mark. The signed question mark does not replace the Question-Maker. It is used to emphasize that a question has been asked and that the signer expects a response.

Question Mark

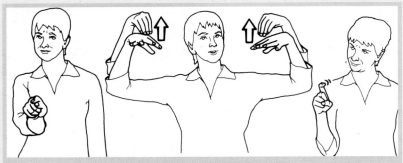

Did you turn off the lights?

Ask him / her, not me.

To ask

The sign *to ask* is directional and follows the rules of directionality, as seen in the examples. The sign *ask me* (plural) means *Do you have any questions?* if paired with the Question-Maker.

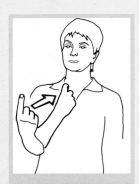

I ask you

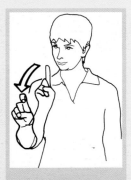

You ask me

I ask everybody

Ask me (plural)

Classroom Exercise

1. *Ask.* Sign the correct form of *to ask.*

   1. *Ask me.*
   2. *I ask you.*
   3. *They ask me.*

   4. *He / she asked you.*
   5. *Any questions?*
   6. *We ask many questions.*

   7. *Don't ask me.*
   8. *Ask him / her.*

2. *Who am I asking?* Sign each sentence using the correct form of *to ask.*

   1. *Ask him to open the door.*
   2. *Ask me later.*

   3. *Sean asked Kris to help him.*
   4. *I asked everybody "How are you?"*

   5. *?*

3. *Using "ask" in conversation.* Sign the following questions to a partner who will respond in ASL. When done, switch roles and repeat the exercise.

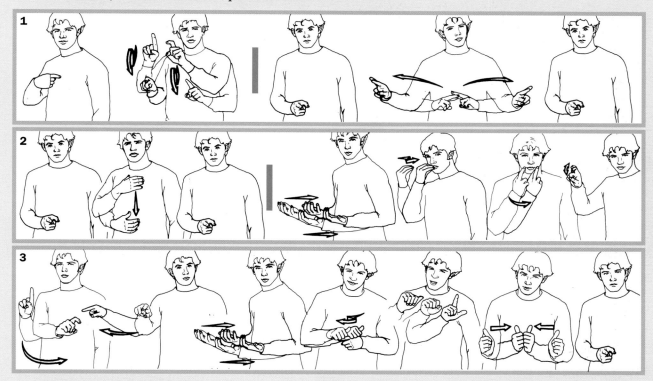

Vocabulary   Making Conversation

| To eat, food | To be hungry | To be ready | Restaurant | With |

Classroom Exercise

1   *Signing ask.* Create a complete sentence using each of the following signs.

   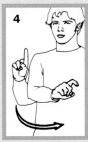 

2   *Sentences.* Sign each sentence in ASL.

1. *I don't know what's for homework. Ask him (or her).*
2. *My ASL teacher asked me to help you.*
3. *Are you hungry? I want to go to a restaurant. Do you want to go with me?*
4. *Don't ask me. I don't know his (or her) name.*
5. *Does everybody understand? Are there any questions?*

FYI Don't worry about the past tense for now. Just use the vocabulary you know already.

3   *Dialogue.* Work with a partner to develop a dialogue using *ask* and other vocabulary you've learned.

I Want to Know . . .

When do I use the Question Mark instead of a closing signal?

In Unit One you learned how ASL sentences are completed by pointing to a person to show that you've finished your thought or question. Similarly, the Question Mark sign shows that the signer has posed a question, but when to use one or the other?

The Question Mark:

• Is best used informally, between friends and people you know well;

• Is not for questions using *who, what, when, why, where, which,* and *how*;

• Is often used to ask general questions to more than one individual;

• Allows an individual to pose a question whose answer can be provided by anyone.

Other closing signals:

• Are required for sentences and questions using *who, what, when, why, where, which,* and *how*;

• Are best used in formal situations between strangers, acquaintances, and student-teacher relationships;

• Allow you to ask specific questions to specific individuals.

Days of the Week

There are two ways to sign the days of the week in ASL. Which way is used by Deaf people in your community?

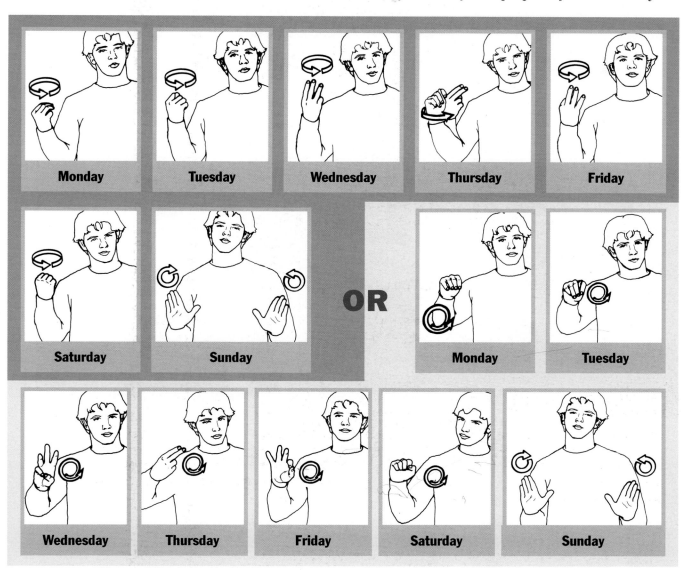

OR

Variation Alert!

Thursday

This variation of the sign *Thursday* is used by some Deaf signers. It is not as common as the other sign for *Thursday*.

FYI Don't sign or fingerspell the English word "on" in ASL sentences involving dates.

Classroom Exercise K

1   *Marc & Kelly's week.* Based on the illustrations below, explain what Marc and Kelly did each day in complete sentences. An example is provided.

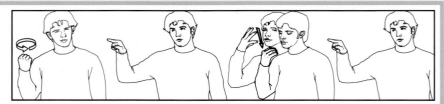

2   *Activities.* Use the vocabulary below to ask a partner what he or she does on a particular day. Follow the example as shown.

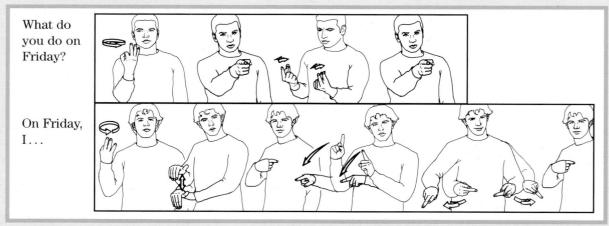

1. *Monday*	4. *Thursday*	7. *Sunday*	10. *Evening*	13. *Today*
2. *Tuesday*	5. *Friday*	8. *Morning*	11. *Tomorrow*	14. *Yesterday*
3. *Wednesday*	6. *Saturday*	9. *Afternoon*	12. *Later*	

3   *Dialogue.* Work with a partner to create a dialogue in which you sign about activities done on at least four different days.

Vocabulary — Signing About Activities

To chat, to hang out

Church

Do-do

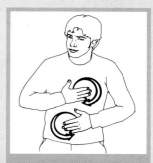

To enjoy, have fun

To kick back, take it easy

Mosque

To play sports

Temple

Yesterday

Eyes on ASL #5

DVD

Signs that show *when* something happened, such as the day of the week, come first in a sentence.

Remember to use *when* signs in their proper position: At the front of the line!

Accent Steps

Do-do is a sign that has many meanings. Use the WH-Face each time you sign *do-do* to ask:

- *What are you doing?*
- *What did you do?*
- *What do you do?*

Homework Exercise 3

A. Practice signing the events that occurred in Kelly or Marc's week, making sure that you sign clearly. Work on achieving a "flow" and avoid signing in a jerky, unpolished format. Be sure to include appropriate facial expressions, directionality, and other features of ASL grammar.

B. What have you done this week? Explain what you've done each day. Work on achieving a "flow" and avoid signing in a jerky, unpolished format. Be sure to include appropriate facial expressions, directionality, and other features of ASL grammar.

C. Write assignments A or B in ASL gloss.

My Routine

My Routine Watch Kris sign in full motion on your student DVD.

DVD

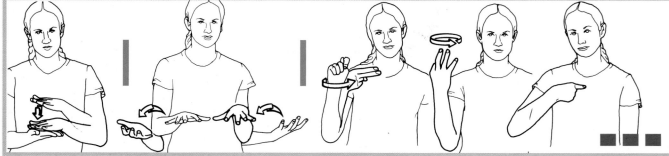

Classroom Exercise L

1   *What does Kris do?* Complete the following sentences in ASL. Don't forget to use ASL Rule #5.

1. *On Thursday, Kris...*
2. *Kris does homework on...*
3. *She works on...*
4. *Every day, Kris...*

5. *Kris hangs out with...*
6. *On Friday, she... .*
7. *Kris chats on..*
8. *On Sunday, Kris...*

9. *She doesn't work on...*
10. *Kris goes to school...*

2   *Comparison.* What do you and Kris do differently? Follow the example to explain how your routines are not the same.

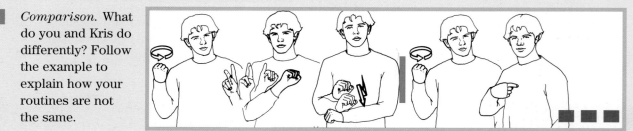

Did you know?

Deaf people use visual signals for doorbells, the telephone, fire, or smoke alarms. There are even visual signals activated by crying babies! The Deaf community has adapted many listening devices to serve visual purposes, and manufacturers now include visual options in a range of products. If you have a silent vibrate option on your cell phone or pager, thank the Deaf community who advocated for the alert! Nowadays, visual alerts for public smoke and fire alarms are required by federal law. Can you find any examples of visual signaling devices in your school, office, or home?

Classroom Exercise M

1   *Weekend activities.* Find out three things a partner does on the weekend, using the ideas below to help you. Prepare to explain what you learn about each other to your classmates.

go to the movies   work

go to a party   eat in a restaurant

sleep   hang out with friends

read   play sports

chat with friends   study

kick back   practice ASL

2   *What do you do?* Create complete sentences for each vocabulary word.

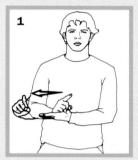

3   *Dialogue.* Remember that *when* signs come first in a sentence. Practice signing the dialogue below with a partner.

Student A   *What do you do on the weekend?*

Student B   *On Saturday, I kick back, study. I work on Sundays. What do you do?*

Student A   *I don't work on the weekend. I enjoy going to the movies with friends.*

Student B   *I like going to the movies. Do you want to go on Friday?*

Student A   *Sure!*

Vocabulary   **When?**

   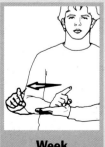  

| **Day** | **Every day** | **Um, uh, well…** | **Week** | **Weekend** | **To work, job** |

Classroom Exercise

1   *What day is it?* Explain which day of the week the date falls on, in a complete sentence.

1. *August 9*	**6.** *August 24*
2. *August 31*	**7.** *August 20*
3. *August 11*	**8.** *August 12*
4. *August 14*	**9.** *August 11*
5. August 1	**10.** *August 3*

SUN	MON	TUE	WED	THU	FRI	SAT
1	2	3	4	5	6	7
8	9	10	11	12	13	14
15	16	17	18	19	20	21
22	23	24	25	26	27	28
29	30	31				

2   *Using the calendar.* Use the calendar to provide information about the day and date of the week asked for.

SUN	MON	TUE	WED	THU	FRI	SAT
1	2	3	4	5	6	7
8	(9)	10	11	12	13	14
15	16	17	18	19	20	21
22	23	24	25	26	27	28
29	30	31				

Yesterday was Sunday.

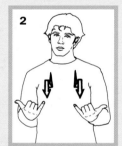

Accent Steps

When you're thinking of something to add to a sentence, use the *um* sign to show you're not finished yet.

❝ Deafness isn't the opposite of hearing. It's a silence full of sound. ❞

— *Mark Medhoff, writer, playwright, producer*

Classroom Exercise

1 *When do you...?* Sign each sentence in ASL, making the changes indicated.

1. *I practice ASL on Monday.* ***(every day)***
2. *We go to school on Saturday and Sunday.* ***(don't go)***
3. *He works Tuesday and Thursday morning.* ***(afternoon)***
4. *She goes to the mosque on Wednesday.* ***(Friday)***
5. *They study every day.* ***(don't study)***

> **FYI** Don't worry about a sign for "and" yet. You will learn more about this in Unit 3.

2 *This weekend, I ...* Select appropriate vocabulary to complete each sentence.

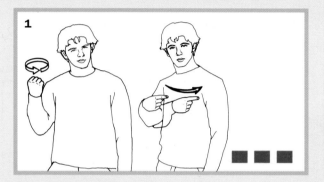

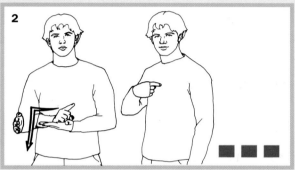

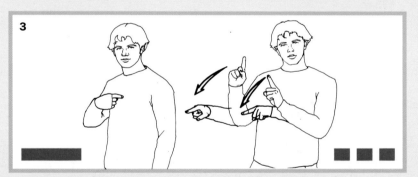

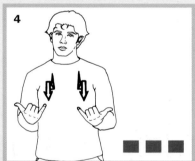

Homework Exercise 4

A Practice signing the date of your next ASL class. Focus on your fingerspelling and numbers, and make sure your signing is smooth.

B Practice signing *My Routine*. Prepare to show your classmates and teacher how well you can sign the narrative.

C Write Classroom Exercise O, Part 2, in ASL gloss.

ASL Up Close

The WH-Signs

All languages have a set of words called **WH-Words** frequently used in conversation. The WH-Words in American Sign Language serve this same conversational purpose, but also have a unique emphasis in the language that isn't found in English. You will learn how to use the **WH-Signs** in more depth in Unit 3. Pair the WH-Face with each of the WH-Signs.

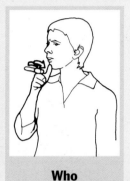

Who

What

Variations

Who

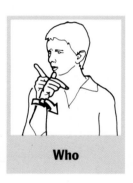

Who

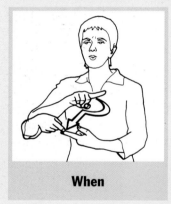

When

Where

Why

Why

Why, because

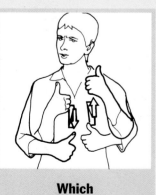

Which

Eyes on ASL #6

WH-Signs go at the end of ASL sentences and must include the WH-Face (see Page 42).

Unlike English sentences, WH-Signs don't occur at the beginning of a sentence. *Who* may occur at the beginning, as long as it also occurs at the end.

Classroom Exercise

1 *What or who is it?* Ask a partner about the illustration in complete sentences. An example is provided. Remember to use ASL Rule #6 correctly.

2 *Using WH-Signs* Ask a partner to respond to the question you ask. Make sure you use the WH-Face. Switch roles and repeat the exercise when done.

Classroom Exercise

1 *Responding to WH-Questions.*
   A partner will ask you each
   a question. Respond in a
   complete sentence. When
   done, switch roles and repeat.

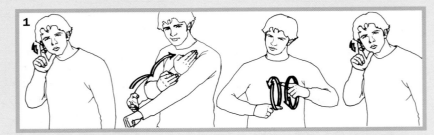

Vocabulary Making More Conversation

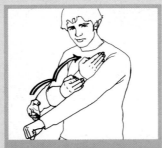 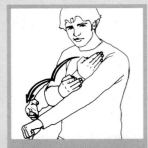 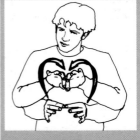 

| To get better | To get worse | Important | Water, water fountain |

Classroom Exercise R

1 *Making conversation.* Your teacher will ask the following questions in ASL. Respond in a complete sentence using the information in parentheses.

1. *Where are you going?* (**home**)
2. *What are their names?* (**?** , **?**)
3. *Do you want the door open or closed?* (**open**)
4. *Why is practice important?* (**I want to get better**)
5. *You play sports every day?* (**No, Tuesday, Thursday**)

6. *What's on the test?* (**I don't know**)
7. *Ask him what's on the test.* (**He knows**)
8. *What's your ASL teacher's name?* (**?**)
9. *When do you work?* (**Monday**)
10. *What are you doing tomorrow?* (**Nothing**)

2 *Asking questions.* Work with a partner to ask and answer five WH-Sign questions. When done, create a dialogue using the questions.

> Don't worry about the signs for *or* and *on*. You will learn about them in Unit 3.

Classroom Exercise S

1 *Comprehension.* Watch Marc's narrative titled *My Advice* on your Student DVD. Respond to the questions below.

1. *What does Marc say about practice?*
2. *What happens if you don't practice your ASL?*
3. *What suggestion does Marc give about practicing?*

4. *What should you not do in a restaurant?*
5. *Give an example of three signs that used a non-manual signal.*
6. *What question does Marc ask?*

2 *My Advice* Practice signing Marc's narrative. Focus on clarity instead of speed, and include non-manual signals when necessary.

Homework Exercise 5

A What are your weekend plans? Prepare to explain what you will do this weekend in at least 3 – 5 complete ASL sentences.

B Practice signing five WH-Sign questions smoothly and clearly. Write the sentences in English, and write an explanation of how the sentences would be signed in ASL.

C Practice the *My Advice* narrative. What are your weak areas? What are your strong points?

D Write assignments A or B in ASL gloss.

Journal Activities

1. All cultures appreciate various forms of art. One famous Deaf artist is Ann Silver, well-known for her mixed media installations featuring the Deaf experience and aspects of Deaf culture. In *A Century of Difference*, Silver charts the evolution of labels applied to the Deaf since 1900. What perspectives do these labels imply? Why do you think Silver chose to work with license plates? What do you think this means? What point does Silver make in *A Century of Difference*?

— *A Century of Difference (2002),* Ann Silver.
Reproduced by permission of artist

2. Most, if not all, minority groups in the United States have experienced a series of identifying labels that have changed over the years, similar to the evolution from *deaf and dumb* to *Deaf*. Using Ann Silver's *A Century of Difference* as a model, create a series of license plates that illustrate another community's experience with evolving labels. What do members of that community prefer to be called now? How has this group's identity and labels changed over the years?

3. Are deaf people disabled, handicapped, both, or neither? Use a dictionary to help you understand the differences between each term. In what ways do you think the terms might apply? In what ways might they not? What would you prefer to be called? What do you think Deaf people prefer to be called?

Unit 2 Review

A   What effects do Eyes on ASL #5 and #6 have on sentence structure in ASL? With that in mind, how does ASL differ from English sentence structure? In your own words, rewrite these two Eyes on ASL to help another ASL student understand how to use each, giving examples to support your explanation.

B   What is an iconic sign? Of the signs below, which are iconic, and what do they mean? How do you know?

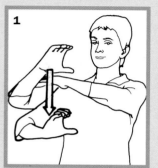
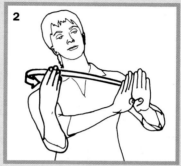
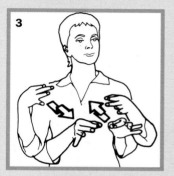

C   Identify and correct the errors in the following sentences. Explain to a partner or friend why the errors are wrong and how to fix them.

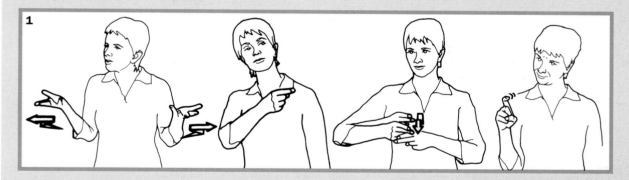

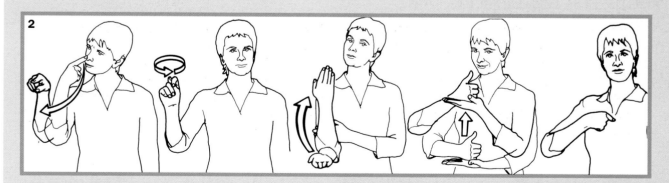

Unit 2 Review

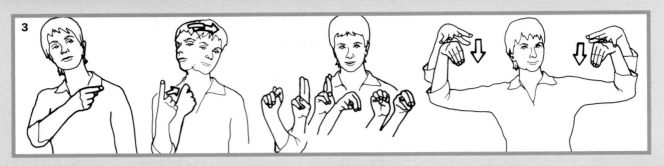

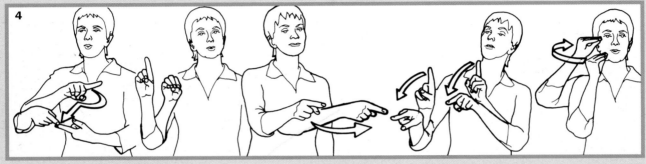

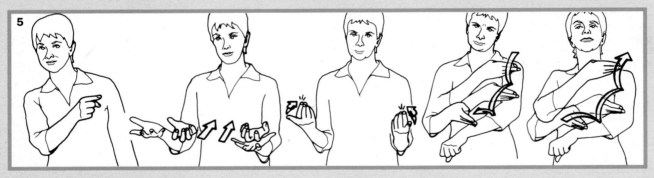

D Do you recognize, understand, and use each of the following ASL principles?

- Directionality (*help, ask*)
- WH-Face (to show uncertainty; also for WH-Signs)
- Closing signals and WH-Signs
- *When* signs in sentences
- Question-Maker and Question Mark
- Non-manual signals
- Eye gaze

E Can you:

- Ask for help and clarification?
- Use the WH-Face and Question-Maker correctly?
- Use *when* signs in the correct order?
- Use WH-Signs in a conversation?
- Sign short paragraphs clearly?
- Understand a signed paragraph?

Getting to Know You

Unit Three Objectives

- To expand ASL skills and topics of conversation
- To understand topic-comment structure
- To incorporate numbers into conversation
- To understand how ASL name signs are made
- To use possessive signs and deixis appropriately
- To talk about favorites

Unit Three Vocabulary

to	Act, show	.94
	Actor	.94
	Address	.99
	America	.78
	April	.104
	At (symbol)	.96
	Atlanta	.82
	August	.104
	Avenue	.99
	Beach	.77
	Birthday (1-3)	.103
	Black	.93
	Blue	.93
to be	Born in	.75
	Boston	.82
	Boulevard	.99
	Brown	.93
	Canada	.78
	Car, to drive	.94
to	Celebrate	.105
	Chicago	.82
	Christmas	.106
	City, town	.82
to be	Close to, near	.83
to be	Cloudy	.110
to be	Cold	.110
	Color	.93
to	Comment	.89
to be	Cool	.110
	Court	.99
	Dark	.94
	December	.104
	Denver	.81
	Depends	.105
	Dot, period	.96
	Easter	.106
	Eid	.106
	Email	.96
	Fall	.105
to be	Far	.83
	February	.104
to be	From	.75
	Gray	.93
	Green	.93
to	Grow up	.75
	Halloween	.106
	Hanukkah	.106
	Here	.75
	His, hers, its	.92

to be	Hot	.110
	Houston	.82
	How many	.105
	Independence Day	.106
	Inside	.109
	Internet	.96
	January	.104
	July	.104
	June	.104
	Kwanzaa	.106
	Labor Day	.106
	Light	.94
to	Listen	.96
to	Live in	.75
	Los Angeles	.82
	March	.104
	Martin Luther King, Jr. Day	.106
	May	.104
	Memorial Day	.106
	Mexico	.78
	Mickey Mouse	.84
	Month	.105
	Music	.96
	Musician	.94
	My, mine	.92
	New Orleans	.82
	New Year's	.106
	New York	.79
	New	.100
	November	.104
	Number	.99
	Ocean	.77
	October	.104
to be	Old	.100
	Orange	.93
	Ours	.92
	Outside	.109
	Page	.96
	Pager	.100
	Passover	.106
	Philadelphia	.82
	Pink	.93
	Purple	.93
to	Rain	.110
	Ramadan	.106
	Red	.93
	Road	.99
to	Rollerblade	.77

	Salt Lake City	.82
	San Francisco	.82
	Season	.105
	Seattle	.82
	September	.104
to	Ski	.77
to	Snow	.110
	Spring	.105
	St. Patrick's Day	.106
	Street (general)	.99
	Street (specific)	.99
	Summer	.105
to be	Sunny	.110
	Telephone	.99
	Television	.94
	Thanksgiving	.106
	That way	.83
	Their, theirs	.92
	Topic	.89
	TTY	.100
	United States	.78
	Valentine's Day	.106
	Vacation	.73
	Veteran's Day	.106
	Videophone	.100
to	Visit	.77
to be	Warm	.110
	Washington, D.C.	.82
to	Watch	.94
	Waves	.110
	Weather (1-2)	.109
	Web page	.96
	White	.93
to be	Windy	.110
	Winter	.105
	Year	.105
	Yellow	.93
	Your, yours	.92
	Yours (plural)	.92
	50 states & provinces of Canada	.78–79

Key Phrases

Love-it	.94
Oh-I-see	.76

Where are you from?

Hi, I'm Kelly, from New York. Where are you from? On my vacations I love to travel and visit friends and family. My favorite vacation spot is Hawaii because of the beautiful weather, the ocean, and the beaches. There's a lot to do over there! What do you do for fun? I hope we can talk some more. Bye!

DVD

Where are you from? Watch Kelly sign in full motion on your student DVD.

Vocabulary — Where are you from?

Other new vocabulary seen in the narrative is presented throughout Unit 3.

 **A lot of**	**To be beautiful, pretty (Unit 4)**	 **To do, action, activity**	 **During, on, in (Unit 6)**
 **Family (Unit 4)**	 **Fun (Unit 8)**	 **You and me, we (Unit 4)**	 **Vacation**

Where Do You Live?

As you socialize with Deaf people, you will be asked questions about your background, especially if you are hearing and new to most people. Deaf individuals will want to know where you are from, why you are learning ASL, and whether you have other Deaf friends or family. Your company will be more valued if you make the effort to ask questions in ASL as well as responding to those asked of you.

Where are you from? Watch Sean and Kelly talk about their backgrounds on your student DVD.

Dialogue Translation

Sean: *Hi! Where are you from?*

Kelly: *I was born in Ohio. Now I live in Utah. What about you?*

Sean: *I was born and grew up in Maine.*

Kelly: *Oh, I see. I want to go there!*

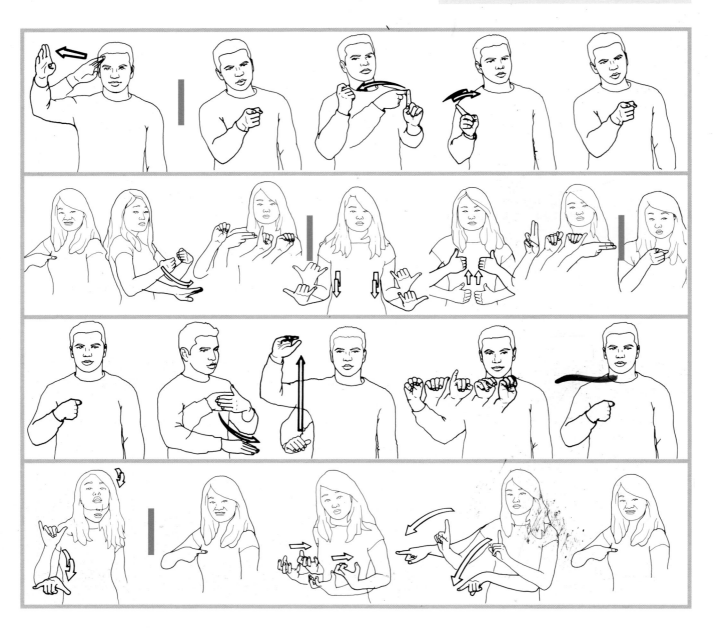

Classroom Exercise

1 *Where are you from?* Ask a partner these questions about his or her background using the example as a model. When done, switch roles and repeat the exercise.

1. *Where were you born?*
2. *Where do you live?*
3. *Where did you grow up?*
4. *Where are you from?*

FYI Don't worry about the past tense. Just use the vocabulary you know. You'll learn how the past tense works in Unit 6.

Where were you born?

I was born in Houston, Texas

2 *Comprehension.* Watch *Where are you from?* on your student DVD and answer the questions below in complete ASL sentences.

1. *Where is Kelly from?*
2. *Where did Sean grow up?*
3. *Who is from Ohio?*
4. *Where was Kelly born?*
5. *Does Kelly live in Utah?*
6. *Does Sean want to go to Maine?*

3 *Dialogue.* Create a dialogue with a partner about a Deaf and a hearing person meeting for the first time. What will they talk about?

Vocabulary — Background Signs

To be born in	**To be from**	**To grow up**	**Here**	**To live in**

Classroom Exercise B

1. *Interviews.* Work in groups and find out background information about each member. Use *oh-I-see* to show you understand what is being signed. You will share the information learned with the rest of the class.

2. *Sharing information.* Use the clues provided to introduce each person. Refer to the map on page 78 for the signs of states, provinces, and countries.

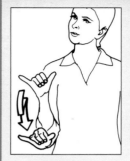

EXPRESSION CORNER

Oh-I-see is an ASL expression that conveys comprehension, sympathy, and concern, similar to sounds like *huh, hmm, oh, aha,* and *I see.* It is often used in conversation.

Oh-I-See

1
Name: Rachel
Born: Massachusetts
Moved to New Hampshire
Goes to school in New Hampshire

2
Name: Dan
Born: Georgia
Grew up: Mississippi
Wants to live in Florida
Likes to water ski

3
Name: Jeff
Born: Canada
Works in: Quebec
Is hearing
Wants to live in: Hawaii

4
Name: Emilee
Born: Oklahoma
Is Deaf
Enjoys playing sports
Wants to visit Alaska

5
Name: Ryan
Born: Texas
Grew up: Texas
Is learning ASL
Likes going to the beach

6
Name: Aundrea
Born: California
Works on the weekends
Knows ASL
Likes to ski, go to the ocean

7
Name: Sam
Lives in: Washington
Grew up: Montana
Is Deaf
Likes to rollerblade

8
Name: Gary
Born: New Jersey
Grew up: New York
Doesn't like sports
Can't ski

Classroom Exercise C

1 *Non-manual signals.* Sign each sentence in ASL, using either the Question-Maker or WH-Face as needed.

1. *Is he from New York?*   **3.** *Who lives in Texas?*   **5.** *Can we go to the beach on*
2. *Where were you born?*   **4.** *Where do you want to go?*   *Saturday?*

2 *Conversation.* You and a Deaf friend are chatting at a party. Sign the first sentence to a partner, who will respond using *oh-I-see* and the given information. When done, switch roles and repeat.

1

I don't like to ski. I like to rollerblade.

2

I want to visit Hawaii. I was born and grew up in Oklahoma. Where does he/she live?

3

Do you want to rollerblade Friday afternoon? Where?

Vocabulary   Interests

| **Beach** | **Ocean** | **To rollerblade** | **To ski** | **To visit** |

Vocabulary · States & Provinces

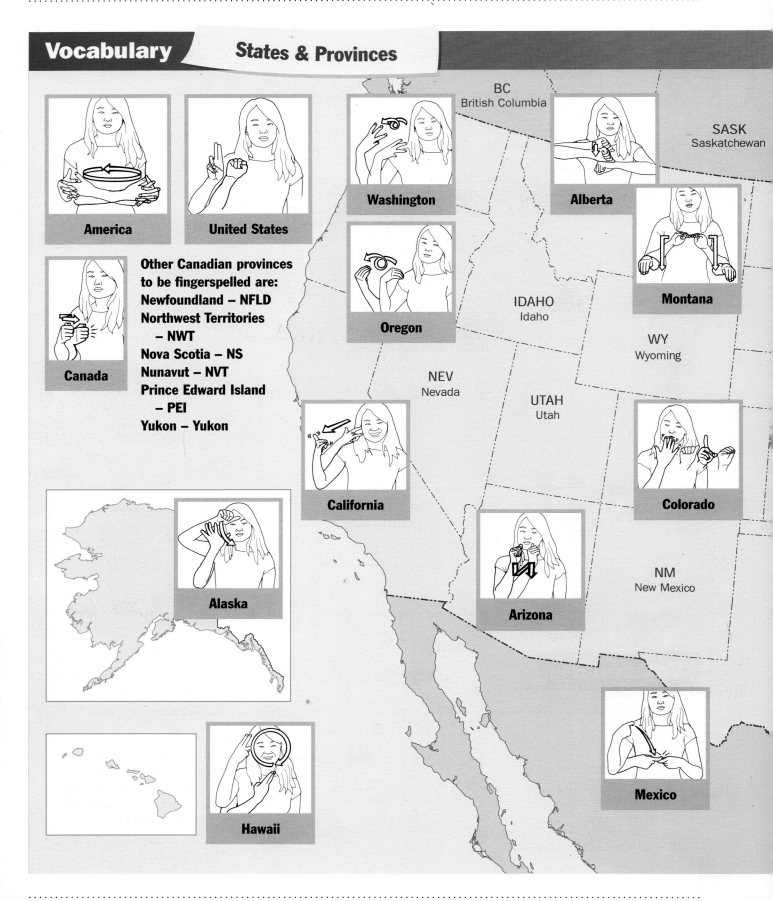

America

United States

Canada

Other Canadian provinces
to be fingerspelled are:
Newfoundland – NFLD
**Northwest Territories
  – NWT**
Nova Scotia – NS
Nunavut – NVT
**Prince Edward Island
  – PEI**
Yukon – Yukon

Washington

Oregon

California

Alaska

Hawaii

BC
British Columbia

SASK
Saskatchewan

Alberta

Montana

IDAHO
Idaho

WY
Wyoming

NEV
Nevada

UTAH
Utah

Colorado

NM
New Mexico

Arizona

Mexico

Manitoba

Ontario

Quebec

NB
New Brunswick

Maine
Maine

NH
New Hampshire

VT
Vermont

New York

MASS
Massachusetts

RI
Rhode Island

CONN
Connecticut

NJ
New Jersey

DEL
Delaware

MD
Maryland

WASHINGTON+DC

West Virginia

ND
North Dakota

MINN
Minnesota

SD
South Dakota

WISC
Wisconsin

NEB
Nebraska

IOWA
Iowa

MICH
Michigan

PA
Pennsylvania

KAN
Kansas

MO
Missouri

ILL
Illinois

IND
Indiana

OHIO
Ohio

KY
Kentucky

VA
Virginia

NC
North Carolina

OKLA
Oklahoma

ARK
Arkansas

TENN
Tennessee

SC
South Carolina

MISS
Mississippi

ALA
Alabama

GA
Georgia

LA
Louisiana

Texas

FLA
Florida

Accent Steps

Most states and provinces are fingerspelled. Fingerspell the state or province name the way it is shown in capital letters on the map. Practice fingerspelling the name of your state/province quickly!

Classroom Exercise D

1 *Dialogue.* Work with a partner to translate each sentence into ASL. When done, practice signing the dialogues.

A

Student A. *I was born in Alaska.*
Student B. *Oh yeah? I'm from Texas.*
Student A. *Do you like Texas?*
Student B. *Yes, I do.*
Student A. *I see. I want to visit Texas.*

B

Student A. *I moved here from Florida.*
Student B. *Why did you move here?*
Student A. *I want to go to school here.*
Student B. *Oh, I see. Do you like it here?*
Student A. *Yes, I do!*

2 *Where?* Based on the illustration, where would you see or do each activity? Respond in complete ASL sentences, following the example.

Homework Exercise 1

A Where do you live? Does your state or province have a sign or is it fingerspelled? Practice fingerspelling or signing the names of three or four states or provinces located near you.

B Sign a presentation about yourself to your classmates. Include background information, places you've lived and would like to visit, as well as places you don't want to visit. Using the vocabulary you've learned so far, sign as much information as you can about yourself. Practice and make sure your signing is confident and smooth.

C Write assignment A or B in ASL gloss.

Names of Cities & Towns

You learned that some place names are fingerspelled while others have signs. Some names of cities have signs, but the majority are fingerspelled or abbreviated. Generally, city name signs are recognized across the country if a large Deaf community is located there. As an ASL student, rely on your local Deaf community and your ASL teacher to show you the signs for towns and cities around you.

FYI A city's name sign is usually known everywhere if it hosts a major-league sports franchise like the NBA or NFL.

Dialogue Translation

Kelly: *I'm from Fremont. It's signed like this.*

Marc: *Oh, I see. Where is Fremont?*

Kelly: *It's in California, near San Francisco.*

DVD *Where is that?* Watch Kelly and Marc sign on your Student DVD.

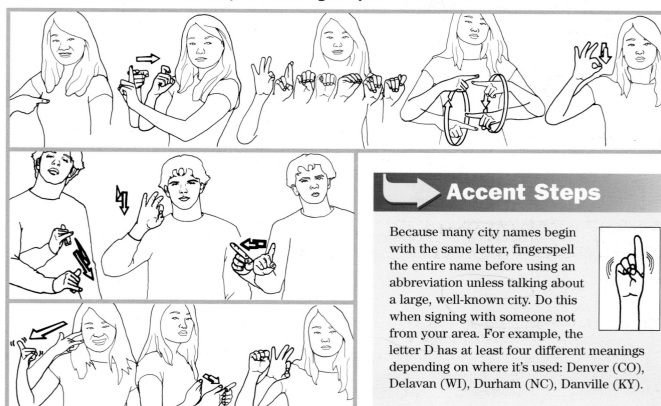

Accent Steps

Because many city names begin with the same letter, fingerspell the entire name before using an abbreviation unless talking about a large, well-known city. Do this when signing with someone not from your area. For example, the letter D has at least four different meanings depending on where it's used: Denver (CO), Delavan (WI), Durham (NC), Danville (KY).

Classroom Exercise

1 *How far away is that?* Sign the name of your hometown and state in a complete sentence. Explain whether the following cities are near or far from you.

1. *Seattle, Washington*
2. *New York City, New York*
3. *Atlanta, Georgia*
4. *Los Angeles, California*

5. *Chicago, Illinois*
6. *Phoenix, Arizona*
7. *Miami, Florida*
8. *Sioux Falls, South Dakota*

9. *Honolulu, Hawaii*
10. *Denver, Colorado*

2 *Where is . . .?* Ask a partner where a city is located. Your partner will respond and use *that way* to point towards the location. Switch roles and repeat the exercise when done. An example is provided.

Where is Miami?

It's in Florida.

City

1. *Houston*
2. *Philadelphia*
3. *Chicago*
4. *San Francisco*
5. *Denver*
6. *Boston*

Possible Locations

Utah
District of Columbia
Colorado
Louisiana
California

Pennsylvania
Massachusetts
New York
Illinois
Texas

FYI Use the sign *New York* for both the city and state.

Vocabulary — Well-Known City Signs

Atlanta

Boston

Chicago

City, town

Houston

Los Angeles

New Orleans

Philadelphia

Salt Lake City

San Francisco

Seattle

Washington, DC

Vocabulary — Distance

To be close to, near

To be far

Accent Steps

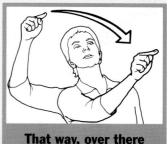

That way is related to deixis. It is used to provide the general direction of an object or location. Emphasize distance by opening your eyes wide while pointing or using the sign *far*.

That way, over there

Classroom Exercise F

1. *Geography.* Ask if your partner lives far from or close to a location below. Your partner will respond in a complete sentence. Switch roles and repeat the exercise when done.

Do you live near New York City?

  1. *Los Angeles*   **2.** *Washington, D.C.*   **3.** *Canada*   **4.** *Mexico*   **5.** *Alaska*   **6.** *?*

2. *Conversation.* Ask your partner the following questions in ASL. Your partner will respond according to the information in bold. Switch roles and repeat.

  1. *Where do you live?* (?)

  2. *Are you from Illinois?* (**No, I'm from ?.**)

  3. *Where do you want to live?* (?)

  4. *Is your city named San Diego?* (**No, I live in ?.**)

  5. *Did you move here?* (**Yes, I moved here from ?.**)

  6. *Do you like living here* (?)

Did you know?

Wave your hands in the air instead of clapping them!

Deaf Culture NOTE

Name Signs

Do you have a **name sign** or know someone who does? A frequent question is "What's the sign for my name?" Name signs are highly valued in Deaf culture. Having one shows you are accepted by the Deaf community because you made the effort to learn Deaf culture and ASL. You may be given a name sign after you've made Deaf friends. There is no sign-for-name match, so two people with the same name will often have different name signs. This is because ASL name signs are a combination of the person's name (usually the first initial) and a location on the head, torso, or hands where the sign will be made. This type of name sign is called **arbitrary**. Some people with short or easily fingerspelled names will spell their name signs. Another type is a **descriptive** name sign, which shows a physical or behavioral trait the individual is known for. The sign for Mickey Mouse is seen below and is a descriptive name sign. It is impolite for a hearing ASL student to create a name sign instead of having one given by a Deaf person. You'll need to socialize with Deaf people if you want a name sign.

Examples of name signs.

Which are descriptive and arbitrary?

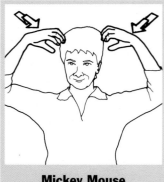   

Mickey Mouse   **"Buck teeth"**   **Any name that begins with "S"**   **Any name that begins with "D"**

Classroom Exercise G

Hometown. Ask a partner each question. When done, switch roles and repeat the exercise.

Classroom Exercise

1 *Using yes & no.* Ask a partner if he or she lives near the location you've chosen. Your partner will respond using *yes* or *no*, following the example.

Do you live near the beach?

Yes, I do. I live in Florida. The beach isn't far away.

1   2   3   4   5   6

2 *Where we live.* Create a dialogue with a partner that includes the information to the right. Do not limit your dialogue to the questions but use your creativity as well.

1. _____ *lives in a state near the ocean.*
2. _____ *lives in a state far from the ocean.*
3. _____ *moved to* _____ *from* _____.
4. _____ *wants to live in* _____ *because* _____.
5. _____ *doesn't want to live in* _____ *because* _____.

Homework Exercise ◄ 2

A Interview a friend of yours and practice signing where he or she was born, is from, and now lives. Did he or she move here? From where? Sign your introduction in complete sentences.

B Use the web to research interesting places across the United States and Canada, selecting at least five you would like to visit. Prepare to explain the selections to your classmates, including the name of the place, its location (city, state/province, country), and a reason why you want to visit.

C Write assignment A or B in ASL gloss.

Deaf Culture Minute

Most Deaf adults live in larger cities across the United States. Jobs, social opportunities, Deaf-interest agencies, schools for the Deaf, and interpreters are more plentiful in metropolitan areas than in isolated rural areas. The metro region of Rochester in New York state features the world's highest per capita population of Deaf people. Are there many Deaf people in your area? Why or why not?

Focus: Is sign language

> **" Where there are deaf people, there is sign language. "** — *George Veditz, 1913*

George Veditz's statement about sign language is as true now in the 21st century as it was in 1913. Many different sign languages are used by millions of Deaf people around the world. There is no universal sign language used by the deaf. When deaf people who use different sign languages come together, communication barriers rarely exist after an initial adjustment period. At large international gatherings of deaf people, such as the World Congress of the Deaf, an artificial means of communication called **Gestuno** is used. Gestuno is not a real language and relies more on basic visual concepts and gestures similar to Esperanto, the spoken hybrid comprised of words from different languages like English, Spanish, and French. While ASL is not a universal sign language, many Deaf people from countries beyond the United States and Canada know and use ASL as a second, third, or even fourth language after coming to the USA for educational purposes. Many return to their native countries after completing their education, bringing ASL with them. Like English, ASL is becoming an international language, but it is far from being universal.

Courtesy: Simon Carmel, International Hand Alphabet charts.

universal?

Compare the French and British Sign Language alphabets. Which alphabet looks familiar? Surprised? You may be surprised to learn that ASL and French Sign Language are closely related while ASL and British Sign Language have almost nothing in common!

Chinese Sign Language for *to walk*

French Sign Language for *to walk*

American Sign Language for *to walk*

French Sign Language alphabet

Japanese Sign Language alphabet

Courtesy: Simon Carmel, International Hand Alphabet charts.

ASL Up Close

Topic-Comment Structure

American Sign Language uses one of two different grammatical structures depending on what is being signed. The first structure is called **topic-comment** and is followed when signing with the WH-Signs (see Page 64). In topic-comment languages the signer presents information and then makes the information either a statement or question by adding a comment. English does not use topic-comment structure often so becoming used to ASL grammar can be a challenge. Keep in mind that while using ASL signs in English word order may be easy to do, it is no different than speaking in Spanish but following English word order — you won't make complete sense in either language.

(What? Its Name)

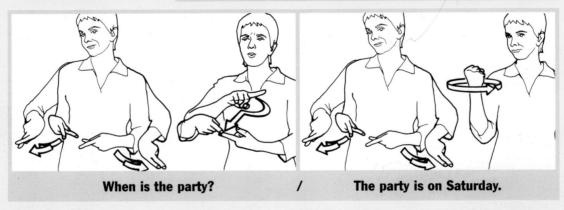

Topic (Its name) **+** Comment (What is it?)

When is the party? / The party is on Saturday.

The second basic structure of American Sign Language is used when WH-Signs are not needed, and follows a **subject-verb-object** (SVO) structure. This format is more familiar to English speakers. However, *why* often acts as a "bridge" or "connector" between two separate SVO phrases. When using *why* this way, raise your eyebrows.

I am not going to school because I'm sick.

Vocabulary / Topic & Comment

To comment

Topic, title

Accent Steps

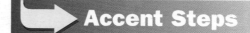

Raise your eyebrows to make the Question-Maker face when using *why* to connect two parts of a sentence.

Classroom Exercise I

1 *Topic-comment.* Select vocabulary from Column A and Column B to make a complete sentence following topic-comment structure.

Column A						Column B	
learn	study	party	ASL	weekend	today	*who*	*where*
test	busy	school	name	tomorrow	don't know	*what*	*why*
ski	do-do	test	from	yesterday	don't want	*when*	*do-do*

2 *Bridges.* Use the *why* sign to connect each sentence together.

1. *She can't go to the party* / **She works.**
2. *He doesn't want a test* / **He didn't study.**
3. *We are very scared* / **Signing is not easy.**
4. *Yesterday I was tired* / **I studied.**
5. *They are going to school* / **They are learning ASL.**
6. *Today I'm happy* / **Tomorrow I'm going to the beach.**

Classroom Exercise J

Eyebrows and mouth. Practice each facial expression, paying attention to the eyebrows and mouth.

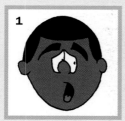

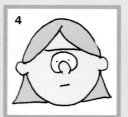

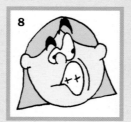

Classroom Exercise

What's missing? Sign each sentence by filling in the blank with a WH-Sign. Choose from *who*, *what*, *when*, *where*, *which*, and *why*.

1

2

3

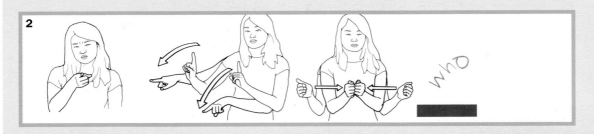

4

5

Classroom Exercise L

1   *The topic is what?* Review Classroom Exercise K and indicate the topic and comment of each sentence.

    1. *Topic:*
       Comment:
    2. *Topic:*
       Comment:
    3. *Topic:*
       Comment:

    4. *Topic:*
       Comment:
    5. *Topic:*
       Comment:
    6. *Topic:*
       Comment:

2   *Word order translation.* Change each of the following sentences into topic-comment structure.

    1. *I'm happy.*
    2. *Please open the door.*
    3. *Who's Deaf?*
    4. *Where's the water fountain?*
    5. *Is the party on Saturday?*
    6. *Who walks home every day?*

    7. *I'm not confused.*
    8. *What are you doing Saturday?*
    9. *Where's my paper?*
    10. *I sleep on the weekends.*
    11. *Is the restaurant over there?*
    12. *Do you mind handing out the papers?*

3   *Sentence creation.* First identify each phrase as a topic or comment, and then create a complete sentence using the phrase.

Homework Exercise 3

A   What English words or phrases describe the facial expressions in Classroom Exercise J? On a sheet of paper, make a list of possible words and explain why each fits the expressions.

B   Write five sentences in ASL gloss format on a sheet of paper to be turned in. Use vocabulary from Units 1 – 3 and make sure each sentence has a topic and a comment.

C   You've been asked to help a friend of yours this coming weekend, but you're unable to help due to several reasons. Practice signing why you can't help, using topic-comment structure and the WH-Signs. Refer to at least five different reasons.

D   Write assignment A, B, or C in ASL gloss.

ASL Up Close

Possessive Signs

Signs for *mine, your, his, hers, theirs,* and *ours* are called **possessives**. Use possessive signs to ask and answer questions, clarify statements, and develop conversations on a variety of topics. Possessive signs follow the same rules as deixis to point towards people and things, including eye gaze (see Page 6).

My, mine

Your, yours

His, hers, its

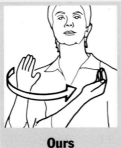

Ours

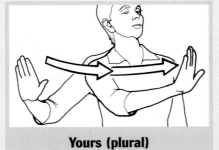

Yours (plural)

Theirs

Example

What's your email address?

Classroom Exercise M

Whose is it? Practice the possessive signs by signing each sentence.

1. *It's my book.*
2. *Our teacher is Deaf.*
3. *No, it's not his. It's hers.*
4. *Your (plural) homework is due today.*
5. *My email isn't working.*
6. *Her teacher is hearing.*
7. *Is this your DVD?*
8. *Her friend is named Glen.*
9. *It's not mine. It's yours.*
10. *?*

Accent Steps

Don't use possessive signs with names. Using them instead of deixis results in ungrammatical sentences like *Mine name Joe* or *Their name Ann and Tomas.* Remember that deixis conveys the verb *to be,* not possessive signs.

Classroom Exercise

1   *Color palette.* Identify each color.

2   Ask a partner what is his or her favorite color, then share that information with your classmates. Other information to determine:

1. *What is the most popular color?*   **2.** *What is the least popular color?*

Vocabulary   Colors

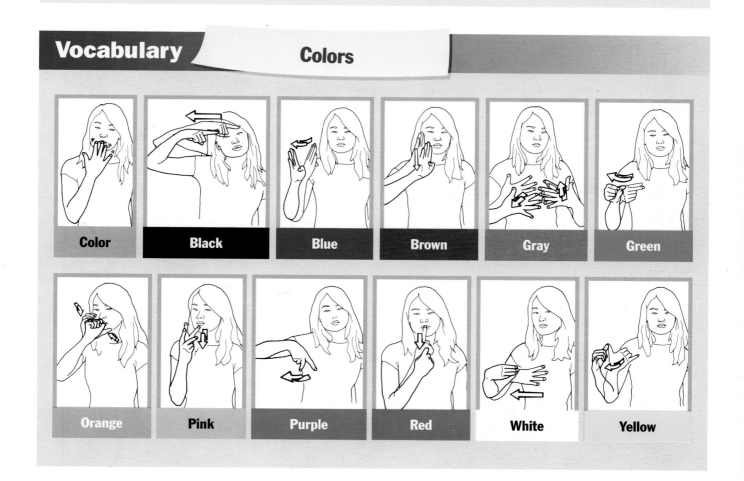

Classroom Exercise

1. *Getting to know you.* Ask a partner the following questions. When done, switch roles and repeat.

1. *I don't like the color bright blue. Do you?*
2. *Who is your favorite singer / musician?*
3. *Who is your favorite actor?*
4. *What color is your car?*
5. *What do you do on the weekends?*

2. *Love-it.* Sign the following sentences and use *love-it* for the bolded terms.

1. *I **like** going to the movies on the weekends.*
2. *I **love** your car!*
3. *They **really like** going to Mexican restaurants.*
4. *She **loved** the movie but I didn't like it.*
5. *What do you **like**?*

Accent Steps

To emphasize the depth or brightness of a color, swing the hand forming the color away from you.

Bright blue

EXPRESSION CORNER

Love-it

Use *love-it* when signing about a non-romantic "love" for things or people. *Love-it* is often used instead of "like a lot" or similar phrases.

Vocabulary   Favorites

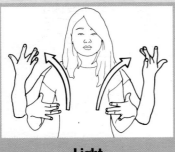

To act, show

Actor

Car, to drive

Dark

Light

Musician, singer

Television

To watch

Classroom Exercise

1   *True or false?* Sign each statement to a partner who will correct the information as shown.

     1. *His favorite color is light blue.* (**No, his favorite color is bright green.**)
     2. *Your last name is Smith.* (**No, my last name is _____.**)
     3. *They aren't listening to music.* (**Yes, they are listening to music.**)
     4. *We're going to the movies on Saturday.* (**No, we're going to a restaurant on Sunday.**)
     5. *They aren't actors.* (**Yes, they are actors.**)

2   *More conversation.* Come up with five different questions to ask your partner. When done, switch roles and repeat the exercise.

I Want to Know . . .

How do I sign "and" and "or"?

Since the word *or* implies a choice, ASL uses *which* to show options.

Does he want a blue or black pen?

The word "and" is used differently in ASL than English. Generally, ASL does not use a specific sign because "and" is implied by a slight pause, head nod, and change of eye gaze.

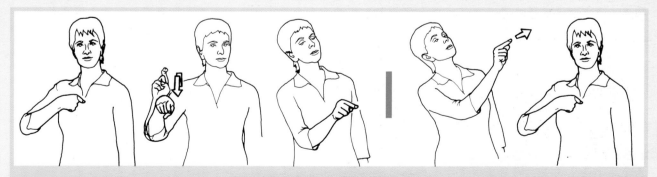

I need this one and that one.

Classroom Exercise

Faces can say a thousand words. Practice each facial expression, focusing on the eyebrows and mouth.

Vocabulary — Email

At (symbol)

Dot, period

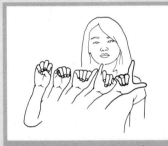

Email, email address

Internet

To listen

Music, to sing

Page

Web page

Accent Steps

To sign *web page* do not sign *www + page*, just sign *www*.

Classroom Exercise

Email & internet addresses. How would you sign each internet address? Follow the example shown below.

My email address is Beach@ave.com

1. *baseballfan@domain.com*
2. *cloud3@ppc.com*
3. *help@vri.org*
4. *http://www.nad.org*
5. *http://www.gallaudet.edu*
6. *traskfamily12@tr.net*
7. *http://www.clerccenter.org*

8. *bluemoon@tuv.edu*
9. *12fan@my2way.com*

 Don't sign the http:// portion of an address.

Homework Exercise 4

A Do you have an email address? Practice signing and fingerspelling your email address using the signs shown in Vocabulary: Email. If you don't have an email address, practice signing the URL of your favorite web site.

B You want to get to know someone better. Develop three questions using the "and/or" concepts. Prepare to ask a partner each question.

C Write assignment A or B in ASL gloss.

Did you know?

One of the pioneers of the internet and World Wide Web, Vinton Cerf, is hard of hearing. A prominent figure in the internet world, he serves on the board of ICANN, the regulating body of the internet. He also serves on the Board of Trustees at Gallaudet University in Washington, D.C. Long interested in communication and technology, his work has had a tremendous impact on people around the world, both Deaf and hearing. The next time you use the internet, remember the work of Vinton Cerf!

To learn more, visit www.icann.org.

Numbers & Questions I

Refer to your Student Companion to practice the ASL number system.
When signing numbers, do not move your hand towards the right or left.

Dialogue Translation

Kelly: *I need your address and telephone number.*

Sean: *My address is 437 Park Blvd., and my telephone number is 555-9226.*

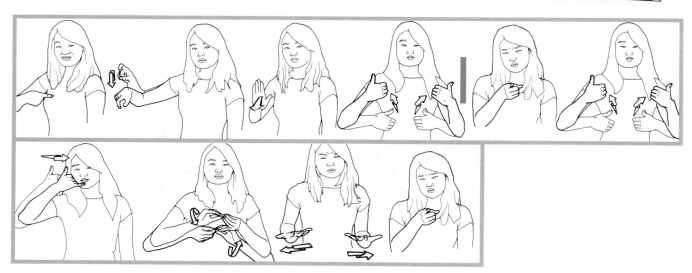

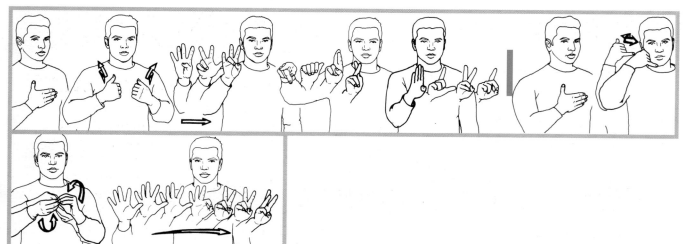

Classroom Exercise

1 *I live on...* How many students live on a:

- *Court / Cul-de-sac*
- *Boulevard*
- *Drive*
- *Road*
- *Circle*
- *Avenue*
- *Street*
- *Lane*
- *Parkway*
- *?*

2 *Addresses.* Sign a complete sentence using the addresses below.

1. *6225 Jarvis Avenue*
2. *34 Brookvale Circle*
3. *576 Lewelling Blvd.*
4. *901 Phoenix Way*
5. *3307 Third Ave. North*
6. *4588 Peralta*
7. *7422 Niles Blvd.*
8. *3000 Evergreen*
9. *39217 Estudillo*
10. *1120 Hollenbeck Lane*
11. *465 Oak Park Blvd.*
12. *100 Tesla Road*

3 *Dialogue.* Work with a partner to develop a dialogue using one or more of the dialogue prompts. Each dialogue should incorporate addresses and telephone numbers. Use fictitious numbers as needed.

1. *where do you work?*
2. *favorite restaurants*
3. *home address / telephone number*
4. *plans to meet at a movie theater*
5. *going to a party*
6. *asking for help*

Eyes on ASL #7

Numbers 1 – 5 always face you except when signing addresses and telephone numbers.

 DVD

When counting in ASL, twist your hand towards you for numbers 1 – 5.

Accent Steps

Don't confuse the signs *to live* and *address*. They are easily mistaken because they look very similar, but the movement of each sign is different.

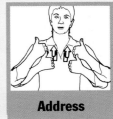

Live   **Address**

Vocabulary — Addresses & Telephones

Address   **Number**   **Street (general)**   **Telephone**

Always Fingerspell

Avenue *(ave)*
Boulevard *(blvd)*
Court *(court, ct)*
Drive *(drive, dr)*
Road *(road, rd)*
Street *(street, st)*

When signing about an unnamed street, route, path or road, use the general *street* sign. If the word "street" is part of the name, such as Street of Dreams, then fingerspell *street*.

Classroom Exercise

1 *What's the number?* Match the name or telephone number to the information fingerspelled by your teacher or partner.

375	**DIRECTORY**	
CAPUTO, Anthony	555-4667	CHANG, Ming Li 555-0215
CAPUTO, Frank	555-9873	CHRISTIE, Robert 555-9807
CARDENA, Rafael	555-8614	CHRISTO, Rolf 555-7546
CARDENAS, Ramon	555-8654	COHEN, Andrea 555-4089
CHANG, Min Li	555-0396	COHN, Andrew 555-2390

FYI Don't forget to pause briefly between the first and last sets of a telephone number. Pause rather than making a dash!

2 *Updating addresses.* A friend of yours is updating information and needs your assistance. In complete sentences explain the information found on each card. Switch roles and repeat when done.

1 Jeff Michaels
29222 Sunrise Avenue
San Diego, California
(619) 555-2000
Email SurfsUp@2sd.com

2 Lori Brace
181 Lamp Road
Calgary, Alberta
Canada

3 Olivia ??
Seattle, Washington
(206) 555-3444 old
(206) 555-5040 new
work (206) 555-9239

4 Dan Olman
7 Pine Blvd
Madison, Wisc. old
new 16 Front Ave.
Atlanta, GA

5 Kelly Trask
3877 Pierce Avenue
New York City
(212) 555-8322 videophone
Pager KellyT

6 Marti Housen
44 Caswell Blvd.
Louisville, Kentucky
Pager M400@kentucky.com
(502) 555-3876 TTY

Vocabulary — Addresses & Telephones

New

To be old

Pager

Video phone

Fingerspell: *TTY*

Classroom Exercise

Using addresses. Use the illustration below to help you answer the following questions in complete ASL sentences.

1. *Where is the Mexican restaurant?*
2. *What is Scott's address?*
3. *Who does Scott live near?*
4. *On what street is the school?*
5. *Where's the party?*
6. *Does Lisa live close to or far from school?*
7. *Is Paul's home close to the restaurant?*
8. *What's near the school?*
9. *Who does Marti live near?*
10. *What is Marti's address?*

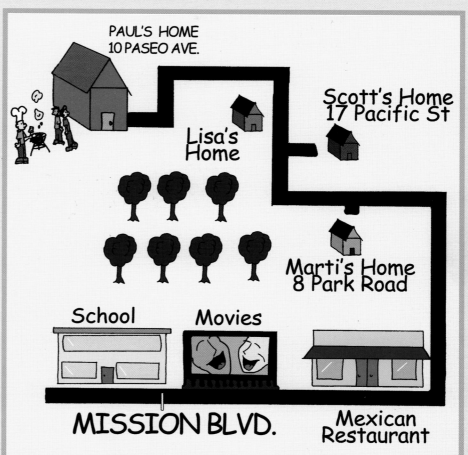

Did you know?

While you use a telephone to reach friends and family, a Deaf person uses a videophone! Videophones allow two Deaf people to converse in ASL as naturally as having a conversation in person. Just like there are different types of telephones to choose from, Deaf people select the videophone that has the features they want. In addition to the videophone, users need a monitor and high-speed internet connection to make calls. Deaf people can call hearing friends by using the videophone to connect to an interpreter who voices what the Deaf caller signs, and signing what the hearing person speaks. Not all Deaf people have videophones. Some prefer to use a TTY, a device similar to a keyboard. A caller types messages into the TTY and the person on the other end reads the message on a built-in screen. Which way of making calls would you prefer?

Courtesy Sorenson Communications

Classroom Exercise

Conversation. Ask a classmate each of the following questions, who will respond in a complete sentence.

Homework Exercise 5

A   Use your local telephone book to find relay service numbers. Does your state use a 1-800 number? 711? Do you have Spanish - English relay options? Write down a list of relay numbers you find.

B   Create a fictitious individual's contact information, including a home address, a minimum of two telephone numbers, and pager and email address. Prepare to sign the information in ASL using pauses, eye gaze, correct number format, and ASL structure in a smooth presentation.

C   Write assignment B in ASL gloss.

Numbers & Questions II

See your Student Companion for more practice with ASL numbers.

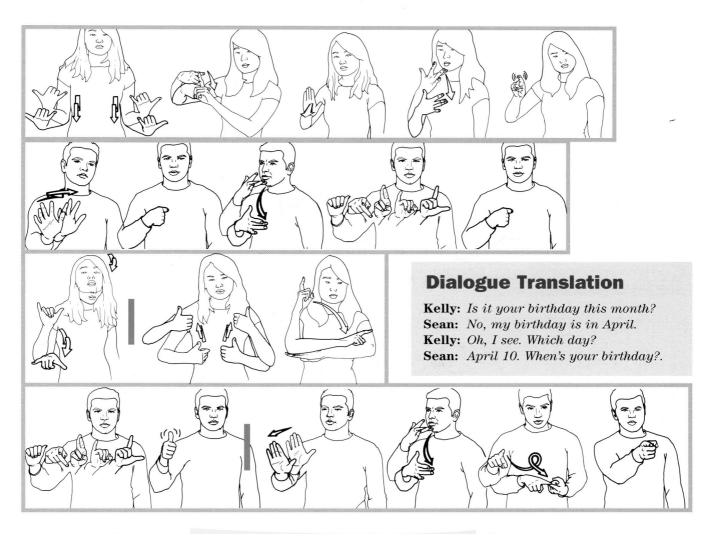

Dialogue Translation

Kelly: *Is it your birthday this month?*
Sean: *No, my birthday is in April.*
Kelly: *Oh, I see. Which day?*
Sean: *April 10. When's your birthday?.*

Vocabulary — Birthday Variations

Remember to use the sign variation preferred by your local Deaf Community.

Birthday (1)

Birthday (2)

Birthday (3)

Classroom Exercise

1 *Birthdays.* Do you share your birth date with anybody else in your ASL class? Find out who:

1. Was born in January
2. Was born in August
3. Was born in November
4. Was born in April
5. Was born in June
6. Whose birthday is this month

2 *Dates.* Develop speed and accuracy switching between fingerspelling and numbers. For additional practice, repeat the exercise by alternating each date with a partner.

1. May 10
2. April 3
3. July 22
4. December 7
5. September 25
6. February 9
7. October 31
8. June 15
9. August 29
10. March 2
11. November 8
12. January 23
13. April 13
14. September 17
15. May 19
16. March 2
17. August 18
18. December 5
19. June 27
20. July 4

Vocabulary — Months of the Year

The months of the year are fingerspelled using their abbreviation or the full word for the month.

Jan

Nov

The months using abbreviations are:
January — Jan
February — Feb
August — Aug
September — Sept
October — Oct
November — Nov
December — Dec

July

April

The months that are fingerspelled are:
March
April
May
June
July

Classroom Exercise

1   *The seasons.* Ask a partner to provide the correct season that corresponds to each month, as seen in the example.

1. November	**4.** December	**7.** March	**10.** April
2. May	**5.** February	**8.** August	**11.** July
3. January	**6.** June	**9.** October	**12.** September

2   *Conversation.* Ask a classmate each question. Use topic-comment structure as needed. Switch roles and repeat.

1. How many months are there in a year?
2. Which season is your favorite?
3. Which months are in the spring season?
4. What are your three favorite months?

5. Which season and month is your birthday in?
6. What season are we in now?
7. Which months are in the winter season?
8. Which months do you go to school?

Vocabulary   Seasons

To celebrate	Depends	Fall	How many	Month

Season	Spring	Summer	Winter	Year

Vocabulary — Major Holidays

Fingerspelled holidays include:

Eid
Labor + *Day*
Martin Luther King, Jr. Day
  (MLK + *Day*)
Ramadan
Veterans + *Day*

Christmas

Easter

Halloween

Hanukkah

Independence Day

Kwanzaa

Memorial Day

New Year's

Passover

St. Patrick's Day

Thanksgiving

Valentine's Day

Classroom Exercise Y

1 *Holidays.* When is each holiday celebrated? Sign *depends* for those holidays not occurring on fixed dates. Raise your eyebrows during the *when* sign. An example is provided.

1. *Kwanzaa* **(December)**
2. *Easter* **(depends)**
3. *Ramadan* **(depends)**
4. *Valentine's Day* **(February)**
5. *New Year's* **(January)**

6. *Hanukkah* **(depends)**
7. *Independence Day* **(July)**
8. *St. Patrick's Day* **(March)**
9. *Martin Luther King, Jr.* **(January)**

10. *Christmas* **(December)**
11. *Passover* **(depends)**
12. *Memorial Day* **(May)**

2 *Dialogue.* Work with a partner to develop a dialogue using one or more of the prompts:

1. *favorite holiday*
2. *least favorite holiday*
3. *seasonal activities*

4. *birthday plans / dates*
5. *meaning of particular holidays*
6. *who celebrates which holidays?*

3 *Holidays and activities.* State when each activity takes place, based on the illustration.

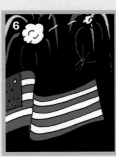

Homework Exercise 6

A   Explain in ASL a specific activity you do during each of the four seasons. What do you enjoy doing in winter, spring, summer, and fall? Practice your presentation.

B   Practice signing today's full date. Refer to your Student Companion for practice exercises. Can you sign the following dates quickly and clearly?

1. *November 7, 1984*   3. *August 15, 1659*   5. *September 23, 1902*
2. *April 21, 1970*   4. *July 4, 1776*   6. *February 18, 2008*

C   What's one of your favorite holidays? Prepare to explain to your classmates in ASL about a holiday or celebration you enjoy. What is its name, when is it, and what do you do? If you do not celebrate holidays, prepare to sign about an activity your family does together.

D   Memorize and sign the paragraph below.

E   Write assignments A, B, C, or D in ASL gloss.

Talking About the Weather

Translation

Today's weather is cool with a bit of rain, with tomorrow's weather being warm and sunny.

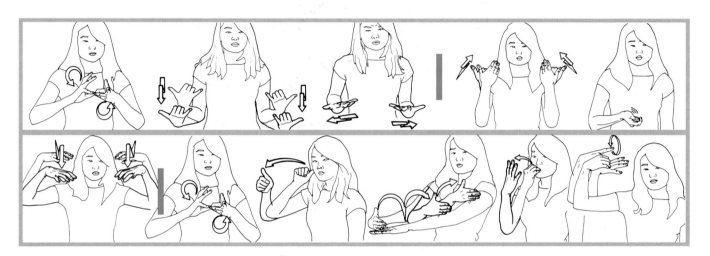

Classroom Exercise Z

Weather. Do the following with a partner:

1. *Create a dialogue incorporating weather signs.*

2. *Discuss activities that can be done inside and outside, depending on the weather.*

Accent Steps

The sign *inside* is a literal sign that means *to be inside of*. Avoid using the sign *inside* for *in December* or *in the future*. You will learn more about how such concepts are signed in later units.

Vocabulary   The Basics

Inside

Outside

Weather (1)

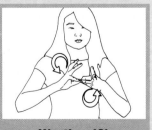

Weather (2)

Classroom Exercise

1 *Today's weather.* Based on the illustrations below, describe the weather in a complete sentence.

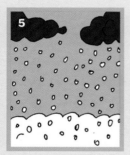

2 *Emphasis.* What kind of facial expression would you add to the correct weather-related sign?

1. *freezing cold*
2. *raining cats and dogs*
3. *very hot / sweltering*
4. *terrible windstorm*
5. *fluffy clouds*
6. *pouring*

Accent Steps

Only a facial expression distinguishes *cold* from *winter*. Beware of slight differences like *rain* and *snow*. What's the difference?

Vocabulary   Weather

To be cloudy

To be cold

To be cool

To be hot

To rain

To snow

To be sunny

To be warm

Waves

To be windy

Classroom Exercise **BB**

1 *Coming back from a walk.* Kelly takes a walk rain or shine every day. Based on the illustrations, explain in complete ASL sentences what she encountered on her walk. Describe as much as you can.

2 *Travel forecast.* You and a friend are making travel plans. What kind of weather can you expect in each location? Select vocabulary from each column to make a complete sentence.

Destination		Season / time of year		Weather	
1. Alaska	6. Hawaii	today	summer	cold	hot
2. Chicago	7. Colorado	tomorrow	winter	rainy	cool
3. Texas	8. New York City	March	December	windy	sunny
4. Seattle	9. North Dakota	fall	spring	snow	snowy
5. Montreal	10. Arizona	August	November	cloudy	

Homework Exercise **7**

A Describe your ideal weather and season. What makes them your favorites? Prepare to explain in ASL to your classmates why you enjoy them.

B Use a newspaper, the television, or the internet to obtain your local forecast for the week. In ASL, explain the types of weather to expect.

C Write Assignment A or B in ASL gloss.

Journal Activities

1. Many people are often surprised to learn that Deaf individuals enjoy the same conveniences as hearing people do, especially with telephones, pagers, and entertainment options. What, if anything, do you think Deaf people cannot do?

2. *Point & Counterpoint:* For several years **Deaf Child Area** signs have appeared in neighborhoods across the United States, brewing controversy. Read both perspectives and then write a response explaining which position you support and the reasons why, and why each position may be right.

Point

Deaf Child Area signs just make sure a Deaf child who can't hear a car horn is safe playing on the street. The signs are what's best for a Deaf child and the public safety because a Deaf child can't hear potential danger and is more likely to be involved in an accident. Drivers are used to seeing signs alerting them to potential dangers, such as icy roads and animal crossing signs, so they remind drivers to slow down and drive with care.

Counterpoint

Deaf Child Area signs don't really ensure the safety of any child playing on the street, whether Deaf or hearing. While such signs are often placed with good intentions, they single out the Deaf child and make him or her more needy than hearing children. Signs like this convey the perception that Deaf people — children or adults — need more care and attention simply because they don't hear. And realistically, it's unlikely such signs encourage bad drivers to think twice.

Unit 3 Review

A   You are going to meet several Deaf people at a party Friday night. What questions can you ask to learn more about the people you talk with? Make a list of questions and answers and practice signing them with a partner. Keep the following topics in mind:

1. The city, state, and country where you live or are from
2. Asking for / exchanging telephone numbers or email addresses
3. Explaining where you live
4. Favorite TV shows and movies
5. Upcoming holidays
6. The weather

B   What is the difference between these non-manual signals? Create five sentences using these non-manual signals correctly.

C   Identify and correct any errors in the following sentences. Explain to a partner or friend why the errors are wrong and how to fix them.

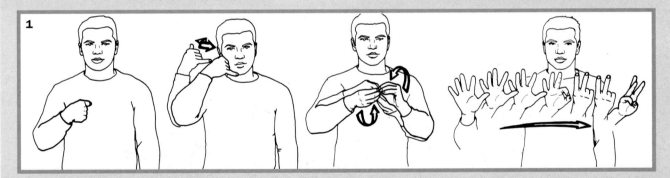

Unit 3 Review

3

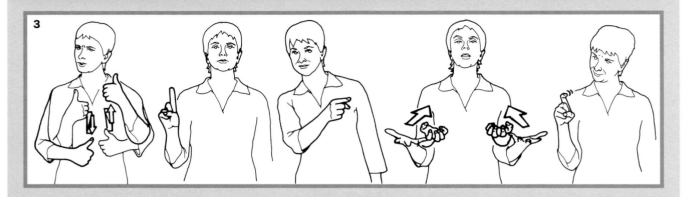

4

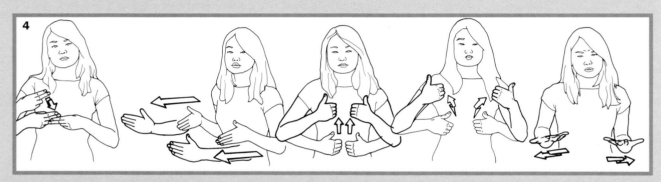

5

D   Sign an example of each skill. Can you:

1. Ask for and provide addresses?
2. Use number signs correctly?
3. Use possessive signs and deixis correctly?
4. Use WH-Signs when needed?
5. Show the difference between topic-comment structure and SVO-structure?
6. Conduct a conversation in ASL?
7. Use eye gaze, pauses, and sign order correctly?

Units 1 – 3 Review

Review Exercise A

1   *Sentence creation.* Complete each sentence in Column A using vocabulary from Column B and/or other signs you already know.

Column A

1. Yesterday, we...
2. Today, you...
3. On the weekend, they...
4. Thursday, I...
5. Monday, s/he...
6. Tomorrow, they...
7. Sunday, you (plural)...
8. Today, I...
9. Tomorrow, their...
10. Yesterday, my...

Column B

Ski	Don't like	Want
Want	Enjoy	Due
Don't want	School	Need
Love-it	Sick	Help me
School	Like	Ask me
Work	Absent	Mexico
Rollerblade	Snow	Valentine's Day
Vacation	Weather	Cold
Study	Go	Hot
Party	Homework	Visit
Friend	Not, don't	Read

2   Sign each of the following sentences in ASL.

1. Do you mind opening the door?
2. What's your telephone number and email address?
3. Do you enjoy listening to music? Can you sing?
4. What's our ASL homework? Is it due Thursday or Friday?
5. They moved here from Washington, D.C.
6. What's the weather today? Is it cool or cold outside?
7. My favorite holiday is Thanksgiving. What's yours?
8. Don't ask him! He doesn't know.
9. Did you see the test yesterday?
10. What are you doing this weekend? I want to have fun.

3   Sign an example of each concept in a complete sentence.

1. WH-Face
2. Question-Maker
3. Head nod
4. Head shake
5. directionality
6. eye gaze
7. topic-comment structure
8. subject-verb-object structure

- Confused when watching ASL? Non-manual signals like facial expressions and eye gaze can reveal a lot of information, even if you don't understand a sign or two. Best bet when you don't understand something: Ask the signer to repeat. Asking a signer to slow down or repeat information is a wise move!

- Rely on context to understand differences between the past and future. If it's Monday and someone is signing about weekend plans, it often refers to the immediate past. Understand the context by looking for *when* signs and other details that help you understand the bigger concept (WH-Signs are on page 64).

- Use topic-comment structure to bring up a topic "out of the blue." When the topic is clear, you can switch to subject-verb-object structure.

Review Exercise B

What's happening? Describe as many details as you can based on each illustration. Use your imagination to help you explain the scenes in complete ASL sentences.

Review Exercise C

Possessives. Insert the correct possessive sign in the space provided.

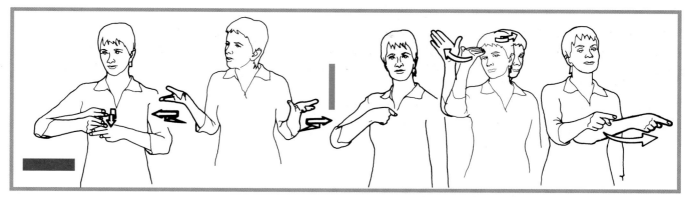

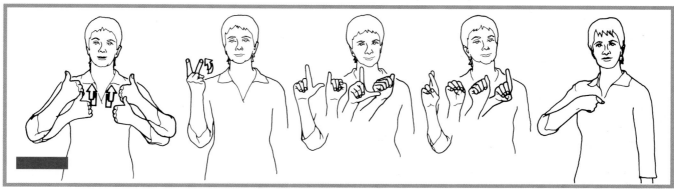

Review Exercise D

Weekend recap. Over the weekend you met several new friends. State what you learned about each in complete ASL sentences using the information provided.

1 Mia is Deaf and lives near you, at 17 Middlefield Road. She goes to school and works at a restaurant. On the weekends she loves to ski with friends and meet new friends.

2 Ryan is Deaf and moved here from New Jersey because he wants to act on TV. His favorite Deaf actor is Phyllis Frelich. He really likes Los Angeles because of the warm weather and enjoys roller-blading near the ocean.

3 Carlos is visiting from Florida. He is happy to see his friends here and enjoys practicing his ASL. He likes to take it easy and watch TV and go to the ocean. His email address is Carlos5@bb5.com and he wants you to visit him in Florida.

4 Shelly is hearing and is learning ASL. You have to sign slow with her because she doesn't understand ASL very well. She asked me to introduce her and she was excited to meet Mia. She wants to practice ASL so she isn't confused!

Review Exercise E

Numbers review. Practice signing each number and number sequence correctly. Refer to Eyes on ASL #7 on Page 99 if necessary.

1. *3, 5, 7, 9*
2. *2, 4, 6, 8, 10*
3. *555-0762*
4. *15, 13, 11, 9, 7*
5. *17 Ridge Road*
6. *1221 Mowry Ave.*
7. *322-9866*
8. *1, 2, 3, 4, 5, 6*
9. *15, 16, 17, 18, 19*
10. *9, 3, 0, 6, 10, 14*
11. *4988 Rose Blvd.*
12. *1818 View Lane*

ASL TIPS

- Frustrated by fingerspelling and numbers? When reading somebody else's fingerspelling, don't try to spell each word letter by letter in your head. Instead, sound out the word as it's being spelled. Try this approach with a long word like *encyclopedia* and see if it works for you!

- Some ASL students learn fingerspelling by looking at the pattern or shape each letter forms, eventually being able to "predict" letter sequence based on the pattern and conversational context. For example, if you and a friend have been talking about food and fingerspell a word shaped like this, what would you guess was spelled? Here's a hint: They come in a variety of colors but red is the most popular to eat.

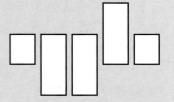

UNIT FOUR

Family & Friends

Unit Four Objectives

- To recognize and use gender distinction in ASL
- To understand and use contrastive structure
- To gain exposure to Deaf art
- To sign about family, friends, and relationships
- To use pronoun signs appropriately

Unit Four Vocabulary

Key Phrases

What's your family like?

Hey, how are you? I want to talk about my family. All together, there are five of us.
I'm fifteen years old and the middle child. I'm the only Deaf person in my family.
I have one brother and one sister. They don't sign very well but are getting better.
We like to play games and sometimes go camping. What's your family like?

DVD

What's your family like? Watch Sean sign in full motion on
your student DVD.

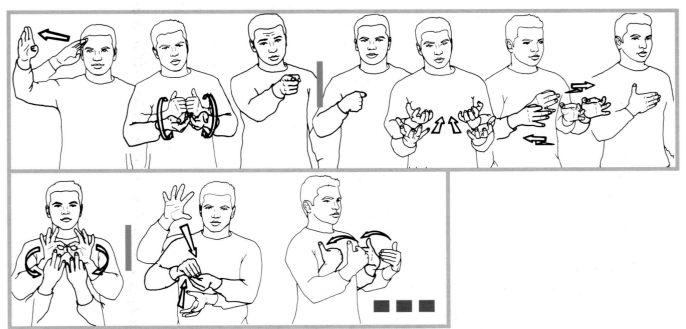

Vocabulary — What's your family like?

Other new vocabulary seen in the dialogue is presented throughout Unit 4.

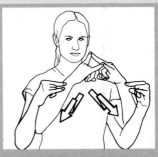

To camp (Unit 6)

To play (Unit 6)

Sometimes (Unit 7)

Signing About Family

Making inquiries about someone's family is a common way to practice and use language. In the dialogue below, notice how each signer exchanges information. Pay particular attention to the phrase "brothers and sisters." What is different about the shoulders?

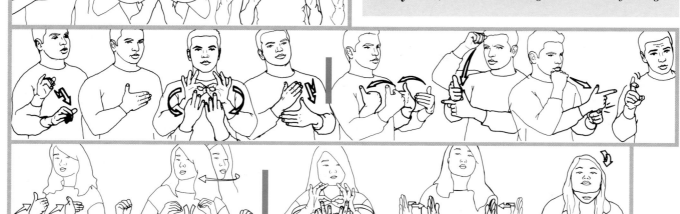

Dialogue Translation

Sean: *What's your family like?*

Kelly: *My family is small.*

Sean: *Oh, I see. My family isn't too big. Do you have brothers and sisters?*

Kelly: *No, I don't have any. It's a small family!*

Vocabulary   Family Size

Big, large

Family

Like, same as

Medium

Only

Small

Classroom Exercise

1 *How many?* What can you say about each family? In complete sentences, explain:

1. How many children are in each family?

2. Who are the hearing and Deaf members of each family?

Their family has two children.

Rand Family: All Deaf

Clark Family

Arroyo Family: Children Deaf

Dart Family: Parents Deaf

2 *Headcount.* Ask a partner how many members are in each family. Your partner will respond using the information shown. When done, switch roles and repeat the exercise. An example is provided.

How many people are in your family?

1. 8 people	**3.** 11 people	**5.** 8 people	**7.** 6 people	**9.** 2 people
2. 3 people	**4.** 5 people	**6.** 4 people	**8.** 4 people	**10.** ?

Vocabulary — **Family Members**

All, everybody

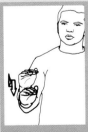
Child

Children

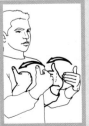
To have

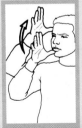
Parents

People

Classroom Exercise B

1 *Have Deaf?* The expression *have deaf* is a common way to ask whether there are Deaf people in your family. If the answer is yes, it is polite to explain who is Deaf in the family. Ask a partner if he or she has any Deaf members in the family, following the example. Your partner will respond using the information shown. Switch roles and repeat the exercise when done.

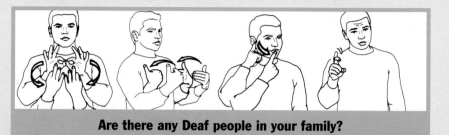

Are there any Deaf people in your family?

FYI Don't sign *who* in sentences like "I have a brother who is Deaf."

Yes, my parents are Deaf.

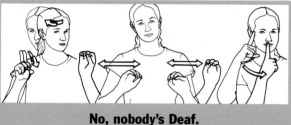

No, nobody's Deaf.

1. *Yes, my mother is Deaf.*
2. *No, there are no Deaf people in my family.*
3. *Yeah, I have a Deaf cousin.*
4. *Yes, my brother is Deaf.*
5. *Yes, my Aunt Claire is Deaf.*

6. *Nobody's Deaf in my family, but my grandfather is hard-of-hearing.*
7. *Yeah, I have a cousin who's Deaf.*
8. *Yes, my sister and brother are Deaf.*
9. *All my family is Deaf.*

2 *Building blocks.* Create complete sentences using information from each column. An example is shown.

My Deaf friend lives in New York.

Column A	Column B	Column C	Column D
1. sister	Deaf	born	sign language
2. cousin	hearing	from	Hawaii
3. parents	hard-of-hearing	lives in	restaurant
4. brother	wants	works	Canada
5. friend	likes	to study	Florida

Vocabulary   **Family Signs**

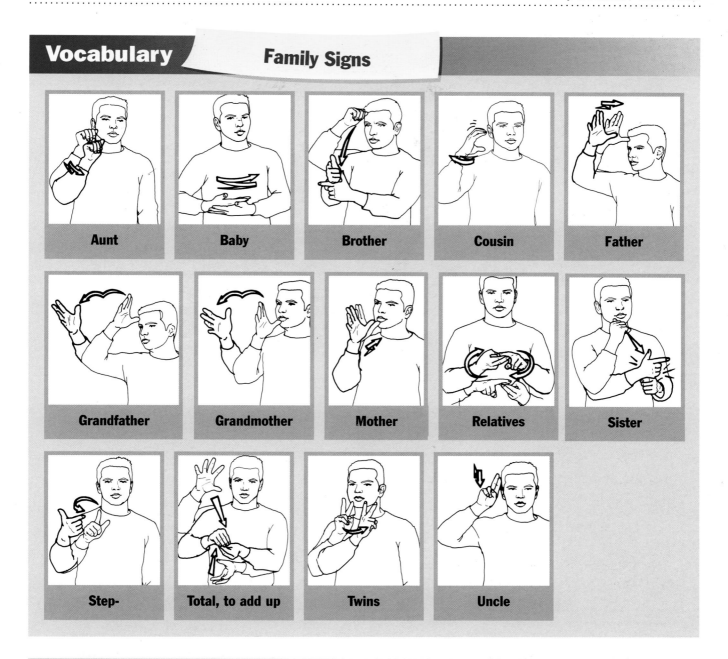

Aunt	**Baby**	**Brother**	**Cousin**	**Father**
Grandfather	**Grandmother**	**Mother**	**Relatives**	**Sister**
Step-	**Total, to add up**	**Twins**	**Uncle**	

Homework Exercise   1

A   Who do you live with? What are their names? Practice signing about your family in a minimum of five ASL sentences. Practice signing clearly and smoothly.

B   Is your family large, medium, or small? Practice signing about your family and relatives, including how many family members you have, names, and where everybody lives. Bring in a photograph to help you explain your family relationships in a minimum of five ASL sentences. Practice signing clearly and smoothly.

C   Write the sentences you practice in ASL for Assignments A and / or B in ASL gloss.

Classroom Exercise C

Chris Lee's family. Answer the questions about Chris Lee's family in complete ASL sentences.

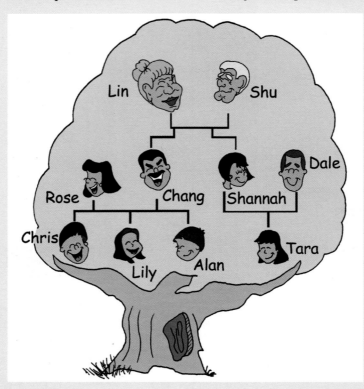

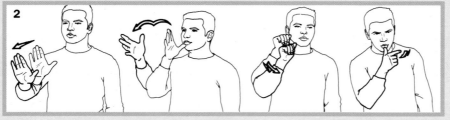

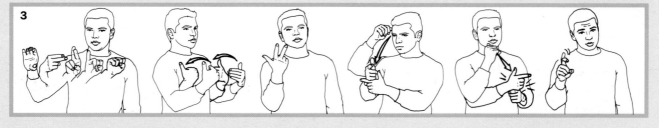

Classroom Exercise (continued)

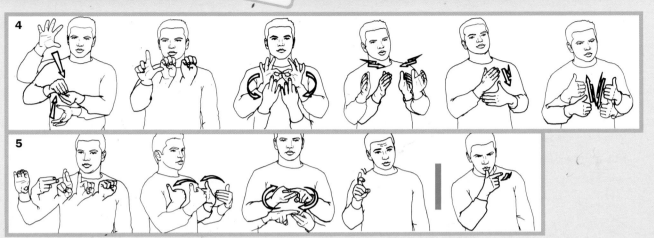

Classroom Exercise

1. *Family information.* Fill in the blanks with names or with signs from Vocabulary: Related Signs to make a complete sentence.

1. *My stepbrother's name is ____.*
2. *Yesterday, their grandfather ____.*
3. *Our ____ cousin lives in ____.*
4. *My uncle ____ is not ____.*
5. *I don't want to ____.*

6. *I have twin ____.*
7. *My younger sister is named ____.*
8. *Their aunt is ____.*
9. *My ____ brother / sister is named ____.*
10. *Are they ____ or ____?*

2. *Dialogue.* Create a dialogue with a partner in which family information is exchanged, including:
1. *asking about any Deaf members of the family;*
2. *asking for and giving the names of at least three family members;*
3. *explaining whether one has older or younger siblings.*

Vocabulary Related Signs

To be dead, missing	**To divorce**	**To marry**	**Older*, tall, adult**	**Younger*, short**

*Use the signs *older* and *younger* as seen, even if an older sibling is shorter or a younger sibling is taller than you.

ASL Up Close

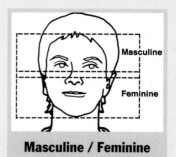

Masculine / Feminine

Gender Distinction in American Sign Language

When you say "my cousin" in English, how do you distinguish between a female or male cousin? English does not have a way to convey the concept of a female cousin in a single word, unlike most languages. ASL distinguishes **gender** aspects of signs by locating a sign in either the masculine or feminine areas of the face, as seen in the illustration. Depending where you place the sign *cousin*, it means *female cousin* or *male cousin*. What other signs do you know with gender distinction?

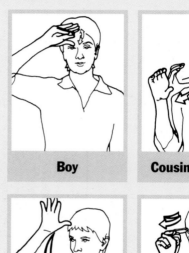
Boy

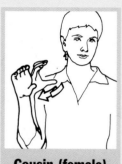
Cousin (female)

Cousin (male)

Daughter

Girl

Man

Nephew

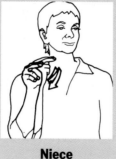
Niece

Son

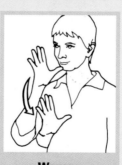
Woman

Classroom Exercise E

1   *Gender distinction.* Sign each sentence in ASL, using the correct form of the gender-specific signs as needed.

1. *My cousin Joseph lives in Florida.*
2. *Her niece was born yesterday.*
3. *My sister married a man who has two daughters.*
4. *Our daughter is named Carrie.*
5. *I have a cousin named Tara.*
6. *My aunt and uncle are divorced.*
7. *My nephew lives in Ohio with my sister.*
8. *My ASL teacher is a man.*
9. *Our daughter's name is Rebekah.*

Classroom Exercise (continued)

2   *Gender signs.* Which gender sign best matches the clues provided?

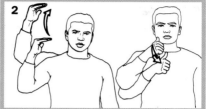

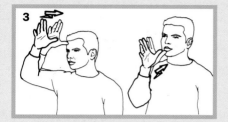

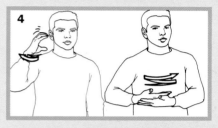

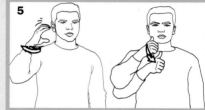

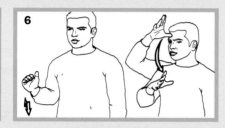

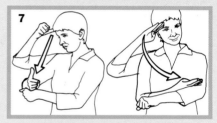

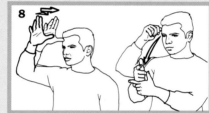

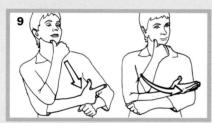

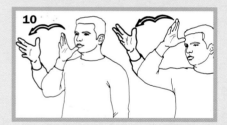

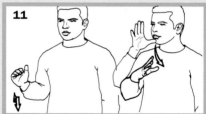

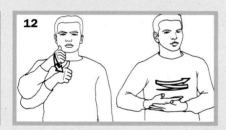

Did you know?

Approximately 10% of Deaf people have Deaf children, which means 90% of Deaf parents have hearing children. A hearing child of Deaf adults is known by the fingerspelled word "**coda**." Though codas are hearing, they are an important part of the Deaf community and culture. Often, a coda's first language is ASL. Contrary to popular belief, hearing children of Deaf parents rarely encounter problems learning how to speak. It can be said of codas that they have the best of both worlds! Many codas cherish ASL and the Deaf community and are proud to have this unique background. To learn more about codas and CODA, an international organization of codas from around the world, visit: http://www.coda-international.org

Contrastive Structure

There are three main uses for Shoulder-Shifting in ASL. In this section, you will use Shoulder-Shifting to ask and answer questions that incorporate more than one detail or piece of information. Using Shoulder-Shifting in this way is known as **contrastive structure.** This generally takes the place of "and."

Dialogue Translation

Marc: *What's your family like?*

Sean: *I have two brothers and two sisters.*

Marc: *Oh, okay. Do they live nearby?*

Sean: *My brother is over in California, and my sister is in South Dakota.*

Classroom Exercise F

1   *And.* Use Shoulder-Shifting for each vocabulary pair.

   1. *Brother and sister*
   2. *4 and 6*
   3. *Married and divorced*
   4. *Deaf and hearing*
   5. *Younger and older*
   6. *Small and medium*
   7. *Cousin (male) and cousin (female)*
   8. *Man and woman*
   9. *ASL and sign language*

2   *Dialogue.* Create a dialogue with a partner that uses at least two examples of Shoulder-Shifting. Prepare to sign the dialogue to your class-

 **Accent Steps**

Don't switch your dominant and non-dominant hands when using the Shoulder-Shift. Simply orient your shoulders in a different direction and continue signing.

ASL Up Close

Using Shoulder-Shifting

The illustration on the right demonstrates **Shoulder-Shifting**, a feature unique to American Sign Language. Related to the concept of deixis in which the index finger points to a person or object which may or may not be visible, shoulder-shifting is a way to distinguish several pieces of information in a signed sentence by slightly moving your head and shoulders in a different direction for each detail. The illustration shown here demonstrates Shoulder-Shifting for three different pieces of information. Shoulder-Shifting is used for:

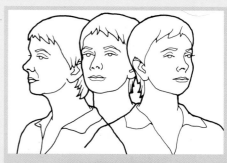

Shoulder-Shifting

- contrasting: Multiple topics or pieces of information in the same sentence;

- comparing: What more than one person says or does;

- separating: More than one idea or concept in the same sentence.

They are married and they are divorced.

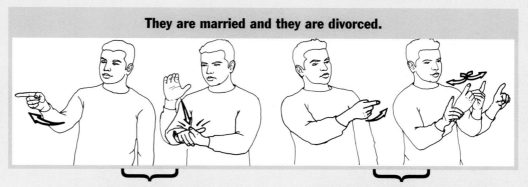

One concept / idea / detail   Second concept / idea / detail

I have three brothers, one sister, and two dogs.

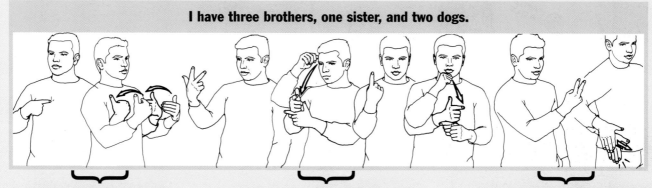

One concept / idea / detail   Second concept / idea / detail   Third concept / idea / detail

Eyes on ASL #8

Use Shoulder-Shifting when signing about more than one person or object.

Eye gaze and shoulder-shifting is used more often than the separate sign for "and."

Classroom Exercise G

1 *Contrastive structure drill.* Sign each of the following sentences, using contrastive structure for the information in italics.

1. *They are:*
   1 man;
   2 women.
2. *I have 2 cousins:*
   Cousin named Sean;
   Cousin named Laura.
3. *I need:*
   hot and
   cold water.
4. *Girl;*
   Boy.
5. *I have:*
   One brother;
   Two sisters.
6. *His:*
   Grandmother is deceased;
   Grandfather is alive.
7. *My:*
   Uncle is watching TV;
   Aunt is sleeping.
8. *My parents are divorced:*
   Father lives in New York;
   Mother lives in California.
9. *My:*
   Mother is Deaf;
   Father is hearing;
   Two brothers are Deaf.
10. She *has:*
    One dog;
    Two cats;
    Two older sisters.

2 *Shoulder-shifting.* Use contrastive structure to describe each illustration.

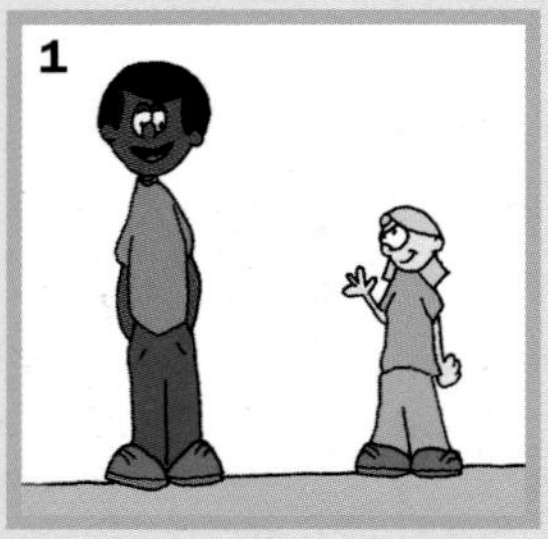

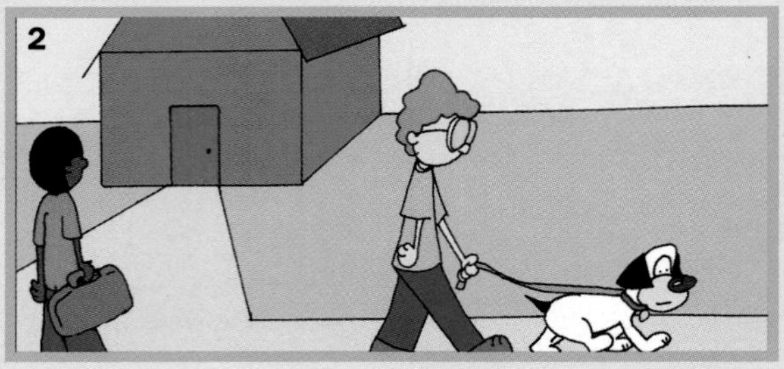

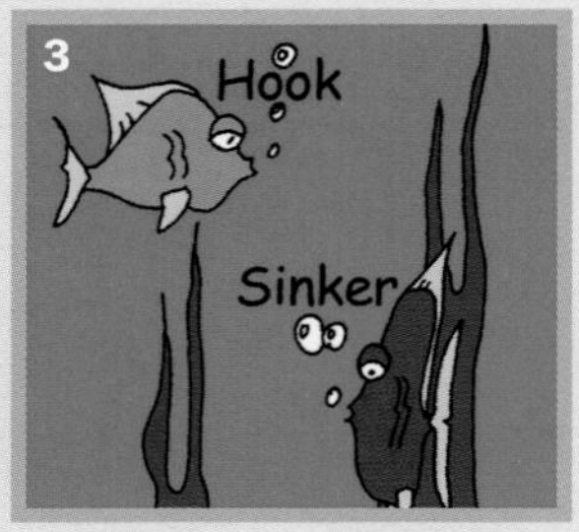

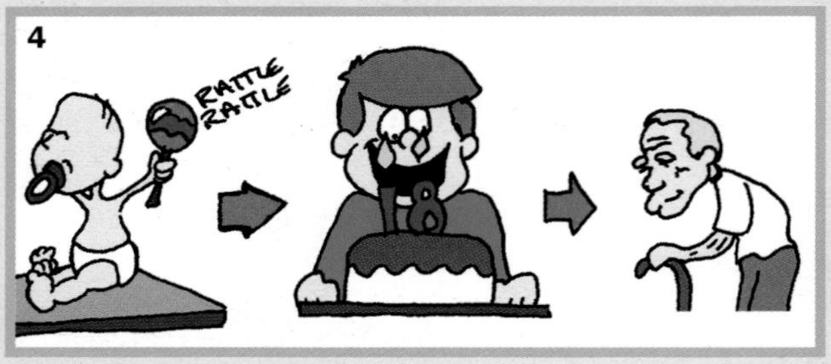

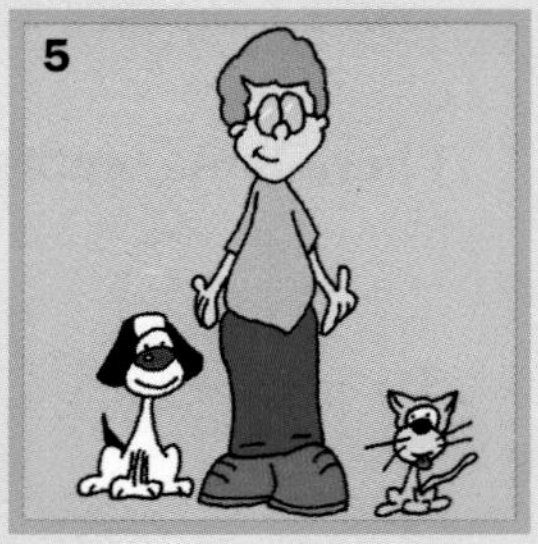

3 *More than one.* Create sentences based on the shoulder-shifting illustrations below.

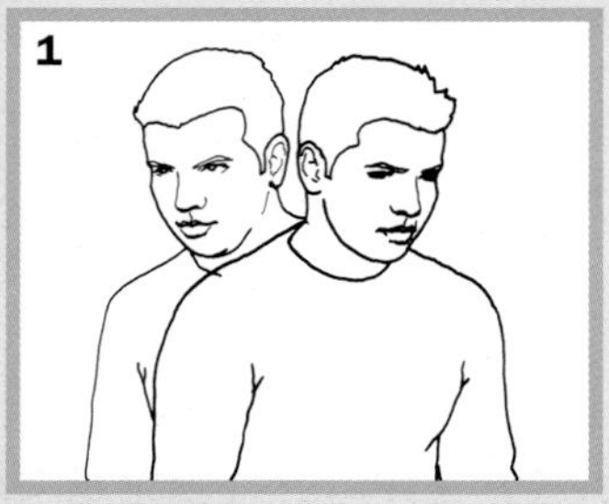

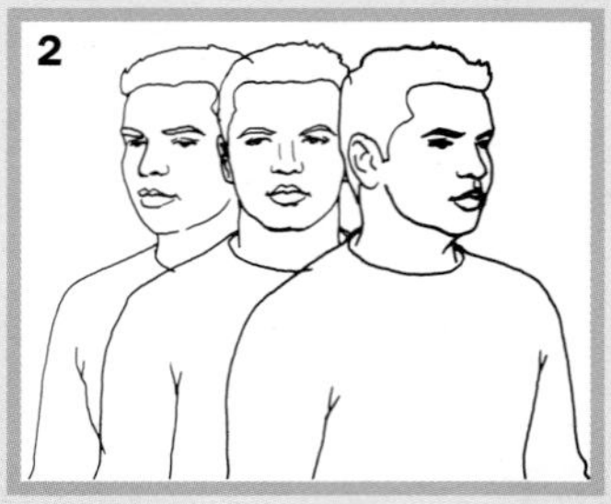

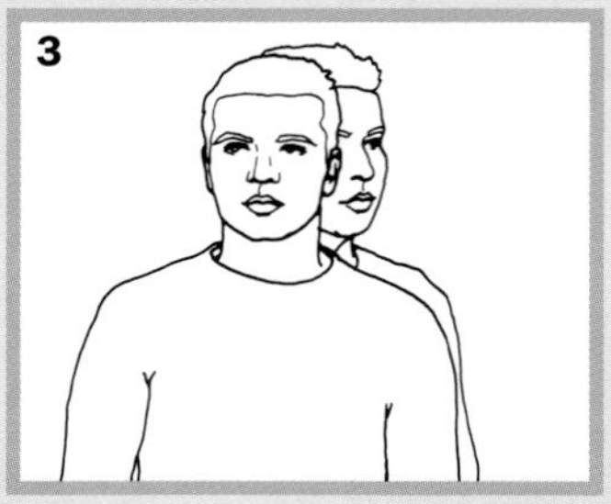

Classroom Exercise

Facial expressions. Use shoulder-shifting with each pair of facial expressions.

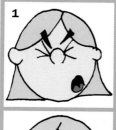    

Accent Steps

Many words in ASL are **compound signs**, which are two separate signs combined to make an additional meaning. Combining the signs for *mother* and *father* creates *parents*, and *sun* plus *shine* means *to be sunny*. When using compounds, sign each portion quickly and smoothly in one motion. Can you think of any other compound signs you know?

Though they are not compounds, *grandparents* and *cousins* are made the same way.

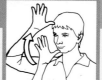 

Vocabulary   Household Pets

Bird

Cat

Dog

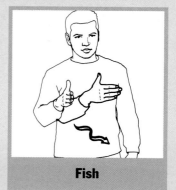

Fish

Homework Exercise 2

A. What did you do this week? For each thing you did, use Shoulder-Shifting to sign its opposite. For example, *I went to school / I didn't go to school.* Practice five sentences using shoulder-shifting.

B. How many brothers and sisters do you have? Cousins? Nieces or nephews? What is the name of a best friend? Your parents, grandparents? Use contrastive structure to sign about a minimum of six different individuals.

C. Write the sentences you practice in ASL for Assignments A and / or B in ASL gloss.

Deaf Culture NOTE

Deaf Family Dynamics

When an ASL student begins to socialize with Deaf people, one certain question is always asked: *Why are you interested in learning ASL?* It is a sincere question deeply rooted in the shared experience of being Deaf in a hearing world. Historically, very few hearing people learned American Sign Language aside from codas and those who worked closely with Deaf people, such as the clergy. Unfortunately, very few others learned how to sign, including hearing family members and relatives. Most Deaf people are from hearing families who don't know ASL but rely on a few signs and improvised gestures called **home signs**. Even today many Deaf children have parents who don't sign, or live in a family where a mother and sibling — usually a sister — can sign.

Because of this background where most hearing people did not want to learn ASL, a sincere question is *Why do you?* Asking this is a way for Deaf people to get to know you and your background, to learn whether you have a Deaf relative or friend, and your motivation to learn ASL. Is it for work reasons, for socialization reasons, for fun? Deaf people are genuinely pleased to see more hearing people learning American Sign Language for many reasons, especially for mutual communication and understanding. Now that ASL is becoming widely respected and studied, more parents are learning ASL for the sake of their Deaf children, a welcome sight in the Deaf community.

Eyes on ASL #9

All age signs originate at the Age-Spot and face outward.

Using separate signs for *10*, *year*, and *old* is sloppy and incorrect.

❝ Communication should begin in the cradle and a mother or nurse should have as nimble a hand as commonly they have a tongue. ❞   —*George Dalgarno, 1661*

Signing Age

Signing somebody's age follows a general pattern of touching a number sign at an area on the chin known as the **Age-Spot**. Being able to use age signs correctly is an important part of making conversation. Note that the WH-Face accompanies the phrase *how old are you?*

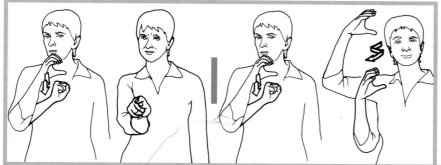

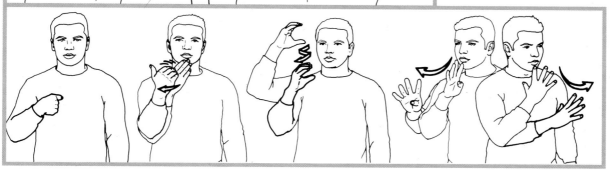

Dialogue Translation

Rita: *How old are you? How old are your cousins?*

Sean: *I'm 15 years old, and my cousins are 4 and 5.*

ASL Up Close

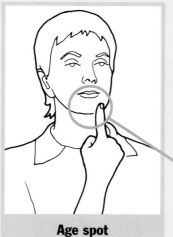

Age spot

DVD

The Age Spot

Place a number sign at the Age Spot and then move the handshape away from the chin in one movement. You do not need to twist your wrist inward for ages involving the numbers 1 – 5. Moving the number away from the Age Spot conveys the meaning *years old*, so you do not need to add separate signs for *year* and *old* after the number.

The Age Spot
The number's movement away from the Age Spot means *years old*, so only one sign is needed to say *two years old*.

Signing Age (continued)

There are four things to know about signing age in ASL:

1. Ages 1 – 9 always follow this format, and is part of the **Rule of 9**.

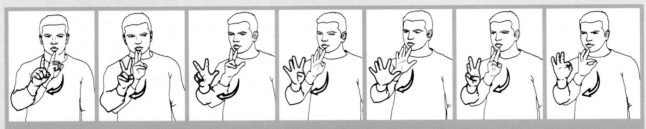

1 year old, 2 years old, 3... 4... 5...6... 9 years old

2. Ages 10 – 100+ except for 13, 14, 15 follow either variation, depending on the style preferred in your area.

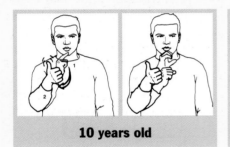

10 years old

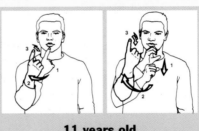

11 years old

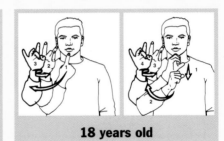

18 years old

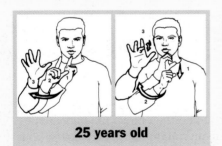

25 years old

3. Generally, age numbers follow the format seen here:

34 years old

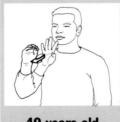

40 years old

65 years old

4. Ages 13, 14, 15 are always signed like this:

13 years old

14 years old

15 years old

Classroom Exercise

1 *Signing age.* Use the correct sign for each age number.

1. 3 years old
2. 10 years old
3. 35 years old
4. 18 years old
5. 20 years old

6. 25 years old
7. 8 years old
8. 1 year old
9. 55 years old
10. 13 years old

11. 40 years old
12. 15 years old
13. 17 years old
14. 2 years old
15. 29 years old.

16. 33 years old
17. 16 years old
18. 5 years old
19. 60 years old
20. 42 years old

21. 9 years old
22. 69 years old
23. 11 years old
24. 17 years old
25. 23 years old

2 *How old is everybody?* Sign each sentence in ASL using the information provided, adding whether the person is a baby, young, a teenager, middle-aged, or old. Follow the example shown.

He is 25 years old. He's young.

1. Chad is 2 years old.
2. Tonya is 33 years old.
3. He is 48 years old.
4. DaShawn is 15 years old.
5. My mother is 42 years old.

6. Ahmed is 20 years old.
7. Kendra is 16 years old.
8. My grandfather is 80 years old.
9. She's 13 years old.
10. Kiernan is 1 year old.

11. Cecile is 30 years old.
12. He is not 1 year old yet.
13. Mike is 17 years old.
14. Tera is 29 years old.
15. I am ___ years old.

3 *Dialogue.* Create a dialogue with a partner that includes the following:

1. greetings
2. asking about one's age
3. exchanging birthdates

4. asking about the age of another family member
5. asking about the age of a friend
6. signing farewell

Vocabulary — Age-Related Signs

Teenager

To be young

ASL Up Close

The Listing & Ordering Technique

Making a visual list of information such as names or ages is called the **Listing & Ordering Technique**. This technique is used most often when providing several details about one or more person or thing. The **non-dominant hand** forms a list with each new bit of information signed by the **dominant hand**.

Example 1
Marc is the first,
I'm the second,
and Lila is
the third.

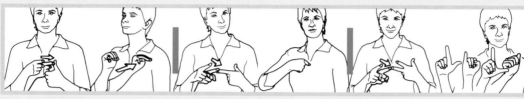

Example 2
He (Marc) is
15, I'm 35, she
(Lila) is 18.

Classroom Exercise J

1. *Age and Shoulder-Shift.* Use contrastive structure to state each set of ages. An example is provided.

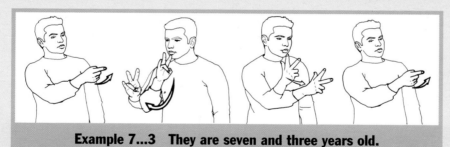

Example 7...3   They are seven and three years old.

1. *6 ... 10*	**6.** *16 ... 20*	**11.** *3 ... 6 ... 9*	**16.** *4 ... 8 ... 12 ... 16*
2. *21 ... 12*	**7.** *8 ... 32*	**12.** *13 ... 14 ... 15*	**17.** *20 ... 5 ... 8*
3. *7 ... 9*	**8.** *17 ... 25*	**13.** *22 ... 26 ... 28*	**18.** *33 ... 15 ... 3 ... 4*
4. *14 ... 16*	**9.** *1 ... 1*	**14.** *19 ... 15 ... 11*	**19.** *17 ... 10 ... 12 ... 18 ... 22*
5. *30 ... 15*	**10.** *42 ... 13*	**15.** *37 ... 57 ... 77*	**20.** *45 ... 50 ... 18 ... 8 ... 6*

2. *Making lists.* Use the Listing & Ordering Technique with each group of information.

1. *10 years old, 5 years old, 25 years old.*	**2.** *Bryan, Leslie, Jason, Lisa, Jeff.*	**3.** *I'm going to: New York, Washington, D.C., Boston.*	**4.** *John is first, Lara is second, and Rick is last.*	**5.** *Megan is 17, I'm ___, and Hannah is 23.*

Classroom Exercise

Context. Use your imagination to create a second sentence that follows the first. Sign both sentences when done.

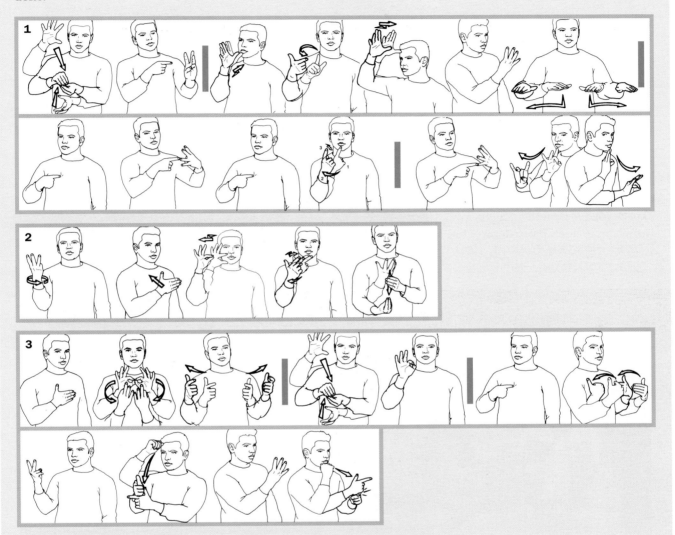

Homework Exercise 3

A What are the names and ages of your family members? Use contrastive structure and the Listing and Ordering Technique to sign about your family. Prepare to share the information with your classmates in ASL.

B You are planning to go out with friends sometime on the weekend. Use contrastive structure and the Listing and Ordering Technique to explain a minimum of five things you would like to do. Prepare to share your plans with your classmates in ASL.

C Use ASL gloss to write down the ASL sentences you practice for Assignments A or B.

Focus: The Deaf Experience

❝ **"They are first, last and all the time, the people of the eye.** ❞   — *George Veditz, 1913*

Part of the definition of culture includes art, which is the expression of human creativity in theater, painting, sculpture, poetry and literature, multimedia, film, drama, and other related forms. The arts are a vibrant and important aspect of Deaf culture, a culture that cherishes the hands and the visual mode of communication. Some Deaf artists focus on deafness and others do not, each preferring to create works ranging from the abstract to the fanciful, the concrete to the utilitarian, aiming to present an interpretation of their unique perspective.

Chuck Baird is a well-known artist highly valued for his fanciful expressions of American Sign Language. Chuck Baird depicts the Deaf experience in *Untitled, 1989.*

Courtesy: Gallaudet University Archives

Courtesy: National Theatre of the Deaf

There are several Deaf theater groups such as the National Theatre of the Deaf and Deaf West Theater that stage performances featuring Deaf actors, writers, and visual themes. Deaf theatre is especially popular with both Deaf and hearing audiences around the world.

Courtesy: National Theatre of the Deaf

and the Arts

Douglas Tilden's (1860 – 1935) sculptures are renowned for their evocative expressions of purpose, seen here in the life-sized *The Bear Hunt*. Tilden is considered one of the finest sculptors of his age.

— *A Tribute to 'Fingershell' by Chuck Baird, II,* Tony Landon McGregor. Reproduced by permission of artist

Deaf Native American artist Tony Landon McGregor fuses traditional art forms with ASL in many of his works.

Deaf actors and writers produce and act in original works for the stage and film, and also appear on television and wide-release movies such as *Love is Never Silent* and *Children of a Lesser God.*

Courtesy: National Theatre of the Deaf

Courtesy: Sandi Inches

Ameslan Prohibited, 1972
Dr. Betty Miller's artwork highlights the oppression Deaf people have experienced, particularly the suppression of American Sign Language, and celebrates the beauty of Deaf culture and ASL. The hands are a cherished focus in Deaf art, a theme passed down between generations of Deaf people.

Classroom Exercise

1 *What's the best age?* At what age do people do the following things? An example is provided.

People tend to graduate high school at 18.

1. *Vote*
2. *Go to college*
3. *Marry*
4. *Have email*
5. *Go to a party*
6. *Learn ASL*
7. *Graduate high school*
8. *Learn to ski*
9. *Start school*
10. *Work*
11. *Have children*
12. *Get a driver's license*
13. *Graduate college*
14. *Understand life*
15. *Learn to read and write*

2 *People should . . .* What should or shouldn't people do?

1. *Visit grandparents*
2. *Be nice*
3. *Practice signing*
4. *Help old people*
5. *Be mean*
6. *Drive tired*
7. *Be absent*
8. *Marry young*
9. *Like their family*
10. *Have a cat or dog*

Vocabulary — Life Events

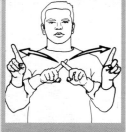
But

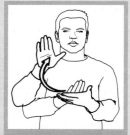
College

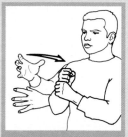
To get (something)

To graduate

High school

License

To pass down, descendants

Should

The difference between *need* and *should* is the NMS. Raise your eyebrows with *should*.

To vote

Narrative: My Family

 My Family. Watch Kris sign in full motion on your student DVD.

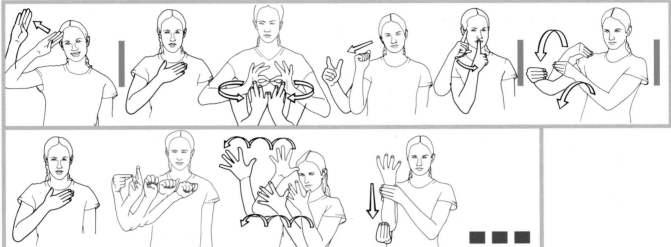

Classroom Exercise M

Comprehension. Respond to the following questions based on the narrative *My Family.*

1. *What does Kris mean when she uses this sign?*
2. *Are Kris' great-grandparents alive?*
3. *What old sign does Kris like? What does it mean?*
4. *What two questions does Kris ask?*

Deaf Culture Minute

All languages, including signed languages, change over time. You can see an example of this by comparing the two signs for *telephone* in Kris' family portrait. Think about the sign *drive*: What kind of signs can you think of that might have been used when people rode in a Model T? What about when riding in a carriage?

Homework Exercise 4

A Practice signing Kris' family portrait in ASL, focusing on facial expressions, pauses, and a smooth delivery. Prepare to sign *My Family* to your classmates.

B Write an accurate translation of *My Family* in English. What differences do you see between the ASL and English versions?

C Write Kris' family portrait in ASL gloss.

Friends & Relationships

The sign *good-friend* can be interpreted several ways, including "best friend" and "buddy." Similarly, *best-friend* is often used to describe a close relationship.

Dialogue Translation

Kris: *Hey, how's it going?*

Sean: *Hi, how are you? This is my buddy Marc. We've been close since we were kids.*

Kris: *Oh, I see. Nice to meet you! Are you visiting?*

Marc: *Yeah, I live in Los Angeles.*

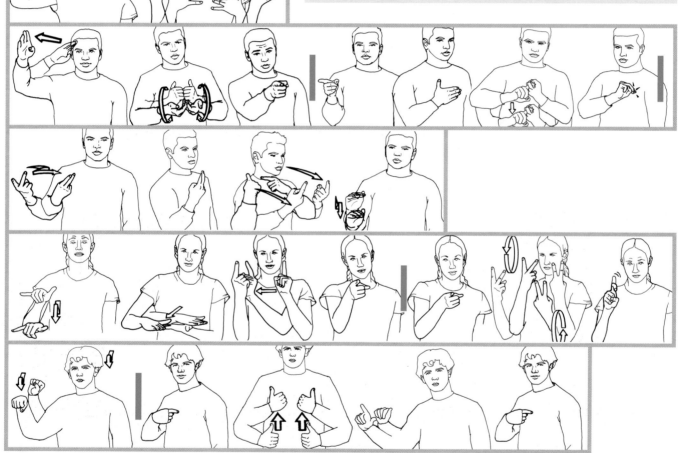

Classroom Exercise

1. *Dialogue 1.* Practice signing the dialogue above with a partner. Use your imagination to expand the dialogue with at least two new sentences and a conclusion.

2. *Dialogue 2.* Create a dialogue with a partner in which you discuss your friends. Who are you close to? For how long? Why are you friends?

Classroom Exercise

1 *Translation.* Sign the following sentences in ASL.

1. *She is my best friend. Her name is Aundrea.*
2. *Do you want to get together tonight?*
3. *I've known him for four years.*
4. *I met my sweetheart at work.*
5. *He wants to go out with her, but she can't.*

6. *On Saturday we are going to the beach.*
7. *We've been buddies since we were 7 years old.*
8. *My good friend is named ___?___.*
9. *I have / don't have a ___?___.*
10. *We want to get together ___?___.*

2 *Information exchange.* Ask a partner the following questions in ASL; when done, switch roles and repeat the exercise.

1. *Do you have a boyfriend / girlfriend? Single / married?*
2. *What is your best friend's name?*
3. *How long have you known your best friend?*
4. *Do you like to get together with friends?*
5. *Who do you want to go out with?*

> **FYI** The sign *to have* indicates the literal possession of <u>something</u>, so you don't need to include *have* when signing "How long have you..."

Vocabulary — Friendship

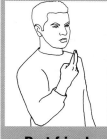
Best friend

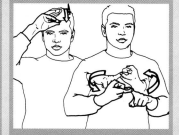
Boyfriend

To get together

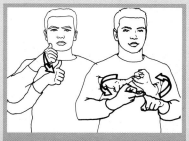
Girlfriend

To go out, leave

Good friend

Since, for

To be single

Sweetheart, honey

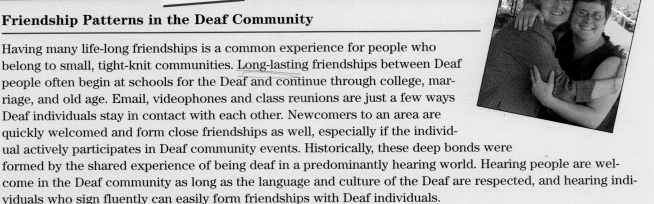

Deaf Culture NOTE

Friendship Patterns in the Deaf Community

Having many life-long friendships is a common experience for people who belong to small, tight-knit communities. Long-lasting friendships between Deaf people often begin at schools for the Deaf and continue through college, marriage, and old age. Email, videophones and class reunions are just a few ways Deaf individuals stay in contact with each other. Newcomers to an area are quickly welcomed and form close friendships as well, especially if the individual actively participates in Deaf community events. Historically, these deep bonds were formed by the shared experience of being deaf in a predominantly hearing world. Hearing people are welcome in the Deaf community as long as the language and culture of the Deaf are respected, and hearing individuals who sign fluently can easily form friendships with Deaf individuals.

How does this differ from your own experience? What benefits do you think the Deaf community gains from being close-knit? Any drawbacks?

Classroom Exercise P

1 *What did you say?* Fill in the blanks with signs chosen from the lists below. Use your imagination to make complete ASL sentences.

They	Me	Friend	High school	Divorce	Homework	Beach
We	He/she/it	Family	Sweetheart	Single	Good friend	Girlfriend
You	Get together	College	Marry	Go out	Close friend	Boyfriend

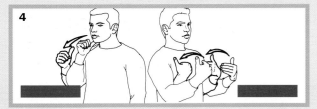

Classroom Exercise (continued)

2 *To go.* Use the singular or plural form of *to go to* when completing the sentence prompt.

1. *I want to go to . . .*
2. *They're going to . . .*
3. *Do you want to go to . . .*
4. *We don't want to go to . . .*

5. *They go . . .*
6. *You (plural) go . . .*
7. *I don't want to go to . . .*
8. *We go . . . . .*

9. *They don't go . . .*
10. *They go to . . .*

Accent Steps

The sign *since* also means "for," but only when signing about a period of time: "I've known him for five years" uses *since*, but not "Tell her for me." *Since* is considered a *when* sign, meaning that depending on the context, it may need to be used with topic-comment structure.

ASL Up Close

Conjugating Verbs: To Go

The basic form of the verb *to go to* is modified when used in the plural form.

To go to

They're going home.

Singular

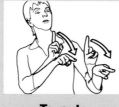
I go

You go

He / she / it goes

Plural

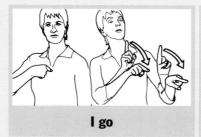
We go

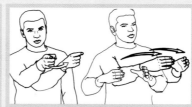
You go (plural)

They go

Classroom Exercise

1 *Relationships.* Sign each of the following sentences in ASL.

1. *Tim fell in love with Angela but they're not dating.*
2. *I have a date on Saturday. Do you?*
3. *No, I think they broke up.*
4. *My older brother loves to flirt.*
5. *I get along with my parents.*

6. *She argued with her best friend. Now, they don't get along.*
7. *Should I date her?*
8. *I love my sweetheart!*
9. *Do you want to go out with us?*
10. *They've been together for 3 years.*

2 *Non-manual signals.* Using only facial expressions and non-manual signals for the meanings shown in bold, how would you sign each concept? Work with a partner and make a list of the ways you can modify the meaning of each sign.

1. *To argue* (**a lot**)
2. *To fall in love* (**repeatedly**)
3. *To break up* (**pleased**)
4. *To be together* (**a very long time**)
5. *To flirt* (**too strongly**)

6. *To go out* (**often**)
7. *To be single* (**happily**)
8. *To be single* (**unhappily**)
9. *To argue* (**a big argument**)
10. *To get along with* (**not by choice**)

3 *Sign selection.* Fill in the blanks with signs from Column A, and then sign the complete sentence.

Column A

1. *Yesterday, I _____ with my _____.*
2. *They do / don't _____.*
3. *We _____ to go to the movies tonight.*
4. *He _____ with her.*
5. *On Friday I did / didn't fight with my _____.*
6. *They _____?*
7. *I _____ _____.*
8. *Are you _____?*

Argue	*Want*
Date	*Don't want*
Verbal-fight	*Flirt*
Parents	*Break up*
Brother	*Fall in love*
Sister	*Together*
Friend	*Relationship*
Girl / boy friend	*Good friend*

Accent Steps

Don't confuse the signs *love* and *love-it*. *Love* is used to for romantic emotions, while *love-it* shows an emotional or sentimental attachment to a person or thing.

EXPRESSION CORNER

Verbal-fight

ASL distinguishes between a literal, physical fight and a heated exchange of words, known as a *verbal-fight*. Look closely at the sign; can you see why the sign is appropriate in a signed confrontation? How do you know?

Vocabulary — Relationships

To argue

To date

To fall in love

To flirt

To get along

Love

Relationship

Together, be together

Homework Exercise 5

A What do you and your friends do during the weekend? Prepare to sign a narrative describing an ideal weekend. What would you do?

B Develop a logical story from the information learned in each illustration. Each story must have a minimum of five complete sentences. Prepare to sign your story in ASL to your classmates.

C Write Assignment A or B in ASL gloss.

Accent Steps

This is one of the more common signs for *to break up*, though there are many others. Look closely at *relationship*: How could you make *break up* using this sign?

To break up

I Want to Know . . .

How do I fix mistakes?

Mistakes are guaranteed to happen, whether you are fluent in a language or not. Knowing how to correct mistakes is an important part of using language well. ASL has several ways to help correct mistakes: The most common corrections are *oops* and *wave-no*. When you make a mistake, use either sign and continue signing. You don't need to over-emphasize the signs or exaggerate facial expressions. The sign *um* shows one is thinking of what to say or trying to remember something. It is also a visual cue to inform those watching the conversation that the signer isn't done. *Wave-no* has several uses in ASL: it draws attention to a mistake (as in Example 2) and also serves as a "stronger" *no* than the sign *no*. Use *wave-no* to correct information ("No, I'm not from California"), to refuse something ("No, I don't want that"), or to signal an objection ("No, you're wrong").

Oops   **Slip-mind**

Um, uh   **Wave-no**

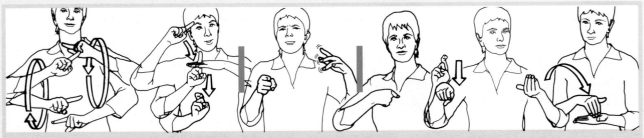

Her name is Kelly — oops, I mean Kris.

No, no — sign it again. / Let me sign it again.

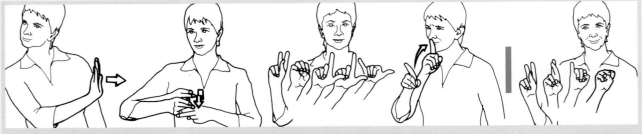

What was I going to say? Umm... I'm going to have to repeat it.

Classroom Exercise R

1 *Sign selection.* Which "fixing" sign best matches the concept shown in italics? Select the best option and sign the entire sentence.

1. *I can't remember the sign . . .*
2. *He's from . . . let's see, uh, I don't know.*
3. *No! I don't want to go out to eat.*
4. *The homework is due Wednesday . . . No, wait . . . It's due Friday.*
5. *Your name isn't Val? Oops . . . It's slipped my mind. What's your name?*
6. *Oh, I need to start again.*
7. *I signed that the wrong way - I meant love, not love-it.*
8. *It's on the tip of my tongue . . .*

2 *Making corrections.* Use *wave-no* to correct the sentences using the information in parentheses. An example is provided.

Is there an ASL party is tomorrow night?

No, the ASL party is Saturday, not tomorrow.

1. *Yesterday I argued with my teacher.* **(With sister)**
2. *He doesn't know.* **(Yes, he does)**
3. *I live on Pine Street.* **(Pine Lane)**
4. *She's hearing.* **(Deaf)**
5. *They don't get along with us.* **(They get along)**
6. *He's 25 years old.* **(29)**
7. *We don't want to go.* **(They do)**
8. *They can't sign.* **(They can)**
9. *Valentine's Day is February 12.* **(February 14)**
10. *It's cold outside.* **(It's hot)**

3 *Dialogue.* Work with a partner to create a dialogue that includes the following:

1. *a conversation that uses wave-no and oops;*
2. *a conversation that uses the plural form of to go to;*
3. *a conversation about friends that uses a "fixing" sign other than wave-no;*
4. *a conversation that uses oops and numbers.*

Pronouns II

In Units 1 and 3 you learned signs for pronouns and possessive pronouns. In this section, you will learn that ASL has a group of pronouns that incorporate number as well. Compare the ASL and English versions of the dialogue below, paying attention to the way ASL identifies an exact number of individuals while English does not.

Dialogue Translation

Kris: *What did you do over the weekend?*

Sean: *On Friday some friends and I went out. What did you two do?*

Kris: *We visited my grandparents.*

Sean: *Oh, how are they?*

Classroom Exercise

1. *Dialogue 1.* Practice signing the dialogue with a partner. Add a greeting, farewell, and at least two new details.

2. *Dialogue 2.* What pronoun signs do you see in the dialogue? What do they mean? Create a new dialogue with a partner using these pronouns.

ASL Up Close

Pronouns and Number

Use the ASL pronoun that shows the particular number of people being talked about whenever possible. When the exact number is unknown, use the general pronouns we, us, or they. Otherwise, use the following pronouns that refer to a specific number of people.

General pronoun: **We, us** (up to 8)	You and I, us two, the two of us		___and I, us two, the two of us		You, me, and ___, us three, the three of us		You, me, and ___, ___, us four, the four of us	
General pronoun: **You** (plural) (up to 8)	You and ___, you two, the two of you		You, ___, and ___, you three, the three of you		You, ___, ___, and ___, you four, the four of you			
General pronoun: **They, them, those** (up to 8)	___ and ___, those two, these two, the two of them		___, ___, and ___, those three, these three, the three of them		___, ___, ___, and ___, those four, these four, the four of them			

Eyes on ASL #10

When using ASL pronouns, the pronoun sign must match the number of individuals talked about.

If you don't know how many subjects there are, then use the generic we, you *(plural)*, and they signs.

Classroom Exercise

1 *Pronoun drill.* What is the correct pronoun sign?

1. *Those four*	4. *You and her*	7. *You, me, and him*	10. *Those two*	13. *Us two*
2. *You and me*	5. *These five*	8. *She and I*	11. *Us five*	14. *You two*
3. *You three*	6. *The six of them*	9. *The five of you*	12. *Two of them*	15. *Those two*

Classroom Exercise (continued)

2 *Using pronouns.* Sign each sentence in ASL, using the correct pronoun. For 8-10, create a sentence using the given pronoun.

1. *Those two are dating.*
2. *The four of us are sick.*
3. *Are you and she in a relationship?*
4. *You three need to study.*
5. *Those two and those two don't get along.*
6. *You and I need help.*
7. *Five of us work on Saturday.*

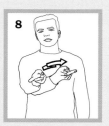

3 *Who?* Create a sentence using the information provided. Use the "Signer" position to select the pronoun sign that best fits the situation. An example is shown.

From Mexico

Those four are from Mexico. / They are from Mexico.

Happy

Learning ASL

1 single, 2 married

1 child, 1 adult

Get along

Want to go skiing

Homework Exercise 6

A You've been invited to join groups of friends, each of whom is doing something different on the weekend. Explain what each group is doing and which group you want to join. Use at least three ASL pronouns and sign a minimum of 5 sentences.

B Write your sentences for Assignment A in ASL gloss.

Classroom Exercise

1 *Conversation.* Fill in the blanks with an ASL pronoun that completes the sentence.

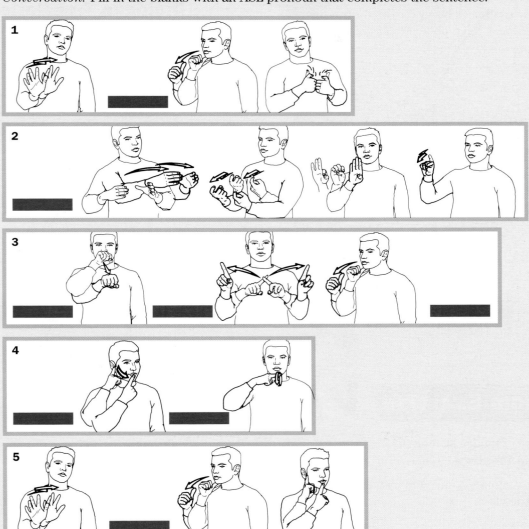

3 *Non-manual signals.* Below are several important non-manual signals in ASL. Practice each, paying attention to the nose, eyebrows, mouth, and lips. Have you noticed your teacher using these NMS?

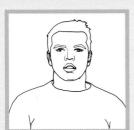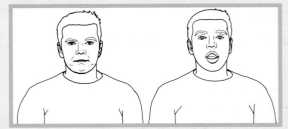

Describing Qualities

In this section you will learn to describe physical and personality traits. Notice that Sean raises his eyebrows for the sign *why*, while Kelly uses the WH-Face. What do you think this means?

Dialogue Translation

Kelly: *Why are the two of you friends?*

Sean: *I love my best friend because she's always funny, she's friendly, likes to go out, and is easy-going.*

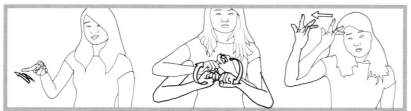

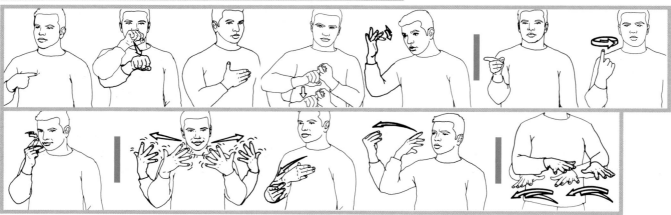

Classroom Exercise V

1. *Dialogue 1.* Practice signing the dialogue with a partner. Expand the dialogue by adding material before and after the sentences above.

2. *Dialogue 2.* Create a dialogue with a partner in which you both explain several characteristics of one or more friends.

Vocabulary — Physical Qualities

To be cute

To be pretty, beautiful

To smile

To be ugly

Classroom Exercise

1. *What are you like?* Ask a partner which qualities apply to him / her. When done switch roles and repeat the exercise. An example is provided.

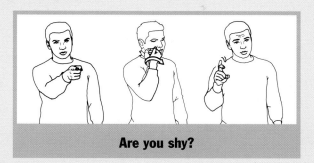

Are you shy?

1. *Like to smile*
2. *Mean*
3. *Shy*
4. *Cute*
5. *Easy-going*
6. *Like to go out*
7. *Arrogant*
8. *Friendly*
9. *Pretty*
10. *Mischievous*
11. *Like to annoy people*
12. *Funny*

2. *Dialogue 3.* Work with a partner to develop a dialogue between two signers that features at least five vocabulary words from the list below. Prepare to sign your dialogue in front of your classmates. Use correct ASL grammar, facial expressions, and remember that the dialogue must make sense.

Vocabulary   Personal Qualities

| To annoy, bother | To be annoyed | To be arrogant | To be friendly | To be funny |
| To laugh | To be mean | To be mischievous | To be shy | To be sweet |

Narrative: Friends

 DVD

Friends. Watch Kelly sign in full motion on your student DVD.

Classroom Exercise **X**

Comprehension. Respond to the questions based on the *Friends* narrative.

1. *How old was Kelly when she met Leon and Rae?*
2. *Are the three friends Deaf?*
3. *What do they do every day?*
4. *Why did Leon dive into the Deaf world?*
5. *How does Leon show Kelly and Rae that he's dived into the Deaf world?*

Classroom Exercise **Y**

1 *Dialogue.* You are single and your parents are waiting for grandchildren, so they want to introduce you to an eligible candidate. You, however, must present reasons why you are not interested in this person. Working with a partner, develop a dialogue between two or three signers.

2 *No, she isn't . . .* Respond to what a partner says about an individual following the clues provided. Use *wave-no* or *yes* as needed.

1. *They are lazy.* (**No, they work hard**)
2. *She is not shy.* (**No, she's outgoing**)
3. *He is friendly.* (**Yes, but arrogant**)
4. *She's interesting and smart.* (**Yes, works hard**)
5. *My mom is nice.* (**Yes, I love her**)
6. *His girlfriend is pretty.* (**Yes, she is not ugly**)
7. *Is he smart or stupid?* (**He is smart**)
8. *Your brother annoys me.* (**Yes, he bothers people**)
9. *Is your cousin a troublemaker?* (**No, he's sweet**)
10. *My best friend likes to work hard.* (**No, he's lazy**)

3 *Multiple meanings.* What do you think the signs are for the following terms? Create a sentence using the corresponding sign.

1. *Handsome*
2. *Amusing*
3. *Cheerful*
4. *Repulsive*
5. *Delinquent*
6. *Eager*
7. *Pessimistic*
8. *Dumb*
9. *Optimistic*
10. *Assertive*
11. *Intelligent*
12. *Kind*

Dive-in describes someone who becomes completely involved with an activity or group. It often refers to hearing individuals who learn ASL and socialize with the Deaf community.

Dive-in & Deaf World

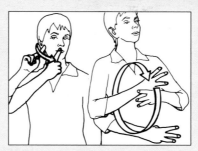

Deaf World refers to the Deaf community's clubs, sporting competitions, and social events where Deaf people form the majority and ASL is the language everybody knows, uses, and cherishes.

EXPRESSION CORNER

Homework Exercise 7

A   Who is your best friend? Explain how and when the two of you met, and include information about his or her character. What you do together? Prepare to present this information to your classmates in ASL in a minimum of five complete sentences.

B   Write an ASL gloss of the *Friends* narrative.

C   Practice signing Kelly's *Friends* presentation, focusing on smooth, clear signing, appropriate facial expressions, eye contact, and pauses.

Vocabulary   More Qualities

To be boring

To be interesting

To be lazy

To be motivated

To be negative

To be outgoing

To be positive

To be smart

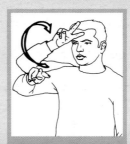
To be stupid

To work hard

Classroom Exercise Z

Opposites. Use Shoulder-Shifting to compare each illustration. An example is provided.

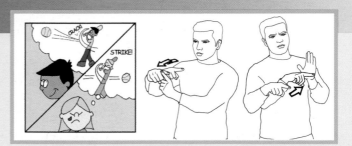

Homework Exercise 8

A. What qualities would the ideal friend have and not have? Using contrastive structure and the Listing & Ordering Technique, describe in detail the qualities of these two individuals. Prepare to sign your presentation to your classmates. You should have a minimum of 8 sentences.

B. Write an ASL gloss of the sentences signed in Assignment A.

Journal Activities

1   What do you think it would be like to have Deaf parents? Imagine the life of a coda and compare it with your own. In what ways would your life be different? How would it be the same? What do you think it would be like to be a Deaf parent with hearing children?

2   Compare the benefits and drawbacks of being Deaf with hearing parents, and Deaf with Deaf parents. What benefits does each arrangement have? Any drawbacks? Is one easier than the other? Why or why not?

3   A hearing couple you know has given birth to a Deaf baby and are unsure about the pros and cons about using ASL. Write a letter to this couple and explain both the manual and oral perspectives on the issue in order to educate them. Why do some parents choose not to learn ASL and others do? Should parents learn to sign, or should Deaf children be raised to speak? What are the pros and cons of each perspective?

4   If you were writing the Table of Contents appearing in Ann Silver's *Clifff's Notetakers: Deaf Culture* book, what topics would you include? What should people know about Deaf culture? Do you have any questions about Deaf culture, ASL, or deafness you would like answered? What are they?

— *Clifff's Notetakers: Deaf Culture* (1999), Ann Silver.
Reproduced by permission of artist.

Unit 4 Review

A A friend is visiting and you are looking through family albums. Describe the members of the Perez and Carter families, and explain what each family was doing when the picture was taken.

B What is contrastive structure? Locate and correct the contrastive structure errors below.

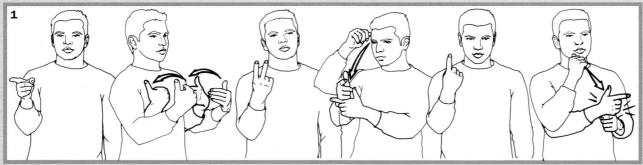

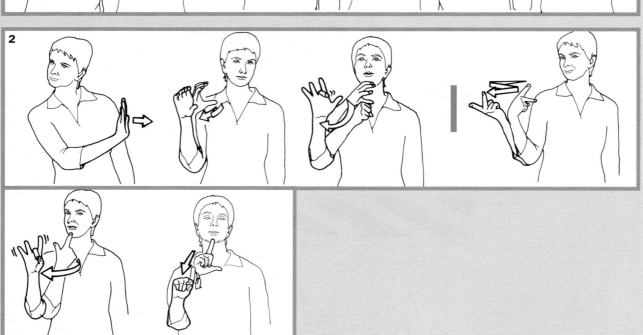

Unit 4 Review

C   Identify and correct the errors in the sentences below. Why are they wrong?

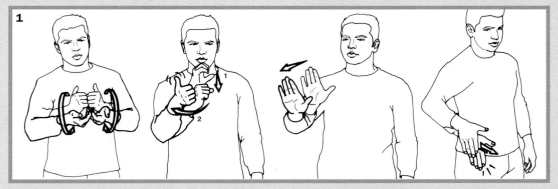

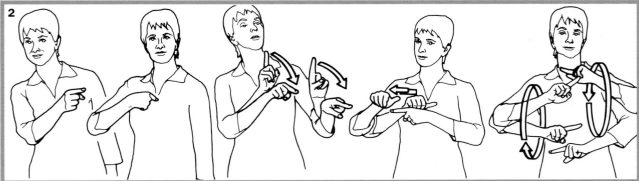

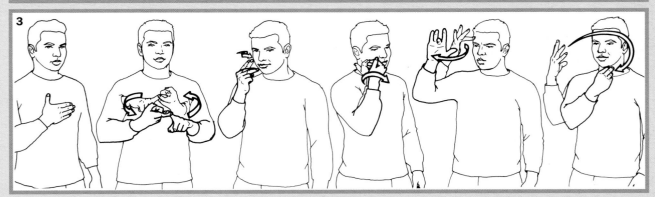

D   Sign each sentence in ASL.

1. *The three of them are 22, 35, and 67.*
2. *I've known her since I was 8 years old.*
3. *The four of us are going to the movies on Saturday night.*
4. *My little sister is cute but annoying. She likes to be mischievous.*
5. *He has two dogs, one cat, and two fish.*
6. *He is a coda; his parents are Deaf but his brother and sister and he are hearing.*

School Days

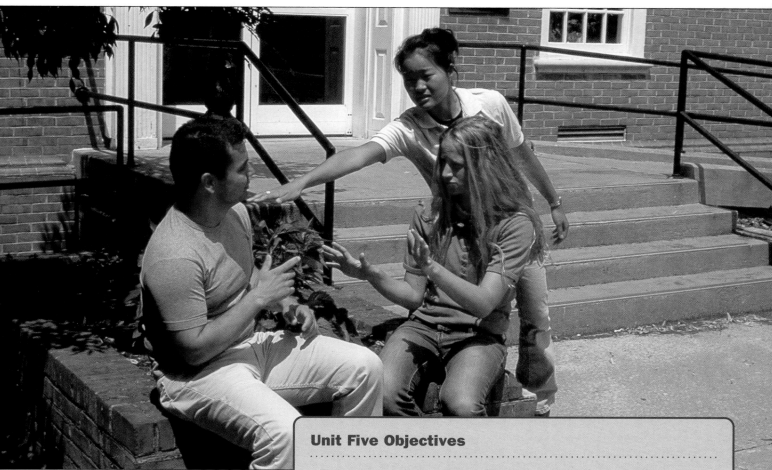

Unit Five Objectives

- To improve conversational skills

- To sign about school and school life

- To identify and use the Agent Marker appropriately

- To understand contemporary Deaf education options

- To understand and use these classifiers: ∧, 1, 3

- To tell time and sign about time-related issues

Unit Five Vocabulary

Key Phrases

Where do you go to school?

Hi, how are you? This year I'm a junior, taking American history, chemistry, and journalism. I play football at the school for the Deaf right over there. I love it there because all the students sign! I'm very involved with student government — I'm vice president of my class. Yikes! I'm late and have to take off. See you later!

Where do you go to school? Watch Marc sign in full motion on your student DVD.

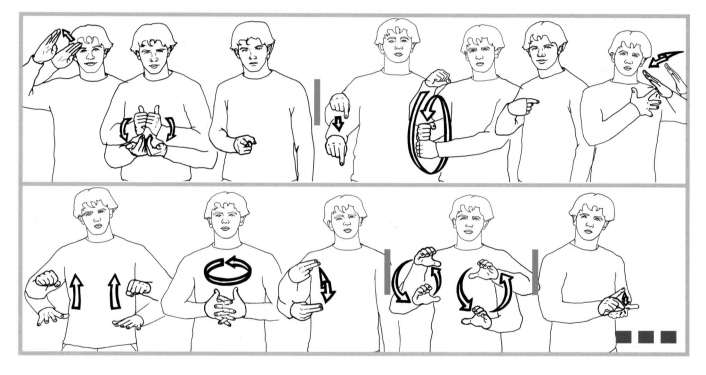

Vocabulary — Where do you go to school?

Other new vocabulary seen in the narrative is presented throughout Unit 5.

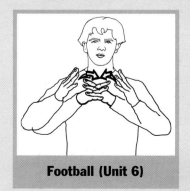

| Football (Unit 6) | Vice-president |

Places Around Campus

Pointing to people is a basic feature of American Sign Language. Just as a signer points to a person who may or may not be present, signers can point to a location whether it is seen or not. If the location is visible, simply point directly towards the area. Modify the point to reflect the actual path someone would take to arrive at the location. Depending on how the point is made, you can sign directions like *over there*, *around the corner*, or *that way*. Look at the way pointing is used in the *Places Around Campus* dialogue shown here.

Places around campus

Dialogue Translation

Marc: *Excuse me, where is the gym?*

Kelly: *It's right around there, near the theater.*

Marc: *Oh, okay. Thank you!*

Kelly: *You're welcome.*

Classroom Exercise A

1   *Pointing.* How would you show the meaning of each direction using the pointing finger?

1. *straight ahead*

2. *around the corner*

3. *far away*

4. *right over there*

5. *towards the left*

6. *very close*

2   *Dialogues.*

1. *Practice signing the "Places Around Campus" dialogue with a partner.*

2. *Sign the "Places Around Campus" dialogue with a partner, but substitute a different direction than the one provided.*

Classroom Exercise B

1 *Giving directions.* Work with a partner to ask where each destination is located at your school. Your partner will point towards its location. When done, switch roles and repeat the exercise.

1. *Student center*	4. *Gymnasium*	7. *Lab*	10. *Men's restroom*
2. *Theater*	5. *Library*	8. *Auditorium*	11. *Pool*
3. *Cafeteria*	6. *Office*	9. *Women's restroom*	12. *ASL classroom*

2 *Misunderstandings.* A visitor to your campus has received incorrect directions. Correct the information your partner signs to you using the information in parentheses. An example is provided.

The office is near the theatre.

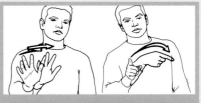

No, it's around the corner

1. *The library is near the student center.* (**near office**)
2. *The cafeteria is near the gym.* (**near theater**)
3. *The pool is far from the gym.* (**near, around gym**)
4. *The tech center is over there.* (**opposite direction**)

5. *The lab is not near the tech center.* (**it is near**)
6. *The office is near the stadium.* (**far from stadium**)

Vocabulary — School Locations

Fingerspell these words: **Lab / laboratory, Pool**

Area (location)

Cafeteria

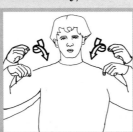

Gymnasium

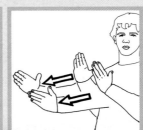

Hallway

Library

Office

Stadium, auditorium

Student center

Technology center

Theater

Classroom Exercise C

1 *Help!* A new student needs help finding his way around school. Respond to your partner in a complete sentence using the information in parentheses. When done, switch roles and repeat.

Excuse me. I'm looking for the office. Where is it?

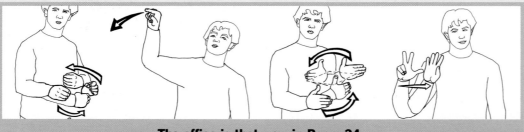

The office is that way, in Room 34.

1. *Bathroom* **(?)**
2. *Office* **(Room 7)**
3. *Tech center* **(Room 24)**
4. *Student store* **(Room 5)**
5. *Women's locker room* **(Room 50, gym)**
6. *Water fountain* **(around corner, down hall)**

7. *Theater* **(Room 227)**
8. *ASL Lab* **(Room 16)**
9. *Cafeteria* **(Room 67)**
10. *Student lockers* **(hallway)**
11. *ASL classroom* **(?)**
12. *Student center* **(Room 23)**

2 *Dialogue.* Create a dialogue with a partner that includes the following details:

1. *two different locations*
2. *a room number*
3. *what's going on at each location?*

Vocabulary — Conversation

Class

Locker

To look for

Room, box

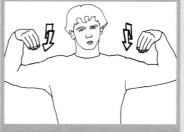

Store

Classroom Exercise D

1 *Around there.* Use the *area* sign in a complete sentence to explain where each location is found.

  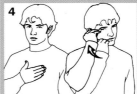 

The bathroom is around there, near the pool. / The bathroom is in that direction, by the pool.

1 2 3 4 5

2 *Compound meanings.* How would you sign the following words using ___ + area? Create a complete sentence for each.

1. *Food court*   **2.** *Neighborhood*   **3.** *Football field*   **4.** *Movie complex*   **5.** *Shopping center*

Vocabulary   Personnel

Coach, boss, dean

Counselor

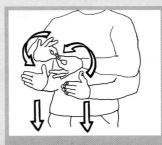
Interpreter

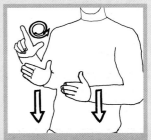
Librarian

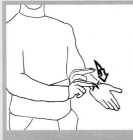
Nurse

Principal

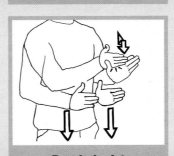
Psychologist

Secretary

School Personnel

In this lesson you will learn vocabulary for people you encounter at school. You will see some signs for school personnel include an added feature called the **Agent Marker**, while others do not. With the exception of a small group of signs, the Agent Marker creates the meaning of someone who does something. In the sentences below, compare the sign *nurse*, which doesn't use the Agent Marker, with *teacher*, which does.

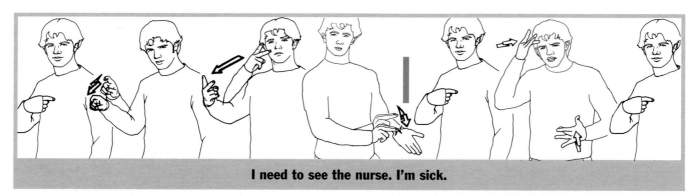

I need to see the nurse. I'm sick.

Is your ASL teacher a man or woman?

Accent Steps

Neighborhood

Adding the *area* sign forms a **compound** meaning, as in home + area: *neighborhood*. Remember this by thinking "an area of / for ___."

Homework Exercise ◀ 1

A Write a dialogue between two people using vocabulary from the "Places Around Campus" lesson. The dialogue must have a minimum of six sentences. Prepare to sign the dialogue for the next ASL class.

B Create a mini-narrative using one or more compound signs using *area*. Your mini-narrative should have a minimum of three sentences.

C Write Assignment A or B in ASL gloss.

Classroom Exercise

1 *Personnel.* Sign each sentence in correct ASL word order.

1. *The interpreter's name is Teri Cassidy.*
2. *My ASL teacher's name is ____ ____.*
3. *The librarian can help you look for the books.*

4. *My boss / coach is named ____.*
5. *Is the nurse here today?*

2 *Go see the nurse.* Your friend is telling you about some problems. Recommend who he or she should see for assistance. When done, switch roles with your partner and repeat the exercise.

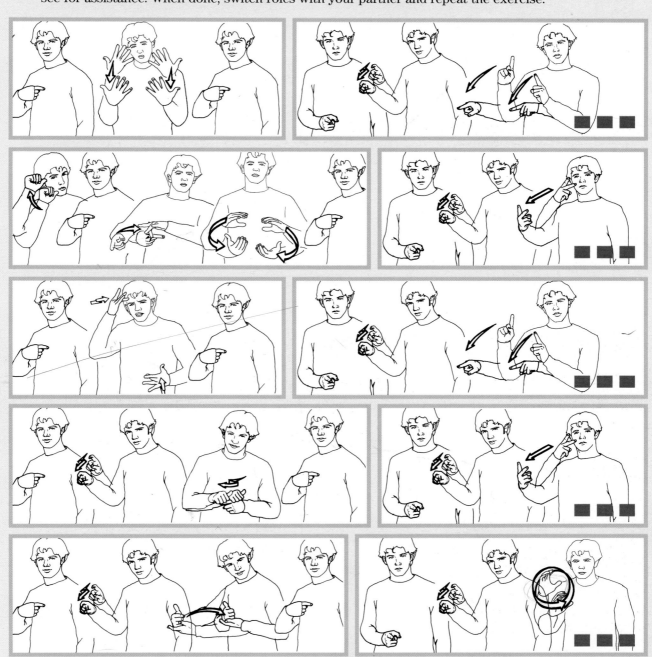

Deaf Culture Minute

There are no signs for Mr., Mrs., or Miss in ASL. Within the Deaf community, an individual is known by his or her name sign and children are permitted to address their elders by name. Titles like Mr. and Mrs. are used to show respect, so signing someone's name with a respectful facial expression achieves the same purpose.

ASL Up Close

The Agent Marker

To learn

Student

The Agent Marker

What is the connection between the signs *to learn* and *student*? The Agent Marker indicates a person who works as, or does, the meaning of the sign. In this example, *one who learns* is a *student*. There are some exceptions to the Agent Marker you need to know, such as the signs for *nurse*, *principal*, and *coach*.

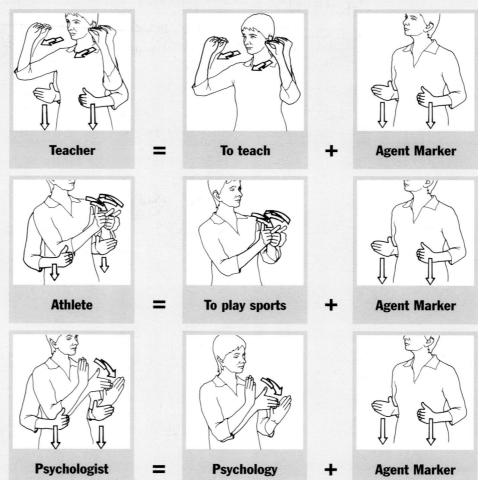

Teacher = **To teach** + **Agent Marker**

Athlete = **To play sports** + **Agent Marker**

Psychologist = **Psychology** + **Agent Marker**

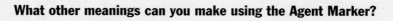

What other meanings can you make using the Agent Marker?

Vocabulary   Activities

To cook

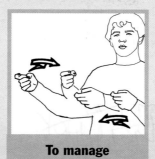

To manage

To pick on

To serve

To write

Classroom Exercise F

1   *How do you sign that?* What signs are paired with the Agent Marker to make the following words? Think carefully about the vocabulary you've learned and their meanings before deciding.

1. *Voter*	4. *Troublemaker*	7. *Employee*	10. *Waiter*	13. *Chef*
2. *Trainer*	5. *Visitor*	8. *American*	11. *Actor*	14. *Writer*
3. *Driver*	6. *Skier*	9. *Canadian*	12. *Manager*	15. *Bully*

2   *Conversation.* Sign each of the following sentences in ASL.

1. *My cousin is a troublemaker. He loves to pick on my little brother.*
2. *I'm not a chef but I like to help my parents cook.*
3. *Where's our waiter?*
4. *Who manages the student store?*
5. *Our coach wants us to go to practice on Saturday.*

3   *Making inquiries.* Ask a partner to respond to each question. When done, switch roles and repeat.

1. *Are you a writer?*	5. *Are you Canadian or American?*
2. *Are you a chef?*	6. *Are you a skier?*
3. *Are you an employee?*	7. *Are you a driver?*
4. *Are you a musician?*	8. *Are you a nag?*

Homework Exercise   2

A   Considering the Agent Marker's influence on the meaning of a sign, make a list of 10 signs you think could be modified by the Agent Marker. Make another list of signs you think cannot use the Agent Marker. What is the difference between them?

B   Write a dialogue between two signers that includes a minimum of three uses of the Agent Marker. The entire dialogue should be at least five sentences long.

C   Write Assignment A or B in ASL gloss.

More Places Around Campus

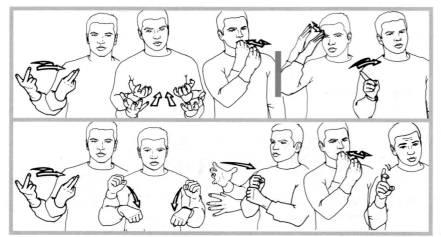

Dialogue Translation

Sean: *We're hungry. Know where we can get something to eat?*

Marc: *Yeah, there's a vending machine down the hall.*

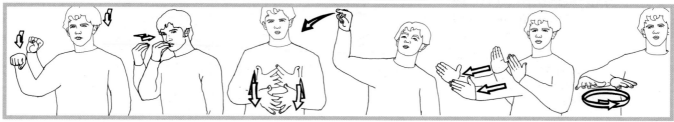

Vocabulary — More Locations

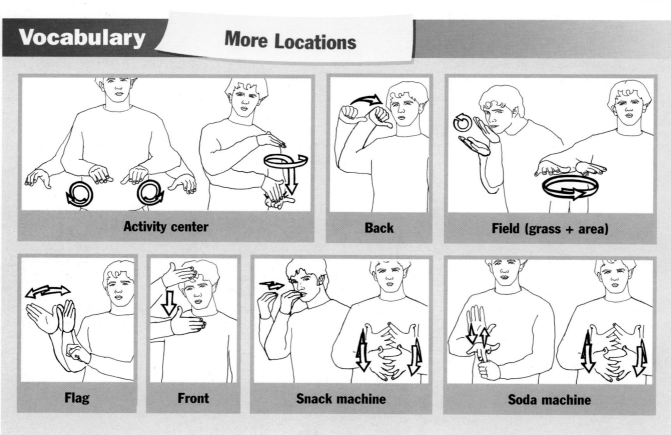

| Activity center | Back | Field (grass + area) |

| Flag | Front | Snack machine | Soda machine |

Classroom Exercise

Dialogue. Work with a partner to accomplish the following:

1 Create a dialogue that expands on the sentences in "More Places Aound Campus" on page 176. How will the dialogue begin and end? Where are they and why are they there? Use your imagination.

2 Create a new dialogue that includes the following:

   1. *Agent Marker*   **2.** *Two locations*   **3.** *Three personnel*

Classroom Exercise

1 *Where is the auditorium?* Ask a partner to explain where items 1-6 are located. When done, switch roles and locate items 7-12. Ask and answer the questions in complete ASL sentences. Refer to the illustration below for each location.

  1. *Where is the soda machine?*
  2. *Where is the ASL classroom?*
  3. *Where is the nurse's office?*
  4. *Where is the flag?*
  5. *Is there a counselor or psychologist?*
  6. *Where are the locker rooms?*
  7. *Does this school have an activity center?*
  8. *Where is the cafeteria?*
  9. *Where is the field?*
  10. *Where is the men's restroom?*
  11. *Does the school have a pool?*
  12. *Where's the snack machine?*

[Map illustration showing: Field, Pool, Locker rooms 43, Cafeteria 39, Activity Center 41, Science 37, English 35, Counselor 33, Office 31, Nurse's office 45 / 29, Auditorium 45, Drama Classes 13 15, Soda and snack machines, ASL Classroom 21 23, Math Class 25, Girl's room 27, Mens room, Flag]

2 *Around campus.* What amenities does your school have? Create a dialogue with a partner in which you discuss different features your school has and where they are located.

Did you know?

Federal law requires equal access to information and services for all people, regardless of disability. For both hearing and Deaf people, sign language interpreters are a popular way to obtain equal access to each other. Have you seen interpreters at public events, on television, or at your school or workplace? Interpreters are required to sign what is heard, and to voice what is signed so everybody has access to the information and services provided. While the majority of interpreters are hearing, don't be surprised if you encounter a Deaf interpreter!

When using an interpreter, remember these tips:
• Talk directly to the Deaf person instead of saying "Ask him" or "Tell her."
• Make eye contact with the Deaf person, not the interpreter.

To learn more about interpreters, visit http://www.rid.org

Classroom Exercise

Feedback. Sign each sentence to a partner, who will respond with an opinion about what should be done. When done, switch roles and repeat.

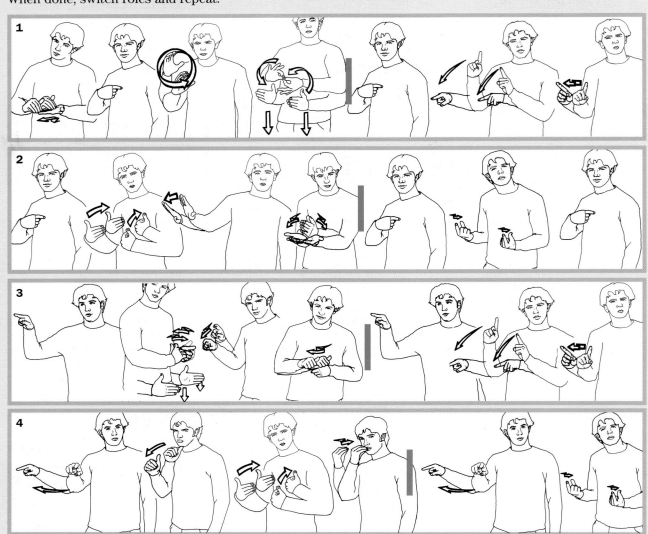

Homework Exercise 3

A Either obtain or draw a map of your school and mark several important locations such as the student center, lockers, telephones, and restrooms. Practice signing directions to the marked locations.

B Where do you spend most of your time while at school? Explain the different places you go to and what you do there, in a minimum of five complete sentences. Prepare to sign this information to your classmates.

C Write Assignment A or B in ASL gloss.

What are You Studying?

 Striking up a conversation about school is one way to get to know somebody better. Like *do-do*, the sign *what year are you* has several meanings depending on the context. When talking about family, *what year are you* is a question about older or younger siblings, but when talking about school it refers to one's level of study in high school and college. Look closely at the sign *what year are you*. Do you see the Listing & Ordering concept? The dialogue here shows you one way to use this sign in conversation.

Dialogue Translation

Marc: *What year are you?*

Kelly: *I'm a junior, taking ASL and economics.*

Marc: *Oh I'm a senior. I'm taking English, math, and governmnet because I want to graduate.*

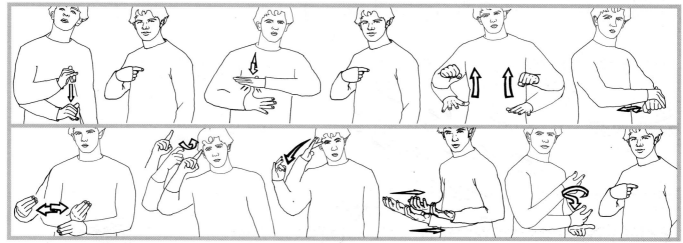

Classroom Exercise J

1   *Dialogue.* Sign the "What are you studying?" dialogue with a partner, adding more conversation and a conclusion.

2   *What year?* Ask several classmates what year of school they are in. Use the WH-Face with the sign *what year are you.*

Classroom Exercise K

1 *What year are you?* Ask a partner what year he or she is in school, who will respond with the information in parentheses. An example is provided. When done, switch roles and repeat.

| **What year is she?** | **She's a junior.** |

1. *Carolyn* (**freshman**)
2. *Kevin Miles* (**senior**)
3. *Shane* (**junior**)
4. *Tisha Leung* (**sophomore**)

5. *Jon* (**freshman**)
6. *Blanche* (**senior**)
7. *Abby Fiore* (**don't know**)
8. *Darrell Jamison* (**junior**)

9. *Brigitte Cowley* (**sophomore**)
10. *Aaron* (**junior**)
11. *Van Nguyen* (**senior**)
12. *you* (**?**)

2 *Taking a survey.* Your campus newspaper is analyzing the results of a survey broken down by class. For each brief biography, state the student's year in school and at least two other details in a complete sentence.

 Angela, 20 years old, junior, majoring in Deaf studies

 Claro, 15 years old sophomore, plays baseball, has 2 brothers

 Sheri, 23 years old, senior, majoring in ASL, wants to teach ASL

 Brent, 17 years old, junior, works at a restaurant, wants to go to college

 Kelly, 22 years old freshman, works as a manager, studying nursing

 Brian, sophomore, has twin brother, doesn't have a major, enjoys acting

Vocabulary   **What year are you?**

    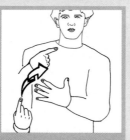

| **Freshman** | **Sophomore** | **Junior** | **Senior** | **What year are you?** |

Classroom Exercise

1   *Education past and present.* Exchange the following information with a partner:

   1. *Name of your favorite teacher*
   2. *Names of all schools attended* (use the Listing & Ordering Technique)
   3. *Two things remembered from elementary school*
   4. *Why taking ASL*
   5. *Going to high school / college / university? Where?*

2   *What is school like?* What are some characteristics typical for each level of education? Include age range and likely activities. Suggested topics are provided.

<u>**Suggested Topics**</u>

   1. *elementary school*
   2. *middle school / junior high*
   3. *high school*
   4. *college / university*

take art   *learning to read*
learn ASL   *moving away from home*
ride a bike to school   *have 1 teacher all day*
play sports   *have a major*
have a locker   *learn to write*

3   *Dialogue.* Work with a partner to sign a dialogue about an experience you remember from earlier school days. Include an opening, at least three details, a conclusion, and a farewell.

Vocabulary   Education

Elementary school	**To forget**	**Junior high school**	**To major in**
Middle school	**To remember**	**To take (something)**	**To think** **University**

Classroom Exercise M

1 *I'm taking . . . .* In complete sentences, sign the following:

    1. What classes are you taking right now? Use the Listing & Ordering Technique to list the courses. Include a comment about each course.

    2. Compare your course load with a partner's. Who is taking the more difficult courses? The easiest?

2 *Favorites.* Ask a partner to list his or her five favorite classes. Do you disagree with any choices? When done, switch roles and repeat the exercise.

3 *Coursework.* Based on the illustrations, explain in complete sentences what the class is, if it is a high school or college class, and whether you would want to take the class.

Vocabulary — Coursework

Art	Auto body	Biology	Business	Chemistry
Computers / Tech (See Page 184 for variations)	Drama	Economics	Education	Engineering
English	Geography	Government	Gym	Physical Education
Health	History	Journalism	Math	Photography
Physics	Physiology	Science	Sociology	Speech

Vocabulary — Coursework (continued)

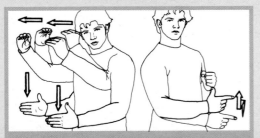

Teacher's assistant

Woodshop

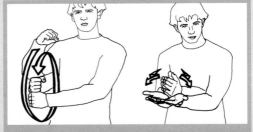

Yearbook

Classroom Exercise N

Coursework. What is each course known for? Explain what people do in the courses below. Note: Raise your eyebrows for the first two signs of the sentence. An example is provided.

What do you do in English? Study literature, reading, and writing.

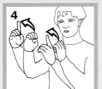

1
2
3
4
5

Vocabulary — Computer Variations

Computer (2)

Computer (3)

Accent Steps

Don't confuse *busy* with *business*. What differences do you see?

Busy

Business

Classroom Exercise

Signing about school. Complete each sentence by filling in the blanks.

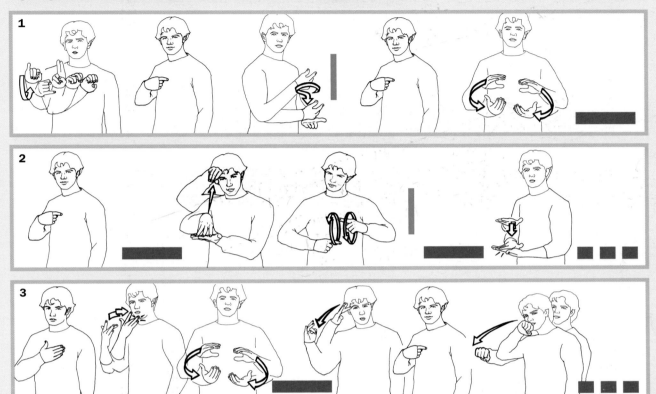

Homework Exercise   4

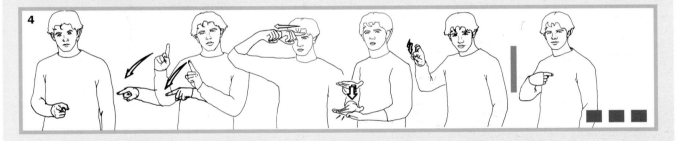

A You will attend a party where most of the people are Deaf. Prepare to thoroughly introduce yourself: What is your name? Where do you live? Where do you go to school? Are you a high school or college student? What year are you?

B What classes are you taking? Explain which courses you're studying and indicate which are your favorites and why, in a minimum of five sentences.

C Write Assignment A or B in ASL gloss.

Focus: Deaf Education . . .

" It is a lamentable fact that, in matters relating to the deaf, their education and well-being, few if any take the trouble to get the opinion of the very people most concerned — the deaf themselves. " —*John H. Keiser*

The American School for the Deaf was the first school dedicated to the education of Deaf children in the United States. Opened in 1817, the school used sign language to educate its students in the **manual method**, many of whom went on to found schools for the Deaf across the United States. There are now several options for Deaf education: Attend a school for the Deaf where ASL is used, attend an oral school where the goal is to teach students how to speak, or be mainstreamed, in which case a Deaf student attends a local public school. Each option has its

**American School for the Deaf
Hartford, Connecticut**
Courtesy: American School for the Deaf

ideological supporters and opponents who believe one form of educating the Deaf to be better than another, leading to much controversy.

School for the Deaf

Schools for the Deaf are environments in which students, teachers, and support staff such as principals, counselors, and coaches generally use American Sign Language. Because there is usually only one school for the Deaf in each state, students stay at school during the week and return home on weekends and vacations. Many Deaf students enjoy all-Deaf sports teams, Deaf teachers and administrators, and having equal access to information and activities where being Deaf is normal.

In many ways, a school for the Deaf is exactly like a hearing school except that students learn and communicate in ASL. Schools for the Deaf have student dances and proms, sports programs that compete against Deaf and hearing teams, and extracurricular activities like journalism, web design, and other social opportunities. The California School for the Deaf in Fremont even has a program where students study and then visit foreign countries like China. Each school strives to educate its Deaf students to be active members of society, just like schools for hearing individuals.

Decisions & Controversies

Oral education

Oral schools believe that deaf people must learn to listen and speak in order to function in the "hearing world" and thus rarely allow students to use sign language. Many years ago oral education used harsh methods to prevent students from signing, though attitudes have greatly changed since then. Oral schools tend to be small and private, with most programs serving students from kindergarten through elementary school, at which point students enter a school for the Deaf or a public school.

Learning to speak when you cannot hear yourself is a long, laborious process that requires much one-on-one instruction and support. With technological support such as hearing aids and FM systems, oral schools strive to train its deaf students to speak and "listen" by lip-reading. As you can see, the manual and **oral methods** of deaf education are completely different philosophies.

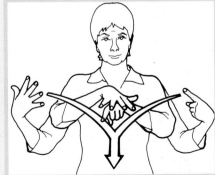

The third option for Deaf education is to be **mainstreamed**, meaning a Deaf student attends a local public school. If there are several Deaf students at the school, they may have their own teacher of the Deaf in a separate classroom, or may take the same classes as hearing students with an interpreter who provides access to the information.

Often, there is only one Deaf student in an entire school which can be lonely and frustrating. The *one in a crowd* sign is used to describe these Deaf mainstreamed students. Compare this sign with *mainstreamed*: Do you see why there are two different signs for the concept? Now that many more hearing students are learning ASL, mainstreamed students may be less isolated.

Mainstreamed

One in a crowd

ASL Up Close

Math

Initialization

Initialization refers to meanings related to a particular root sign, such as the sign for *math*. The signs for *algebra, calculus, geometry,* and *trigonometry* are all related to the basic *math* sign, except for the initials added to each. An initialized sign is one that incorporates a fingerspelled letter as part of the sign. What other initialized signs do you know? Consider *science* and compare that to the signs *biology* and *chemistry*. Are they related?

Algebra

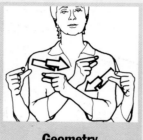

Calculus

Geometry

Trigonometry

Classroom Exercise

1   *Math?* Ask a partner whether he or she is taking a math class. Your partner will respond using the information below. When done, switch roles and repeat. An example is provided.

Are you taking math?

Yes, I'm taking math.

1. *Yes, I'm taking algebra.*
2. *No, I'm not taking math. I'm taking economics.*
3. *No, I don't need to take math.*
4. *Yes, I'm taking geometry and Algebra 2.*
5. *Yes, I'm studying calculus.*

6. *No, I'm majoring in history.*
7. *Yes, we're taking trigonometry.*
8. *No, I'm not taking math.*
9. *Yes, I'm taking ...*
10. *No, I'm not ...*

2   *Dialogue.* In groups of three or more, create a dialogue that includes the initialized math signs. Your dialogue should also include greetings and farewells.

To be good at   **To be bad at**

To be Good or Bad at (something)

The expressions *to be good at* something and *to be bad at* something are often used in ASL conversation. They refer to one's skill in a given area. What are some English synonyms for the phrases *to be good at* and *to be bad at?*

EXPRESSION CORNER

Classroom Exercise Q

1   *Synonyms & Antonyms.* Work with a partner to develop a list of English words and phrases that mean *to be good at* (something) and *to be bad at* (something). Prepare to share the list with your classmates.

2   *Skills.* Ask a partner whether he or she is good at doing the following things. When done, switch roles and repeat. An example is shown.

Are you good at sports?

Yeah, I'm good at sports.   **No, I'm not good at sports**

1. *Are you good at math?* **(?)**
2. *Are you good at cooking?* **(?)**
3. *Are you good at writing papers?* **(?)**
4. *Are you good at facial expressions?* **(?)**
5. *Are you good at science?* **(?)**

6. *Are you good at taking tests?* **(?)**
7. *Are you good at signing?* **(?)**
8. *Are you good at algebra?* **(?)**
9. *Are you good at art?* **(?)**
10. *Are you a good singer / musician?* **(?)**

3   *Opposites . . .* You and a friend have opposite opinions on several issues. Sign each sentence to your partner, who will respond with the information in parentheses. When done, switch roles.

1. *I think s/he's a terrible actor.*
   (No, s/he's a very good actor!)
2. *I think college is boring.*
   (No, college is exciting and fun!)
3. *I think he's a lousy teacher.*
   (No, he's a great teacher!)

4. *I'm not a good signer.*
   (No, you're a very good signer!)
5. *I'm no good at math.*
   (No, you're a math genius!)
6. *I think s/he's a great singer.*
   (No, s/he's a terrible singer!)

Classroom Exercise

I want to be ... You and some friends are talking about future careers. Explain what people must be good at in order to reach the goal.

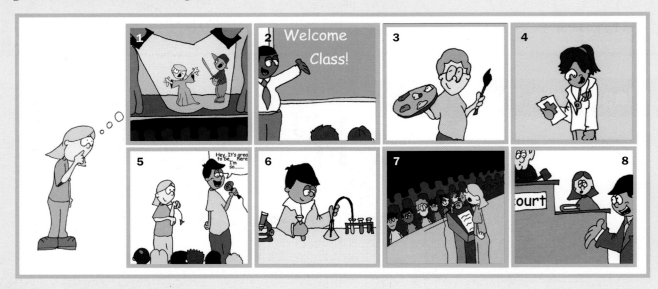

Deaf Culture NOTE

Gallaudet

Gallaudet University

Founded in 1864 and chartered by President Abraham Lincoln, Gallaudet University is the world's only liberal arts university specifically designed for Deaf and hard of hearing students. Located in Washington, D.C., Gallaudet teaches all courses in American Sign Language and hosts international students from around the world. A limited number of hearing undergraduates are accepted each year if they can demonstrate fluency in ASL, though students can study for a semester as visiting students and many hearing graduate students pursue advanced degrees at Gallaudet.

Gallaudet University and the Deaf community became well-known to the hearing world in 1988 when Deaf people around the world campaigned for a Deaf president at Gallaudet University, protesting the philosophy that Deaf people were not capable of governing themselves. After worldwide attention, Gallaudet installed Dr. I. King Jordan as its first Deaf president. His comment that "Deaf people can do anything . . . but hear" has been an inspiration to many. Gallaudet is the pride of the Deaf community and a beacon for Deaf individuals around the world denied educational opportunities in their home countries.

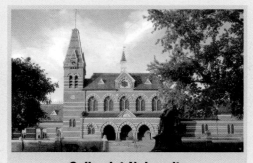

Gallaudet University
Courtesy: Gallaudet University

I Want to Know . . .

How do I sign grades?

To sign a grade in ASL, place a letter onto the palm of your hand, as shown in the examples. The concept behind these signs is a letter grade on a piece of paper. When signing about letter grades in general, fingerspell *grade* or *grades*.

An A grade

An F grade

I didn't study so I failed the test. / I didn't study so I got an F on the test.

Classroom Exercise S

1 *Facial expressions.* Practice making each facial expression below.

2 *Meanings.* What do you think each facial expression conveys? Hostility, pleasure, and amusement are a few different meanings shown above. Discuss the facial expressions with a partner and write down a list of sentences which would use each expression.

Homework Exercise 5

A Practice signing five sentences that incorporate the signs *good at* and *bad at*. Some ideas: What are your areas of strength or weakness? What are your favorite or least favorite school subjects?

B Create a dialogue between two or more people that uses the signs *good at* and *bad at*. The dialogue should have at least five sentences and include an opening, a main body, and a conclusion.

C Write Assignment A or B in ASL gloss.

Classifiers

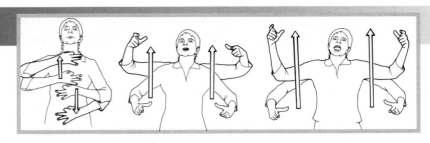

There is a large body of ASL handshapes that convey multiple meanings depending on their use and context. These handshapes are called **classifiers** because each reflects a class of shared characteristics. The English language has a small group of classifiers, especially when describing groups of animals, as in the sentence "A gaggle of geese." However, ASL has a far larger and much richer use for classifiers that influence signs and sign choices, depending on what exactly the signer is communicating. Classifiers are a beloved feature of ASL literature and are often eagerly awaited in a storytelling competition as spectators enjoy classifiers being used in new and unique ways.

Dialogue Translation

Kelly: *What are you two doing?*

Marc: *There's a classifier competition on Friday. We're practicing for it.*

Kelly: *Oh, I see. Have fun.*

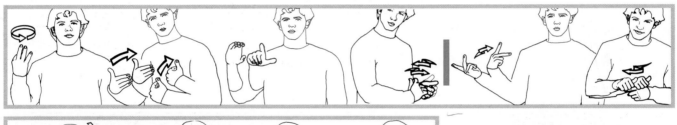

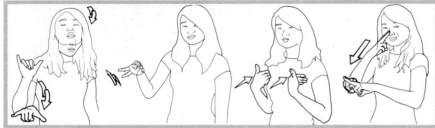

Classroom Exercise T

1. *Dialogue.* Select from the options below:

   1. Recreate the dialogue above by adding new material in at least four new sentences, including greetings and farewells.

   2. How does the dialogue end? Continue the dialogue from above, adding a conclusion.

2. *Classifier stories.* View one or more of the classifier stories on your student DVD. Choose from:

   DVD

   1. ABC Story — *Deafula*

   2. Classifier Story — *Story Using "5"*

   3. Number Story — *Symphony*

ASL Up Close

Classifiers

One of the more challenging aspects of ASL is the concept of the **classifier** (CL), a handshape that reflects particular characteristics. This concept is perhaps the most visual element that is both **iconic** and **abstract** in nature, which often confuses ASL students. In its most basic form, a classifier is a handshape that conveys details contributing to the overall concept of a sign, in addition to the sign's meaning. For those fluent in ASL, using and understanding classifiers is nearly instinctual. As an ASL student, begin developing your classifier skills by closely observing why specific handshapes are used for signs and the meanings those handshapes suggest. Below are some signs that should be familiar, along with one that is unfamiliar. Based on the classifier concept, can you guess the unknown sign's meaning?

Different Uses of CL: B

- Concept: Wide, flat surfaces on my body moving back and forth
- Meaning: I walk

- Concept: Four wide, flat surfaces in rectangular shape
- Meaning: Walls / room

- Concept: Wide, flat, vertical surface that swings open
- Meaning: Door / open

- Concept: Wide, flat, horizontal surface that moves in a wave-like fashion
- Meaning: ?

Vocabulary — Classifiers

 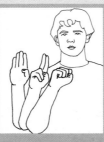  

Accident | **Bus** | **Classifier** | **To dance**

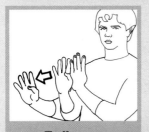   

To line up | **To look at** | **Motorcycle** | **To ride a horse**

CL: 1 An individual

CL: 1 generally represents an individual and its location, action, and manner. Manipulate the sign to reflect details such as walking slowly, hunched over, moving quickly, falling down, or other characteristics. CL: 1 depicts up to five individuals engaged in the same action simultaneously; for larger crowds, CL: 5 must be used (see Unit 6). CL: 1 also refers to cylindrical objects as well, including logs or poles.

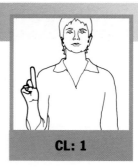

CL: 1

The meaning of Example 1 can vary depending on the characteristics incorporated into the classifier. In this example, it is clear someone is going to the office in a hurry because the classifier is signed quickly. Compare this meaning with Example 2.

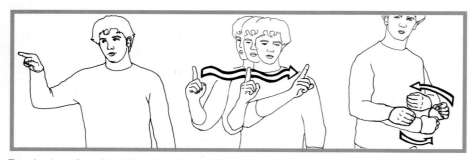

By signing the classifier slowly, a different meaning is conveyed. In Example 2, it is clear someone is going to the office slowly, or not in a rush.

FYI Use eye gaze to show the beginning and end points of the moving person.

Eyes on ASL #11

Because classifiers have different meanings, it is important to identify the object being represented by a classifier.

Classifiers are noted with the abbreviation CL, followed by the sign, as in CL: 1.

DVD

Classroom Exercise U

1. *CL: 1.* Using only CL: 1, how would you sign each meaning below? Keep in mind that facial expressions are an important component as well.

   1. *He's hunched over.*
   2. *They ran that way!*
   3. *She's moving at a snail's pace.*
   4. *He turned around.*
   5. *They went that way, then went in another direction.*

   6. *He's in a rush!*
   7. *She fell down.*
   8. *He's walking very slowly.*
   9. *The three of them are moving towards me.*
   10. *The two people bowed to each other.*

2. *Using CL: 1.* Sign several sentences using CL: 1 to a partner. How many different meanings can you make with the classifier?

CL: ∧ A person's legs or eyes

CL:∧ represents the actions of one individual's legs or eyes. Non-manual signals are especially important when using the classifier to depict the eyes, because facial expressions distinguish between *a dirty look*, *curiosity*, and other meanings. CL:∧ should be used when describing the body as a whole, as in *laying down*. Use this classifier to show others walking, but not yourself — use the sign *I walk*.

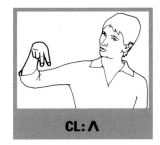

CL:∧

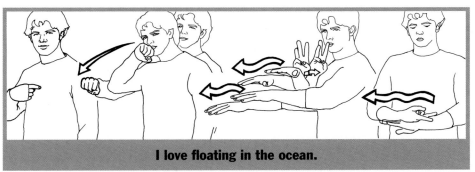

I love floating in the ocean.

Deaf Culture Minute

Classifiers play an important role in ASL literature, especially in classifier stories. A classifier story is one in which the signer only uses a specified classifier to tell an entire story, something that cannot be done in English.

Classroom Exercise

1   *CL:∧* Using only CL:∧ for the words in bold, how would you sign each sentence below? Keep in mind that facial expressions are an important component as well.

1. *He gave me a dirty look.*
2. *She's walking home.*
3. *He was walking and fell on the ground.*
4. *I like to look around.*
5. *They're standing across from each other.*
6. *I'm watching you like a hawk!*
7. *I want to lay down.*
8. *Children like to play hopscotch.*
9. *He keeps looking at me and looking away.*
10. *They're staring at each other*

2   *Using CL:∧* Sign several sentences using CL:∧ to a partner. How many different sentences can you make with the classifier?

3   *Using CL:∧ & CL: 1.* Sign each sentence below using both CL: 1 and CL:∧ for the words in bold.

1. *Can you* **walk on a balance beam?**
2. *The mother* **examined the boy from head to toe.**
3. **He walked over to the man laying on the floor.**
6. **Don't trip on that thing.**
5. *I'm learning how to* **logroll.**

❝ No written or spoken sentence can reach the mind as swiftly . . . as the thing seen . . . . The language of images. ❞ — *Douglas Tilden, sculptor*

CL: 3 Vehicles

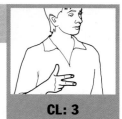
CL: 3

CL: 3 represents the actions of wheeled vehicles such as bicycles, cars, and motorcycles, after the vehicle has been identified. Manipulate the classifier to reflect important details including direction of travel and / or speed, and include facial expressions and other non-manual signals as needed. CL: 3 is an example of a classifier that is not iconic.

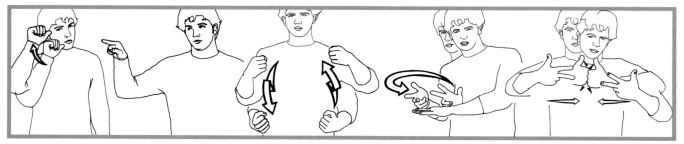

How would you translate this example into English? How many different ways can you think of to explain what happened?

Classroom Exercise W

1 *CL: 3.* Use the signs *bus*, *motorcycle*, and *car* with CL: 3 in a complete sentence. An example is provided.

1. *The bus ...*
2. *The motorcycle ...*
3. *The car ...*
4. *The two cars ...*
5. *The two motorcycles ...*

The motorcycle went over a bumpy road.

2 *Using classifiers.* Create complete ASL sentences based on each classifier below. Remember to state what the classifier will represent, following Eyes on ASL #11.

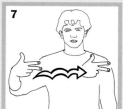
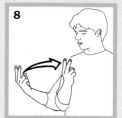
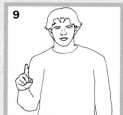
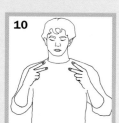

Classroom Exercise W (continued)

3 *Constituent parts.* Work with a partner to identify the classifier parts to each sign. Are numbers 9 and 10 classifiers? How so? What do you think they mean?

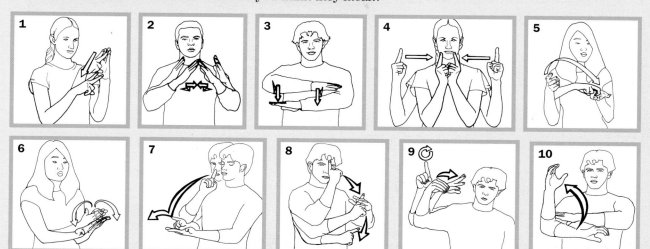

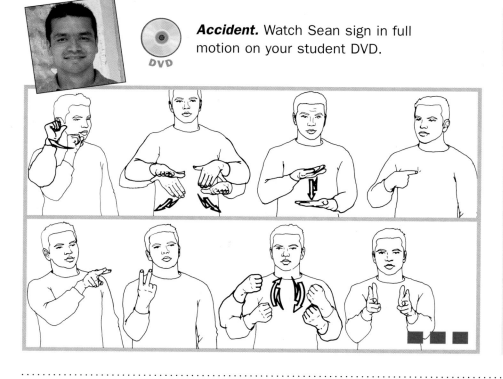

4 *Dialogue or narrative.* Use one or more of the following prompts to create a dialogue or narrative to share with your class.

1. *A mishap or accident*
2. *An encounter between two or more people*
3. *An encounter between one person and a vehicle*

Accident. Watch Sean sign in full motion on your student DVD.

DVD

Deaf Culture Minute

Legend holds that the sign for *America* derives from "log cabin." Is this sign a classifier? Why or why not?

America

Classroom Exercise

Comprehension. Use *wave no* to correct the errors below based on Sean's narrative in *The Accident.*

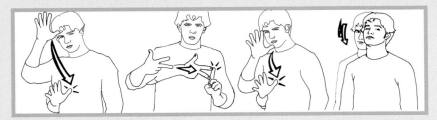

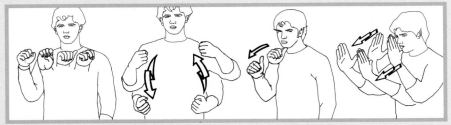

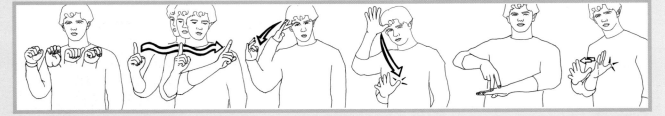

Homework Exercise ✏ 6

A   Develop at least three sentences that use each of these classifiers within the sentence. Practice signing the sentences correctly, including facial expressions as needed.

B   Develop a narrative that includes the CL: 1, CL: 3, and CL: ∧ classifiers. Your narrative should have a minimum of five sentences and tell a logical story or description of an event.

C   Practice signing Sean's *Accident* narrative to present to your classmates. Focus on signing the narrative smoothly and clearly, and incorporate non-manual signals as needed.

D   Write Assignments A, B, or C in ASL gloss.

Signing Time

Signing time combines the **Time Spot** with a number sign to communicate the hour, or a number sign paired with the *minute* sign. Look at the ways time is shown in the dialogue below.

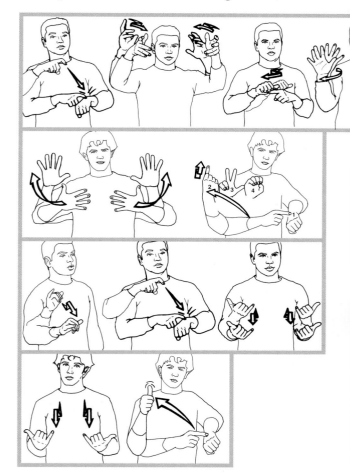

Dialogue Translation

Sean: *What time is basketball practice over?*

Marc: *It's done at 11:30.*

Sean: *Oh, okay. What time is it now?*

Marc: *It's 10:00.*

Eyes on ASL #12

Time signs are also *When* signs, so they come first in a sentence.

All time signs face outward, including numbers 1–5.

Classroom Exercise Y

1 *Dialogue.* Work on the following with a partner:

   1. *Practice signing the dialogue above*
   2. *Expand the above dialogue with more details and a conclusion*

Vocabulary   Time

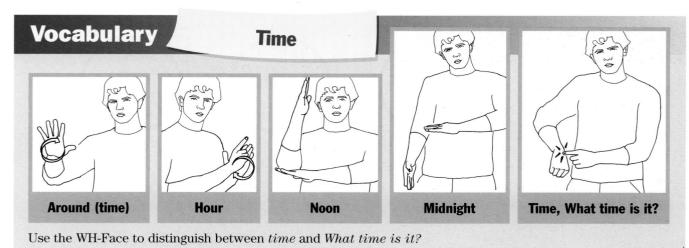

| Around (time) | Hour | Noon | Midnight | Time, What time is it? |

Use the WH-Face to distinguish between *time* and *What time is it?*

ASL Up Close

The Time Spot

The area where most people wear a watch is known as the **Time Spot**, and it is used to sign time in ASL. Hold your non-dominant hand to create a base for the number sign made by your dominant hand, with the number sign touching the Time Spot. The pattern for hours 1 - 9 is shown in Example 1. When signing an hour higher than 9, simply touch the Time Spot with your index finger before making the number sign. For times that combine both the hour and minute, see Example 2.

The Time Spot

 　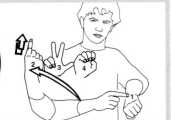

Classroom Exercise Z

1　*Telling time.* Provide the time when asked by a classmate. Switch roles and repeat when done.

2　*More time.* Provide the correct sign for each item below.

1. 2:00	**5.** *around 10:00*	**9.** *11:45*	**13.** *6:45*	**17.** *12:05*
2. *midnight*	**6.** *3:15*	**10.** *2:21*	**14.** *9:15*	**18.** *9:10*
3. *6:30*	**7.** *7:20*	**11.** *4:00*	**15.** *15 minutes*	**19.** *6:00*
4. *1:00*	**8.** *noon*	**12.** *5:00*	**16.** *around 8:30*	**20.** *7:00*

Classroom Exercise AA

1   *What time?* Ask a partner the following questions, who will respond using the information in parenthesis. Switch roles and repeat the exercise when done. An example is provided.

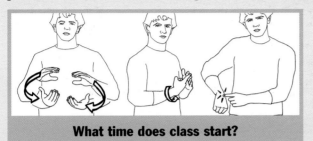

What time does class start?

Class begins at 6:00.

1. *What time do you start work?* **(8:00 Monday)**
2. *What time is it now?* **(?)**
3. *What time is class over?* **(9:45)**
4. *What time do you go home?* **(?)**
5. *What time is your ASL class?* **(?)**
6. *What time does your ASL class finish?* **(?)**

2   *Arrivals & departures.* ASL has several signs for the concepts of *to arrive* and *to depart*, which are based on who / what is arriving or departing. Provide the correct sign for the phrases in bold.

1. *I need to **take off**.*
2. *The plane **lands** at 6:00.*
3. *We **got there** at 9:00.*
4. *She needs to **get going**.*
5. *The train **leaves** at 2:45.*
6. *They need **to go**.*
7. *The **bell rings** at 7:15.*
8. *The bus **departs** in 10 minutes.*
9. *They'll **be here** at noon.*
10. *I'm **going to hit the road**.*

FYI   Use the sign *go out* when referring to the departure of CL: 3 vehicles.

Vocabulary   Beginnings & Endings

Alarm, bell

To arrive (person)

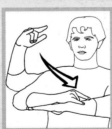

To arrive (plane)

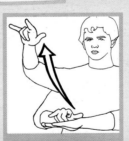

To depart (plane)

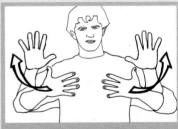

To finish, to be done

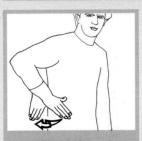

To be late

To start, begin

To take off (person)

Train

Classroom Exercise BB

1 *Running late.* Ask a partner why he or she is late, following the example. Your partner will respond with the information provided. The past tense is shown via context so don't worry about past tense signs. Switch roles and repeat.

Why did you get here late?

1. *I walk slow.*
2. *The bus was late.*
3. *I had to see the nurse.*
4. *I finished work late.*
5. *My ___ class finished late.*
6. *I had to go to the bathroom.*

7. *I was chatting with a friend.*
8. *I was looking for my book.*
9. *The train was late.*
10. *I wanted to finish eating.*
11. *I left home late.*
12. *There was a line in the cafeteria.*

2 *What's going on?* Describe the events in each illustration in complete ASL sentences.

Deaf Culture Minute

The next time you're running late to class or meeting a Deaf friend, be prepared to explain why you were running behind. In formal situations like school, a Deaf teacher will likely ask why you are late — and expect you to respond with a thorough explanation! Doing so is polite and a part of Deaf culture.

ASL Up Close

Multiple Meanings

Beginning ASL students often miss differences in the abstract and literal senses of a sign, usually because the signer chooses the first sign that comes to mind in English. However, ASL and English are not interchangeable. To sign fluently, you need to be able to distinguish between meanings and concepts of ideas and their signs. This skill is known as **conceptually-accurate signing**.

Be aware of and memorize the concept of a sign rather than how to fingerspell them in English. For example, the sign *to break* is the literal breaking of an object in half, compared to the abstract meaning of *taking a break*. Look at the sign *half hour*. Is it literal or abstract? How do you know?

  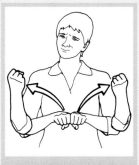 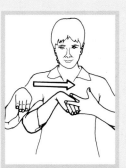 

| To take (abstract) | To take (literal) | To break (literal) | Break (abstract) | Half hour |

Classroom Exercise CC

1 *Multiple meanings.* Sign each sentence in conceptually-accurate ASL.

1. *I have breaks at 10:00 and 1:00.*
2. *Are you taking chemistry and drama?*
3. *My telephone is broken.*
4. *I work at a restaurant on the weekends. I get two half-hour breaks.*
5. *My mother said I can take her car.*

2 *Conceptual signing.* Work with a partner to make a list of 10 English words or phrases that have multiple meanings, and show the sign that best matches the concept. The list has been started for you.

1. *I'm running behind*   3. _____   5. _____   7. _____   9. _____
2. *broken heart*   4. _____   6. _____   8. _____   10. _____

3 *Dialogue.* Create a dialogue with one or more partners that includes the following:

1. *Time*
2. *An arrival / departure*
3. *A mulitple meaning*

Classroom Exercise DD

Sentence creation. Create a complete ASL sentence based on the prompts below.

We leave at 10:00. / Our flight leaves at 10:00.

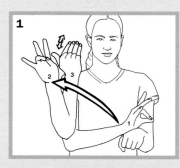

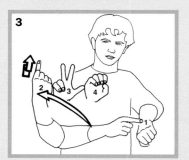

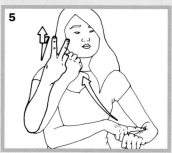

Homework Exercise 7

A Where are you or what do you usually do at the following times? For each time, practice signing a complete ASL sentence.

1. *6:15 p.m.*   3. *Midnight*   5. *7:00 a.m.*
2. *8:30 p.m.*   4. *Noon*   6. *8:30 a.m.*

B Prepare several questions incorporating time into an interview you will sign to a classmate. Practice signing a minimum of five questions.

C Practice signing Marc's narrative, *Where do you go to school?* Be sure your signing is clear and smooth and includes the appropriate non-manual signals. Prepare to sign the narrative to your classmates.

D Write Assignments A, B, or C in ASL gloss.

Journal Activities

1 Deafness is often called the "hidden disability" because people don't "look" or "act" deaf. In what ways is this good or bad? How does this "hidden disability" affect encounters or relationships between Deaf and hearing people?

2 Discuss the educational options available to deaf students. What are the pros and cons of the manual / oral philosophies? Why do you think this is an emotional controversy? Refer to the two perspectives below in your discussion.

> *A teacher said to me, "Teaching deaf children through the means of oralism is the best method to adopt because: The majority is hearing and it is up to the minority like you to join them. Being able to speak is likely to help you people be accepted into the world." So I spent my life trying to be like the others and I can speak, and read lips. And I wonder, now, how valuable it is that we must always try to be like others. My deafness is . . . myself, it is not something that I must fight against, or hide, or overcome.*
>
> — *Freda Norman, actor*

In 1880 educators assembled at a convention in Milan, Italy and announced reasons why the oral method was preferred over the manual:

The Convention, considering the incontestable superiority of articulation [speech] over signs in restoring the deaf-mute to society and giving him a fuller knowledge of language, declares that the oral method should be preferred to that of signs in the education and instruction of deaf-mutes.

http://Search

Research the following subjects on the internet:

- Speechreading/lipreading
- Prelingual deafness
- Certified Deaf interpreter
- Postlingual deafness
- The 1880 Milan Conference

Unit 5 Review

A Tara and Scott have come to talk with their school counselor about courses to take that will help them achieve their goals. Explain to each what courses he or she should take, and why.

B Grades have come out and a group of friends are comparing how well each did. Describe which courses were taken and the grades earned. Use the Listing & Ordering Technique.

Report Card	
Reading	F
English	F
Math	F
Art	D
Gym	D

Report Card	
Reading	B
English	B
Math	A
Art	C+
Gym	A-

Report Card	
Reading	A
English	B
Math	B
Art	B+
Gym	B-

C Describe each scene using the appropriate classifiers.

D What time is it?

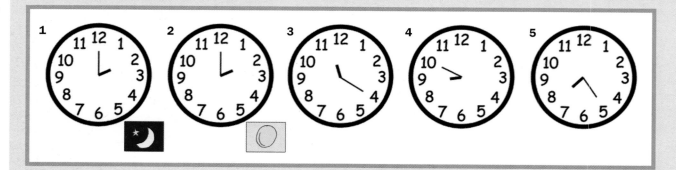

Unit 5 Review

E   Identify and correct the errors in the sentences below. Why are they wrong?

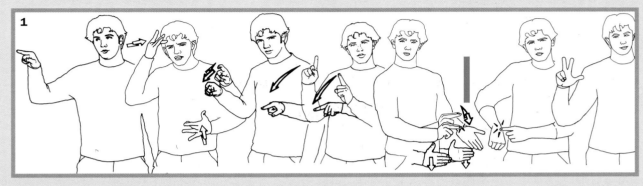

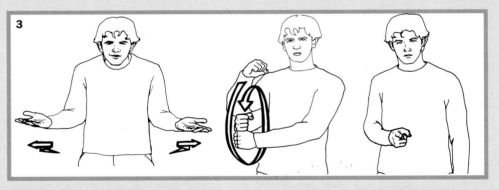

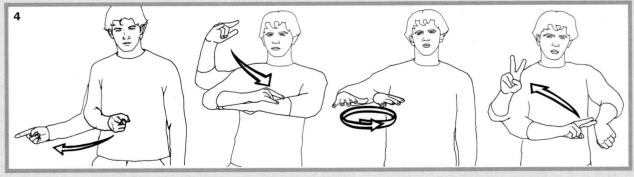

Sports & Activities

Unit Six Objectives

- To sign about sports
- To understand the Five Parameters of ASL
- To understand the different types of ASL literature
- To expand classifier skills
- To use the past, present, and future tenses
- To understand and use the Rule of 9

Unit Six Vocabulary

Key Phrases

The Storytelling Competition

Hey, what's up? Tomorrow evening I'm part of an ASL storytelling competition. A lot of people will be there to watch skits and classifier and handshape stories. I will be signing three stories, a number story and two classifier stories. You should come! You'll have a great time. See you there!

DVD

The Storytelling Competition. Watch Kris sign in full motion on your student DVD.

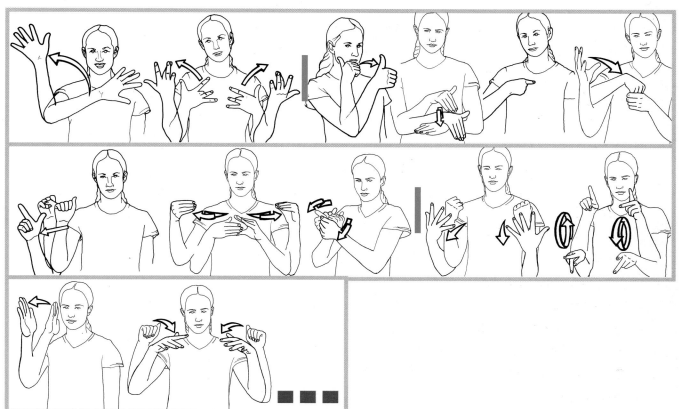

Vocabulary The Storytelling Competition

Other new vocabulary seen in the narrative is presented throughout Unit 6.

Come on

The sign *come on* is an informal way to sign *to join* or *come over here.* Use this sign to say *come on!* to encourage somebody to hurry up.

Involve, to be included

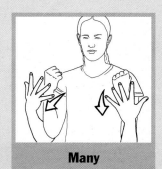

Many

Sports & Activities

Participating in sports or attending sporting events is a popular activity in the Deaf community, which organizes many athletic events and tournaments. In this section, you will learn vocabulary to help you sign about sports and other activities.

Dialogue Translation

Sean: *What do you do after school?*
Kris: *Every day after school I usually run for a half-hour.*
Sean: *Oh, okay. I play basketball with friends.*
Kris: *Oh yeah? I'm not good at basketball.*
Sean: *You should practice with us. It'll be fun!*

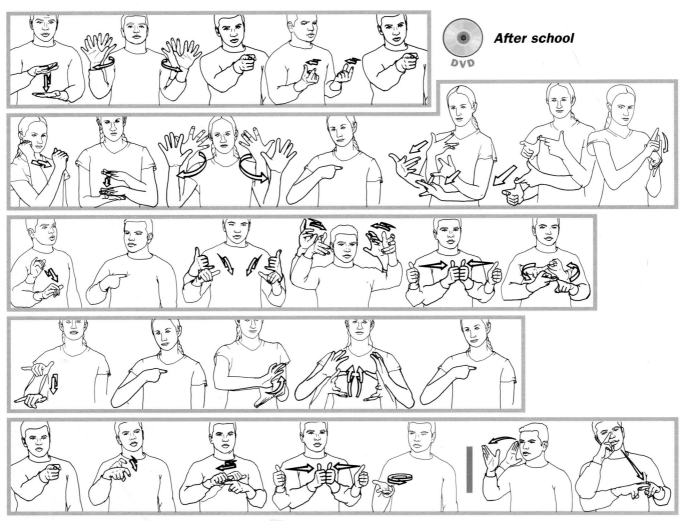

DVD **After school**

Classroom Exercise A

1   *Dialogue.* Practice signing the dialogue above with a partner.

2   *Analysis.* Identify the following language features in the dialogue. Explain the purpose of each feature.

   1. *Closing signals*   **2.** *When signs*   **3.** *Pronouns*   **4.** *Non-manual signals*

3   *After school.* Ask a partner what he or she does after school.

Classroom Exercise

1 *Activities.* When do people play certain sports? Follow the example shown.

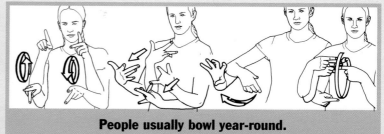

People usually bowl year-round.

2 *Surveys.* Ask classmates to rate their skill with the following sports, using the signs *to be good at* and *to be bad at.* Prepare to share the information with your class.

1. Are you good at ____?
2. Are you bad at ____?
3. Do you play ____? Are you good at it?
4. Do you play ____? Are you bad at it?
5. What's your favorite sport?

Sports

baseball	gymnastics
football	softball
swimming	volleyball
bowling	hockey
basketball	soccer

Accent Steps

Use *during* to talk about a non-specific time when something occurs. *During* is used much the same way as "in" and "on" are used in English to talk about events.

Vocabulary   Signing About Sports

All year, year round	During, in, on (time)	To play	Team	Tend to, usually

Vocabulary

Sports

Baseball	Basketball	To ride a bike	Bowling	Football
Golf	Gymnastics	Hockey	To ice skate	To jog
Karate, martial arts	To scuba dive	To snowboard		Soccer
Softball	To surf	To swim		Tennis
Volleyball	Volleyball (2)	Water polo		Wrestling

Classroom Exercise C

1 *Using during.* The sign *during* is used to explain the general time an action occurs. It is a *when* sign, meaning it comes first in an ASL sentence. Words using *during* are underlined in the English sentences below. Sign each in ASL, placing *during* in the correct location. An example is given.

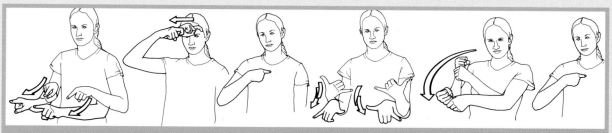

Over the summer I play baseball. / I play baseball in the summer.

1. *In winter they play hockey.*
2. *When it rains, people don't play golf.*
3. *On the weekends, I play soccer.*
4. *We learned to swim in the fall.*
5. *In nice weather I ride to work.*

6. *During the week I practice ice skating.*
7. *People should not swim in bad weather.*
8. *I have volleyball practice on Thursday.*
9. *Over the weekend we take karate.*
10. *I work on the weekend.*

2 *Sports seasons.* You and a Deaf friend are thinking about joining a sports team. In a complete sentence, explain the time of year when people usually enjoy the following activities.

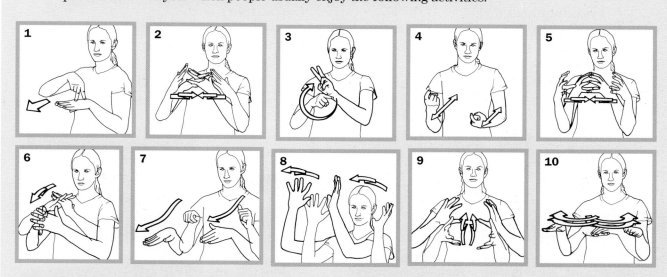

3 *Dialogue.* Work with a partner to develop a dialogue using one of the prompts below. Your dialogue should include a greeting, at least six sentences, a conclusion, and a farewell.

1. *Make weekend plans.*
2. *Compare and contrast the difficulty level of two different sports.*
3. *Debate which sport is the best to play.*

Classroom Exercise D

1. *Conversation.* Ask a partner the following questions, who will respond using the information provided. When done, switch roles and repeat.

   1. *Does she like to play tennis?* **(yes)**
   2. *Do you like to watch golf?* **(no, because it's boring)**
   3. *Are you a hockey player?* **(yes, I play hockey)**
   4. *Which football team is your favorite?* **(?)**
   6. *Are you a good swimmer?* **(yes, I swim very well)**
   7. *Does he play soccer?* **(no, he plays baseball)**
   8. *Is he a gymnast?* **(no, his sister is a gymnast)**
   9. *I think she plays softball.* **(yes, she does. She's very good)**

2. *Who's on the team?.* Following the example, ask a partner to confirm or negate who's on the team. When done, switch roles. An example is provided.

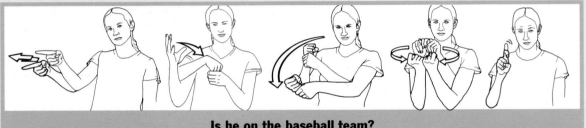

Is he on the baseball team?

   1. *Are those two on the volleyball team?* **(yes, they are)**
   2. *Is she on the basketball team?* **(yes, she is)**
   3. Is he on the golf team? ? **(no, he's not on the team)**
   4. *Are the five of you on the soccer team?* **(no, us four)**
   5. *Are they on the gymnastics team?* **(yes, they are)**
   6. *Is she on the softball team?* **(no, she isn't)**

3. *What are they doing?* Explain the activity occurring in each scene in a complete ASL sentence. Use ASL pronouns where necessary.

Did you know? Equal Through Sports: The Deaflympics

Sports and athletic competitions are just as important in the Deaf World as they are to hearing people. Deaf athletes are organized into local, state, regional, national, and international associations representing a wide variety of sporting interests. Every four years, Deaf athletes and spectators gather to participate in the Deaflympics, the international games for Deaf players. The Deaflympics began in 1924 and are modeled after the Olympic Games, providing the opportunity to compete in an environment that does not penalize or limit achievement due to deafness. For example, starting cues are visual rather than audible, featuring flashing lights rather than the sound of a starting pistol or whistle. Thousands of Deaf players and fans descend on the Deaflympics, turning the sporting venue into a mosaic of sign languages from all over the globe. As Deaf athletes break down social and attitudinal barriers and compete against hearing peers, the ideals of competition and the Deaflympics becomes clear: *Equal Through Sports*.

To learn more, visit: http://www.deaflympics.com

Classroom Exercise E

1. *Who's who?* Match information from each column to sign a complete sentence explaining which sport each athlete is known for, and your opinion of his or her skill level.

Athlete	Sport	Skill level
1. *Tiger Woods*	*basketball*	*very good*
2. *Tara Lipinski*	*golf*	*poor*
3. *Magic Johnson*	*ice skating*	*extremely talented*
4. *Pele*	*?*	*lousy*
5. *me*	*soccer*	*so-so*

2. *Interview.* Find out a partner's top three favorite sports, and why he or she enjoys them. Use the Listing and Ordering Technique. Prepare to share the information with your classmates.

Homework Exercise 1

A. Kris and Sean want to make weekend plans, but are unsure about the weather. What activities can they plan to do depending on the weather? For each weather forecast, explain one or two activities Kris and Sean can do.

B. What are some of your favorite sports and activities? Explain two of your favorite activities, indicating your skill with each and reasons why you enjoy them. You should sign a minimum of five complete sentences in ASL.

C. Write assignments A or B in ASL gloss.

Classroom Exercise

1 *Who needs practice?* Based on the illustration, explain in a complete sentence whether more practice is needed. An example is provided.

She doesn't need practice because she's a very good ice skater.

2 *Conversation.* Ask a partner the following questions, who will respond in a complete sentence. When done, switch roles and repeat the exercise.

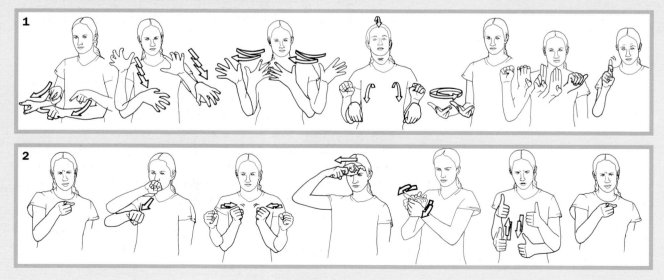

Classroom Exercise (continued)

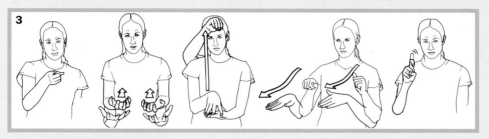

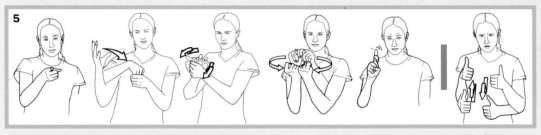

3   *Language comparison.* Write an interpretation of the sentences in Part 2. What differences do you see between ASL and English? Discuss your interpretation with another student.

Deaf Culture

The football huddle

The football huddle was invented in 1892 by a Deaf student at Gallaudet University named Paul Hubbard. Concerned about opposing players being able to see his team's signs and planned plays, Paul urged his teammates to huddle up. Quickly, the concept spread across college campuses and today, the football huddle is an important part of the game. The Deaf community's contributions to the sport of football didn't end with the huddle: Professional Deaf football players like Bonnie Sloan and Kenny Walker and Deaf cheerleaders Mona Vierra and Lisa Fishbein demonstrate that Deaf athletes are as skilled as their hearing counterparts.

ASL Up Close

To experience

Asking *Have you . . .*

American Sign Language uses the signs *to experience* and *finish* to ask questions about whether someone has or has not done something. These types of questions often begin with "Have you..." in English, but in ASL the question is asked without using the sign *have*. Recall that the sign *to have* is literal and indicates possession of something, so using it to ask "Have you gone bowling?" is incorrect. Instead, the concept of the sign *to experience* asks "Do you have any experience with bowling?" In the examples below, look carefully to see how *to experience* and *finish* are used in conversation.

**Have you gone scuba diving? /
Do you know how to scuba dive?**

**Yes, I've gone scuba diving. /
Yes, I know how to scuba dive.**

Another way to respond to a "Have you . . . " question is to use *finish*, to show you've already experienced what was asked.

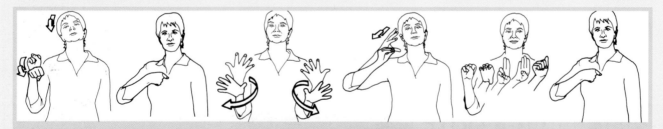

Yes, I've gone scuba diving.

To respond negatively to a "Have you . . ." question, use the *late* sign and the non-manual signal of slightly sticking your tongue out. This combination means *not yet* or *I haven't*.

No, I haven't gone scuba diving.

Classroom Exercise G

1. *Using experience.* What are the best conceptual matches for the English phrases below? Select from to *experience*, *finish*, and *not yet*.

   1. I haven't ...
   2. Did you ...
   3. He did it yesterday ...
   4. Have you tried ...

   5. It's over ...
   6. I haven't gone ...
   7. She knows how to ...
   8. I already did ...

   9. Not yet ...
   10. Have you already tried ...
   11. It's not ready yet ...
   12. It's not done yet ...

2. *Have you?* Ask a partner whether he or she has tried the following activities. Your partner will respond following the cues provided. When done, switch roles and repeat.

Question	Response	Activitiy

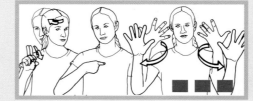

NMS Alert

The sign *finish* is always accompanied by a specific NMS: move your lips as if saying "fish."

EXPRESSION CORNER

Crazy for & Not crazy for

Crazy for

Not crazy for

Crazy for and *not crazy for* are two ASL expressions that refer to a strong like or dislike towards an activity or person. *Crazy for* reflects more intensity than *love it*, and *not crazy for* is less impassioned than *hate*.

Vocabulary — Signing About Activities

To bungee jump

To camp

To exercise, lift weights

To fish

To hike

To play cards

To skateboard

To skydive

Classroom Exercise H

1. *Translation.* Work with a partner to sign the following sentences in ASL, focusing on word order and concepts including *when* signs, *during*, *finish*, *not yet*, and *experience*.

   1. *I haven't gone camping since the summer.*
   2. *Over the weekend my family plays games.*
   3. *I've played soccer since I was four years old.*
   4. *We love winter because it snows and we can snowboard and ski.*
   5. *They already had football practice.*

2. *Dialogue.* Create a dialogue with one or more partners that includes the signs *finish* and *experience.* Some suggestions are below.

   1. *Marriage*
   2. *Experience with a particular sport*
   3. *Discuss a unique or favorite experience and when it occurred*

Key Concepts

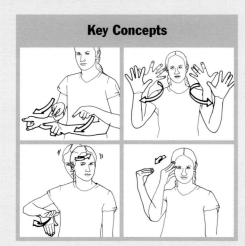

FYI How many classifiers can you find among sports signs? Try to analyze the meaning behind each.

Classroom Exercise I

1 *Discerning differences.* Below are several phrases in English. Select the ASL sign from Column A that best shares the meaning of the English phrase.

1. *I can't stand it . . .*
2. *I'm not big on the idea . . .*
3. *I really like that . . .*
4. *I'm hooked on . . .*
5. *I like it okay . . .*
6. *It's not too bad . . .*
7. *She's not my favorite person . . .*
8. *It's great!*
9. *I go nuts for . . .*
10. *I don't like it at all!*
11. *I absolutely love this!*
12. *I'm not keen on that . . .*

Column A

Love it	*Not crazy for*
Crazy for	*Don't like*
Like	

2 *Sentence creation.* For each illustration, explain how much you enjoy the activity. Use the signs *love it, crazy for, not crazy for, like,* and *don't like* in a complete sentence.

3 *Meanings.* Practice making these facial expressions. Sign a sentence whose meaning matches each facial expression.

Homework Exercise ✏ 2

A Prepare a narrative that focuses on clear, smooth signing, ASL grammar, and appropriate non-manual signals. Your narrative should include these details:

1. *What are two sports or activities that you enjoy? Why?*
2. *What is one sport you'd like to try, and what is one you do not want to try? Why?*

B Select at least four sports signs that you think are, or include, classifiers. Analyze each and explain how and why you feel each is a classifier. Contrast the four you select with four other sports signs that you feel are not classifiers. What makes these signs classifiers? How do you know?

C Write Assignment A or B in ASL gloss.

ASL Up Close

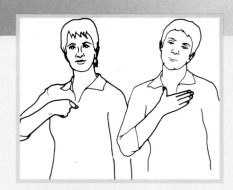

The Five Parameters of ASL

Each sign in ASL can be broken down and analyzed into five separate features called the **Five Parameters of ASL.** If one parameter is wrong, then the meaning of a sign can be drastically affected - or even disappear and leave people trying to understand what's being signed. Signing clearly and precisely takes time and practice, and being aware of the Five Parameters can help improve your ASL skills.

The Five Parameters of ASL:

Correct parameter	Incorrect parameter

1. Handshape: *Me* vs. *My*
The handshape difference between *me* and *my* is simple to identify. When signing *me*, does your thumb stick up? If so, you have a parameter error!

Common hand-shape errors: 1/D, D/F, E/O.

2. Palm Orientation: *Table* vs. nonsense sign
Palm orientation errors are easy to make: Is the palm supposed to face up, down, left, or right? Signing while nervous or without practice may cause palm orientation errors. Often, these mistakes are "big" and obvious.

What are three examples of palm orientation errors?

3. Location: *To see* vs. nonsense sign
Avoid location errors in ASL by remembering most signs are made in front of your body in a comfortable location. If your arms feel awkward, it's one sign the location is off. Some signs are directional and are directed towards your body while others, like *to drive to*, move away from it.

Location errors cause an unpleasant "ASL accent."

4. Movement: *To enjoy* vs. *Happy*
Movement affects meaning, as seen in the examples. Practice and paying attention are key. If your hands and arms feel awkward or constricted, check the sign's movement for parameter errors.

Can you think of three signs that differ only in their movement parameter?

5. Non-manual signals: *Haven't* vs. *Late*
Specific NMS change the meaning of a sign. Facial expressions, head nods/shakes, the eyebrows, nose, eyes, and lips each have particular meanings that can be attached to signs. Your NMS will improve with practice and use of ASL.

Which NMS do you use regularly?

Classifiers

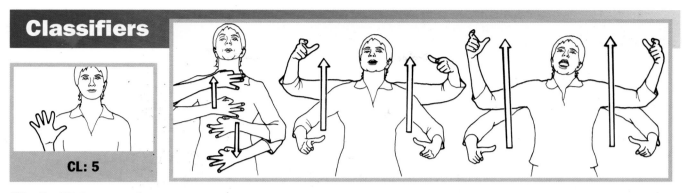

CL: 5

CL: 5 Many people

CL: 5 is related to CL: 1 and represents at least five or more people engaged in an activity such as walking. The concept of CL: 5 is more people than can be easily counted, unless you're talking about a certain group of five individuals. CL: 5 can be preceded by a number sign, as shown in the example.

Thirty-five people are going to the party.

Classroom Exercise J

Translation. Sign each sentence in ASL. Use CL: 5 where indicated in bold.

1. *How many people **went** to your house on Friday?*
2. *The hallway **is crowded** near the office.*
3. ***Huge crowds went** to the movie.*
4. *Why is the sign **popular** a classifier?*
5. *I couldn't see because people were **walking in front of me**.*

Vocabulary CL: 5

Crowded

To flock to (not in a group)

Flock to and *go to (plural)* share a similar concept. However, *flock to* is best used to describe large numbers of people.

Popular

Focus: The Literature of

Both hearing and Deaf people create and enjoy literature, artistic works such as stories, poetry, riddles, and more. The literature of most cultures is written, though cultures that do not use or have a written language also produce a specific type of literature. This type is called **oral literature**, meaning stories are preserved and passed down only by the act of storytelling. The literature produced by the Deaf culture is part of this tradition since it relies on the act of live or recorded storytelling for transmission, even though ASL literature is not spoken but signed. Poetry, ABC stories, classifier stories, handshape rhymes, number stories, narratives, and humor form a highly-regarded body of signed, visual literature passed down from generation to generation.

The Major Forms of the Literature of American Sign Language:

- *ASL poetry:* Covers a broad spectrum of genres and topics, performed by a Deaf poet. Deaf poets such as Clayton Valli and Ella Mae Lentz are cherished for their poetry reflecting the shared Deaf experience.

- *Classifier stories:* Works that use only one or more specific classifiers to tell a complete, plot-driven story.

- *Handshape rhymes:* Works in which the signer tells an entire story using only one handshape, often incorporating meter, or rhythm, based on the story's plot.

- *ABC stories:* Using only the letters of the alphabet in sequence (either A – Z or Z – A), the signer tells a complete story. ABC stories combine elements of classifier stories and handshape rhymes.

- *Number stories:* Similar to ABC stories, the signer uses specific number signs to tell a story. Number signs can be made in sequence like ABC stories (numbers 1 – 10, for example), in a challenging pattern (numbers 7, 5, 7, 5, for example), or in reverse order.

- *Narratives:* Signed in formal ASL, narratives often relate events and aspects of the shared Deaf experience, especially humorous tales of being Deaf in a hearing world. ASL narratives often highlight Deaf history, famous Deaf persons, and Deaf accomplishments or triumphs over adversity.

Performances of ASL literature are popular events for both Deaf and hearing members of the Deaf community.

American Sign Language

Don't confuse the signed literature of American Sign Language with the plays, poetry, and novels written in English (or other languages) by Deaf individuals. In addition to ASL literature, which is always performed in ASL, there is a rich contribution by Deaf authors to the field of written literature in many languages. Some well-known Deaf writers are Robert Panara, Rex Lowman, Laura Searing, Linwood Smith, Gil Eastman, Bernard Bragg, Eugene Bergman, Douglas Bullard, and many others. Have you read any works by these or other Deaf authors?

Here is an example of a simple ABC story transcribed into English.

The Haunted House

A: "knock on door"

B: "door opens"

C: "signer looks around"

D: "signer hears something"

E: "signer is frightened"

F: "signer looks around carefully"

G: "signer sees someone running away"

H: "signer decides to depart"

I: "begins imagining things"

J: "notices artwork on the wall"

K: "portrait of a man with cigar"

L: "signer outlines portrait on wall"

M: "signer hears sound"

N: "signer looks closer at portrait"

O: "signer notices a hole in portrait"

P: "signer sees a person swinging in the air"

Q: "it is the queen"

R: "hanging by a rope"

S: "she is dead"

T: "all of a sudden"

U: "signer glances to the right"

V: "sees someone standing there"

W: "person says something to the signer"

X: "signer's legs shake"

Y: "person tells signer to stay"

Z: "signer escapes"

Watch examples of ABC, classifier, and hand-shape stories on your student DVD.

The story below can be both a classifier story and a handshape rhyme. Use your imagination to complete the story using only CL: B.

Sleeping Puppy

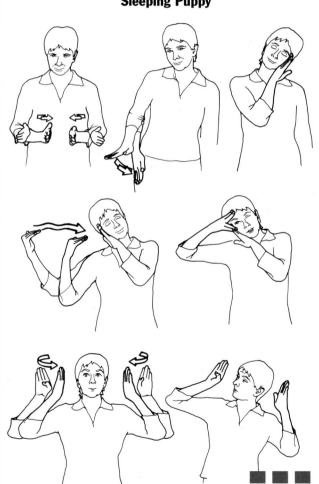

CL: Bent V Seated Position

CL: Bent V

CL: Bent V represents a pair of human legs in a seated position, animals, and insects. When using CL: Bent V it is essential to remember Eyes on ASL #11 (see Page 194) because the classifier doesn't distinguish between sizes of animals or insects. Refer to Unit 10 for animal signs.

My dog tends to jump on me. / My dog tends to jump on people.

CL: B & Base B Flat Objects

CL: B

CL: B represents large, flat objects (see Page 193). When CL: B is used as a flat surface and another classifier placed on top, it becomes CL: Base B. In addition to flat objects, CL: B provides a bird's eye view of objects normally shown with CL: 3. Use CL: 3 when describing a vehicle in which you are not involved, but use CL: B if you were a passenger or driving the vehicle.

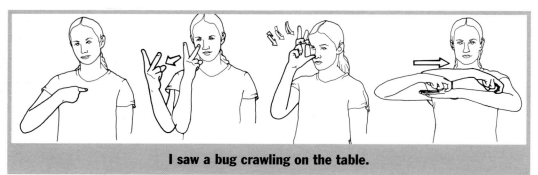

I saw a bug crawling on the table.

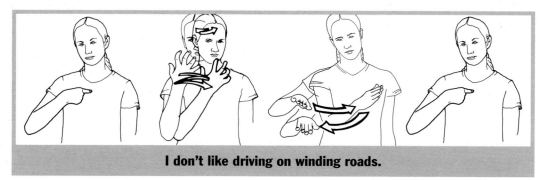

I don't like driving on winding roads.

Classroom Exercise K

1 *Classifier concepts.* Use classifiers to describe each illustration. Don't forget to apply Eyes on ASL #11.

1

2

4

5

6

7

8

9

9

10

2 *Sentence creation.* Sign a complete ASL sentence using the provided classifier.

1

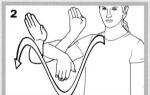
2

3

4

Accent Steps

You can use classifers to describe actions of a boat in addition to the boat sign. Pair CL: 3 with CL: Base B to show the action of a boat seen from a distance, or use CL:B for a first-person or bird's eye perspective.

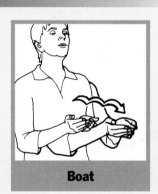

Boat

Vocabulary — Classifiers

Bug, ant

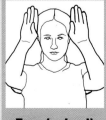
Ears (animal)

To jump (animal)

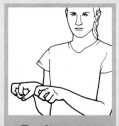
To sit next to

Winding road

Vocabulary — ASL Storytelling

ASL poetry	Handshape	Poetry	Story, to tell a story

Classroom Exercise L

1. *Interview.* Interview a classmate and find out the following information. Prepare to share what you learn with your classmates. When done, switch roles and repeat.

   1. *Have you gone to an ASL poetry show?*
   2. *Do you enjoy ASL literature? Why or why not?*
   3. *Have you signed a handshape story?*
   4. *Do you like storytelling? Do you know an ASL story?*
   5. *Do you like signing or reading poetry?*

2. *Dialogue.* Practice signing the dialogue with a partner, paying attention to ASL grammar and structure.

Student A	*What did you do yesterday?*
Student B	*My family and I went to an ASL storytelling competition.*
Student A	*Oh, did you have fun?*
Student B	*Yes, I did. I loved the ASL poetry and handshape stories.*
Student A	*I haven't seen ASL poetry, but I want to see classifier stories.*
Student B	*I don't mind going again tonight. Do you want to go?*
Student A	*Sure!*

Deaf Culture Minute

Did you notice there are two different signs for *poetry*? The two signs differentiate between poems produced by hearing culture and those produced by Deaf performers. Over the years, Deaf poets felt the general sign *poetry* did not fully capture the depth of expression that is part of ASL poetry, and eventually the sign *express myself / let it out* became known as *ASL poetry*.

Homework Exercise 4

A. A friend of yours was sick and unable to attend the ASL storytelling competition, so you are explaining what you saw and your impressions of the event. What did you enjoy or not enjoy? How many people were there? What did you like? What kind of ASL literature did you see? Your narrative should have a minimum of eight ASL sentences.

B. Create a short narrative based on one of the illustrations. Use at least three classifiers. Your narrative should have a minimum of eight ASL sentences.

C. Write Assignment A or B in ASL gloss.

ASL Up Close

Past, Present & Future: The ASL Tenses

All languages have ways of talking about present, past, or future periods of time. Distinguishing periods of time is called **tense**. In ASL, tense is formed by the addition of certain signs called **tense markers** to the beginning of a sentence that is then understood to be in the past or future tense. If there are no tense markers, then the sentence is in the present tense. The **ASL Timeline** diagram illustrates how tense is formed in ASL. This timeline divides your signing space into three regions: The present, past, and future areas. Tense markers for the past end their movement towards or over the shoulder while those for the future tense complete their movement ahead of the body. The further back or forward a sign is completed corresponds to the length of time into the past or future.

| Past tense: *ago* | Present tense: *now* | Future tense: *will* |

The American Sign Language Timeline

Distant past — Recent past — Near Future — Distant Future

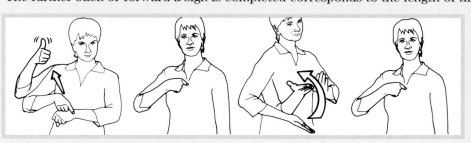

I leave at 10:00

Present Tense: *I leave at 10:00*.
Because there is no tense marker, the sentence is in the present tense.

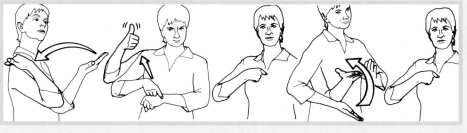

Past Tense: *I left at 10:00*.
The past tense is formed by adding the past tense marker, called *ago*.

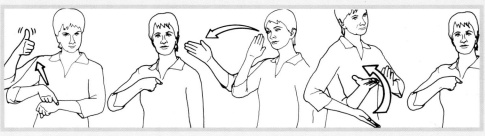

Future Tense: *I will leave at 10:00*.
The future tense is formed by adding the **future tense marker,** called *will*.

DVD

Eyes on ASL #13

Tense markers are generally located in the beginning of a sentence. Absence of a tense marker indicates the present tense.

Tense markers may include: Days of the week, time signs, *ago*, and *will*.

Signing in the Past Tense

Signing in the past tense requires at least one tense marker. Past tense markers may be included in a sign, or they may be independent. One of the most common past tense markers is *ago*. In the dialogue below, look how *ago* influences the past tense. How does the past tense change to the present tense?

Dialogue Translation

Marc: *What are we doing in class today?*

Kris: *Last Tuesday we watched stories in class. Today we're going to practice ASL poetry.*

Marc: *Oh, ok. Thanks! See you there!*

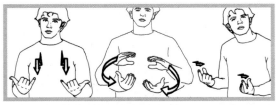

Classroom Exercise

1. *Dialogue.* Practice signing the above dialogue with a partner. Include the following:

   1. *A greeting*
   2. *Explain why Marc doesn't know what happened last week.*
   3. *Another use of a past tense marker*

2. *Analysis.* How do the tense markers affect meaning? Compare the ASL and English translations. What differences do you see?

I Want to Know . . .

How do tense markers work?

Look closely at the parameter changes in the signs *yesterday* and *tomorrow*. The beginning location of each sign is situated on the present tense area of the ASL Timeline, but the final locations differ: *Yesterday* moves toward the shoulder, forming the past tense, and *tomorrow* moves ahead of the body, forming the future tense. Once a tense is formed, you don't have to keep adding the same tense markers because the context is clear. However, when you change tenses you must use a new tense marker.

Yesterday

Tomorrow

Classroom Exercise

1 *Ago.* Using *ago*, change each sentence from the present to the past tense.

Present tense	**Past tense**
1. *I am learning ASL.*	*I learned ASL.*
2. *I have a motorcycle.*	*I had a motorcycle.*
3. *I go to school at 9:00.*	*I went to school at 9:00.*
4. *I live in California.*	*I used to live in California.*

2 *Today & yesterday.* Use terms from Vocabulary: The Past to help sign each word pair.

1. *I go ... I went*	**5.** *This month ... Last month*	**9.** *A month ago ... A year ago*
2. *They do ... They used to*	**6.** *Today ... Yesterday*	**10.** *A week ago ... A month ago*
3. *This year ... Last year*	**7.** *Now ... Before*	**11.** *Last year ... Very recently*
4. *Very recently ... Long ago*	**8.** *This week ... Last week*	**12.** *I finished ... I just finished*

3 *When?* Ask a partner when he or she did each activity. Switch roles when done. An example is provided.

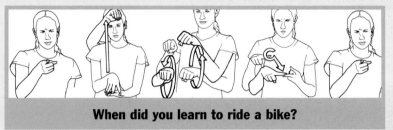

When did you learn to ride a bike?

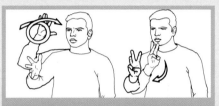

Back when I was 6 years old.

1. *When did you learn to swim?*	**5.** *When did you learn to walk?*
2. *When did you begin learning ASL?*	**6.** *How old were you when you learned*
3. *How old were you when you first flew on a plane?*	*how to skateboard?*
4. *Did you eat recently? When?*	

Vocabulary — The Past

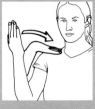

Ago, past

Just, very recently

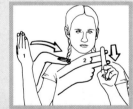

Last month

Last week

Last year

Long time ago

Recently, a little while ago

Used to, before

Accent Steps

The signs *last month*, *last week*, and *last year* can be interpreted as "a month ago," "a week ago," and "a year ago." Sign *used to* to say "When I was..."

Classroom Exercise 0

1 *Context cues.*
Which past tense
marker best fits
the meaning of the
sentence? Select a
past tense marker
and sign the com-
pleted sentence.

2 *Past events.*
Sign a complete
sentence using
the provided
past tense
markers.

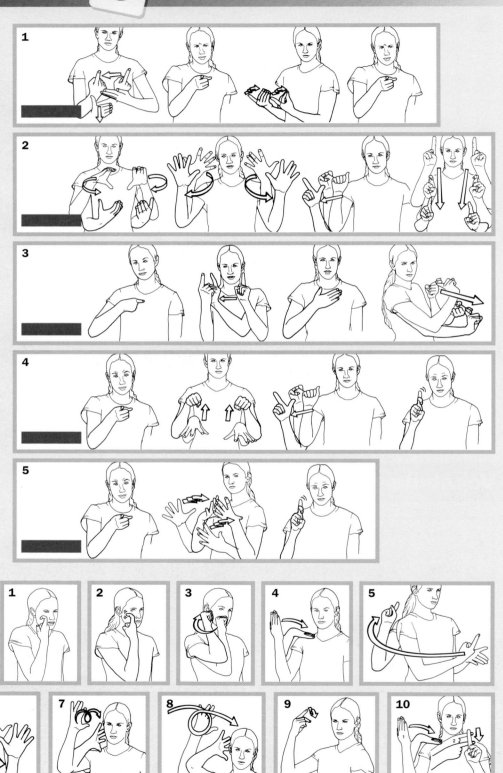

Narrative: Dummy Hoy

Dummy Hoy. Watch Sean sign in full motion on your student DVD.

Classroom Exercise

1 *Comprehension.* Answer each question in a complete ASL sentence.

1. *When did Dummy Hoy join the baseball team?*
2. *Why were Deaf people called dummy?*
3. *Was Dummy Hoy a good baseball player?*
4. *What words did Dummy Hoy need to hear? What did he do instead?*
5. *Did Dummy Hoy play on a school or professional team?*

2 *Analysis.* Answer each question in a complete ASL sentence.

1. *How do you think Dummy Hoy communicated with his team?*
2. *Can Deaf athletes play on pro teams? Why or why not?*
3. *What are some barriers for Deaf athletes?*
4. *Are Dummy Hoy's signs still important to baseball? Why?*
5. *What are some challenges you think Dummy Hoy had?*

Homework Exercise 5

A Describe an event or activity that occurred in the past in a minimum of five complete ASL sentences. Some ideas are provided.

1. *Last weekend's activities*
2. *An event from your childhood*
3. *An event that happened a year ago*

B Practice signing the *Dummy Hoy* narrative smoothly and clearly, including appropriate non-manual signals, pauses, eye gaze, and fingerspelling.

C Write Assignment A or B in ASL gloss.

Vocabulary — Dummy Hoy

To call (a name)

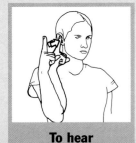
To hear

To talk

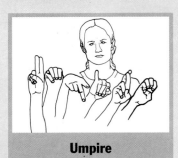
Umpire

Signing in the Future Tense

Similar to the past tense, the future tense relies on tense markers. Many signs, such as *next week* or *next month*, include tense as part of the sign. Being familiar with these signs will enhance your command of ASL. In the dialogue below, notice how the signs *next week* and *will* are used.

Dialogue Translation

Kris: *What will we do in class next week?*

Rita: *We will practice numbers and take a quiz.*

Kris: *Oh, I see. I will be absent because I'm part of a play.*

Rita: *I see ...*

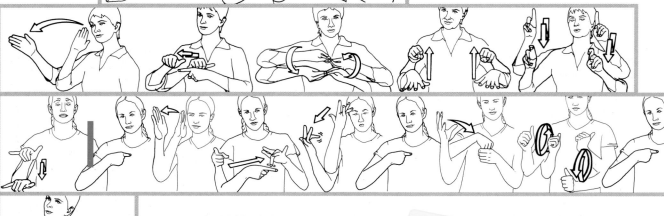

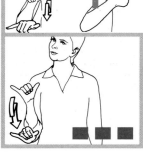

Classroom Exercise Q

1 *Dialogue.* Practice signing the above dialogue with a partner. Include the following:

1. *At least two more future tense markers*
2. *A conclusion: How does the dialogue end?*

2 *Dialogue II.* Change the tense of the above dialogue to the past. What changes are necessary? Sign the revised dialogue with a partner.

Classroom Exercise

1 *How long from now?* Ask a partner when he or she thinks the following events will happen. Fingerspell the underlined terms. Switch roles and repeat when done. An example is provided.

When do you think we will have a woman vice president?

Soon, it's not far off.

1. *When do you think people will live on __Mars__?*
2. *When will you get married?*
3. *When will you graduate?*
4. *When will you have a day off?*
5. *When do you think people will live under the ocean?*
6. *When do you have a vacation?*

2 *Concept comprehension.* Provide a future tense marker that best matches each word or phrase.

1. *In a while*
2. *A year from now*
3. *As soon as I can*
4. *A long time from now*
5. *Day after tomorrow*
6. *A week or so later*
7. *Later on*
8. *In 30 days*
9. *Not in a million years!*
10. *In the future*
11. *Just a few days from now*
12. *Some day*

Vocabulary — The Future

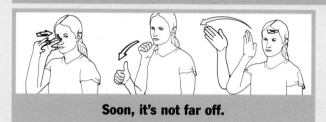

Distant future	**In a few days**	**Next week**	**Next year**

Soon	**Will, future, it will be**		**Variations for *soon***

Classroom Exercise S

1   *Conversation.* Ask a partner each question in ASL, who will respond using the information provided. Switch roles and repeat when done.

1. *When is the homework due?* **(in a few days)**
2. *Is the test this week?* **(no, next week)**
3. *Do you want to get married?* **(someday)**
4. *When is his birthday?* **(next month)**
5. *When will you graduate?* **(next year)**
6. *What time does the game start?* **(soon)**

7. *When is school done?* **(long time)**
8. *What are you taking next year?* **(ASL II)**
9. *When is the ASL story competition?* **(next month)**
10. *When is summer vacation?* **(?)**

2   *Which day?* Sign the following phrases in ASL.

1. *next Wednesday*
2. *tomorrow afternoon*
3. *next weekend*
4. *next Friday night*
5. *next week Monday*

6. *next Sunday morning*
7. *next Thursday*
8. *a week from now*
9. *next year*
10. *next summer*

Accent Steps

Phrases like "next Tuesday" or "next weekend" are signed like this:

Next Tuesday

3   *Signing about the future.* Sign a complete sentence using each future tense marker.

Classroom Exercise T

1   *Non-manual signals.* Use shoulder-shifting to show both the provided facial expression and its opposite.

Classroom Exercise U

Error detection.
Locate and fix any errors in the following sentences before signing them.

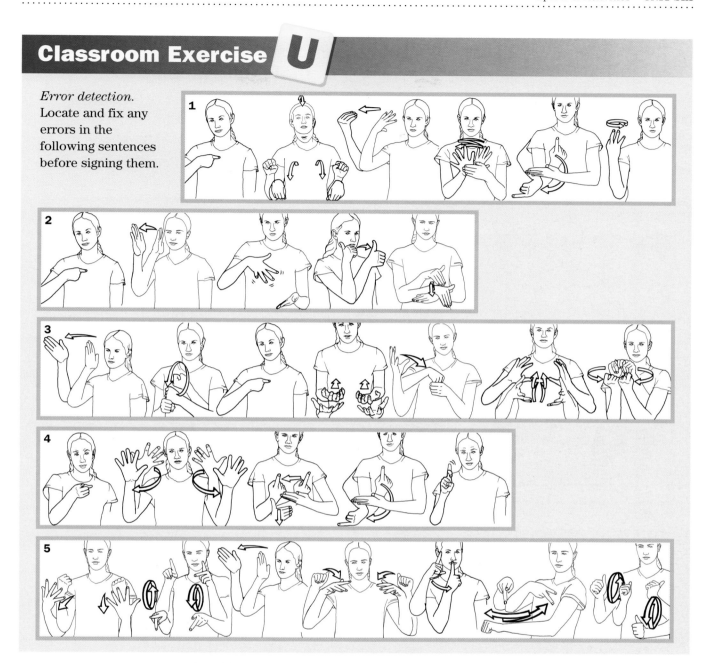

Homework Exercise 6

A Do you have any future plans on your calendar? What will you do? Prepare a narrative that includes the following future tense markers. Your narrative should have a minimum of eight complete sentences.

  1. *Next weekend*   **2.** *Tomorrow afternoon*   **3.** *Next month*

B What are five things you'd like to accomplish in the future? Describe what you'd like to do and when you'd like to accomplish them by, using at least five future tense markers. Prepare to share your thoughts with your classmates.

C Write Assignment A or B in ASL gloss.

The Rule of 9

You already know and use parts of the Rule of 9, an important feature of ASL grammar. The Rule of 9 combines the base meaning of a sign with a specific length of time to form a new meaning. In the dialogue below, can you identify which sign uses the Rule of 9?

Dialogue Translation

Kris: *Soon I will visit my grandmother and grandfather.*

Sean: *How long will you be gone?*

Kris: *I will be gone for two weeks.*

Going Away

DVD

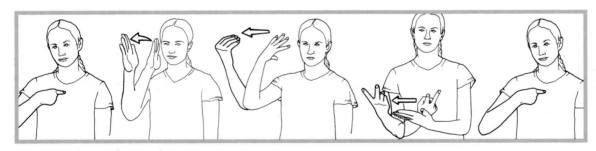

Vocabulary — Duration

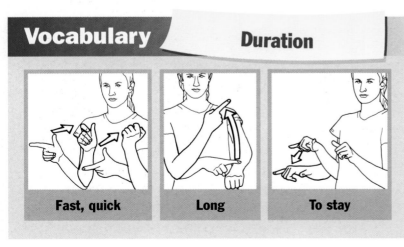

Fast, quick   **Long**   **To stay**

Classroom Exercise V

Dialogue. Sign the dialogue above with a partner, adding the following details:

1. *Greetings*
2. *At least three new details, such as where Kris' grandparents live*
3. *A conclusion and farewell*

ASL Up Close

The Rule of 9

The Rule of 9 is a pattern that influences a concept's **duration**, or how long something lasts. It is used when signing about a specific period of time or age. This period is included with the base sign, so that the difference between *week* and *nine weeks* is the incorporation of the number nine into the dominant hand. Only numbers up to 9 may be incorporated into a sign. Look at the examples below to help you understand this concept.

Use the Rule of 9 with:
Age
Specific time of day
Specific number of hours
Specific number of minutes
Specific number of days
Specific number of weeks
Specific number of months
Specific amounts of money (see Unit 9)

EXAMPLE: DAYS

Base sign: *Day* + **Duration** = ***Four days***

EXAMPLE: AGE

Base: *Age Spot* + **Duration** = ***One year old***

EXAMPLE: MONTHS

Base: *Month* + **Duration** = ***Three months***

Classroom Exercise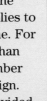

1   *The Rule of 9.* Use the Rule of 9 to provide the correct sign for each item.

1. *3 days*	**4.** *4 hours*	**7.** *1 year old*	**10.** *2 minutes*
2. *5 years old*	**5.** *3 weeks*	**8.** *5 days*	**11.** *7 years old*
3. *6 months*	**6.** *5 minutes*	**9.** *6:00*	**12.** *3 hours*

2   *More Rule of 9?* The Rule of 9 only applies to numbers up to nine. For durations longer than nine, follow a number with the desired sign. An example is provided.

We've been dating for 10 years.

1. *10 days*	**4.** *12 hours*	**7.** *45 minutes*	**10.** *12 weeks*
2. *15 minutes*	**5.** *14 days*	**8.** *10 hours*	**11.** *13 months*
3. *36 months*	**6.** *10:00*	**9.** *21 days*	**12.** *30 days*

Classroom Exercise

1 *How long?* Ask a partner how long each person has been or will be away, following the example. Your partner will respond with the information provided in parentheses.

How long have they been gone?

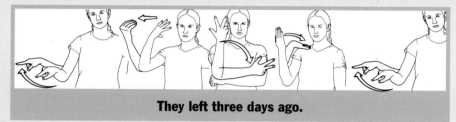

They left three days ago.

1. *Sean* (He hasn't left. He will leave next week.)
2. *Kris* (She took off three weeks ago.)
3. *Marc* (He leaves tomorrow. He will stay for a month.)
4. *Kelly* (Already left. She's been gone since last Monday.)
5. *They* (They will leave in two months.)

2 *Dialogue.* Work with a partner to sign a dialogue about being out of town. How long will you be gone? Where will you go? Your dialogue should have a minimum of eight sentences.

ASL Up Close

Using Tense with the Rule of 9 Incorporating the Rule of 9 with tense can be confusing: There are several exceptions to the general rule that take time and experience to learn. Whether using the past or future tenses, most incorporate the duration, base sign, and tense simultaneously. Look at the examples using *week.* Do you see

1 week

2 weeks

2 weeks ago

how the signs incorporate tense and the Rule of 9?

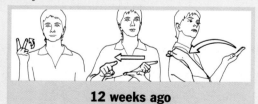

12 weeks ago

Durations longer than 9 must add a separate tense marker indicating the past or present tense. For the past tense, the tense marker goes after the duration. For the future tense, the tense marker precedes the duration.

In 10 months

Some exceptions include *days* and *years*, which include parts of tense and the Rule of 9, but not every number. For now, learn and use these signs:

2 days ago

2 years ago

Classroom Exercise Y

1 *Tense practice.* Sign each phrase, applying the Rule of 9 and tense correctly.

1.	*in 6 weeks*	**5.**	*in 4 hours*	**9.**	*in 8 years*
2.	*2 years ago*	**6.**	*5 minutes*	**10.**	*1 hour*
3.	*5 days*	**7.**	*the year before last*	**11.**	*2 weeks from now*
4.	*3 months ago*	**8.**	*next year*	**12.**	*day before yesterday*

2 *Setting goals.* Complete each sentence by adding an appropriate tense marker and a comment.

In three months I will be good at hockey.

1.	___ *I will be good at* ___.	**6.**	___ *I wasn't good at* ___.
2.	___ *I will* ___.	**7.**	___ *I want to go to* ___.
3.	___ *I will experience* ___.	**8.**	___ *I didn't want to* ___.
4.	___ *I haven't / didn't* ___.	**9.**	___ *I was bad at* ___.
5.	___ *I will take* ___.	**10.**	___ *I will* ___.

Classroom Exercise Z

Signing with tense. Complete and sign each sentence.

1.	*When I was 10, I loved* ____.	**6.**	*I will* _____ *next week.*
2.	*Next summer, I want to* ____.	**7.**	*The weekend starts* _____ *days from now.*
3.	*Two years ago, I* _____.	**8.**	*When I was a child, I played* _____.
4.	*In two weeks, the date will be* _____.	**9.**	*One hour ago, I* _____.
5.	*I used to* _____.	**10.**	*In 3 hours, I will* _____.

Homework Exercise 7

A Starting on today's date, explain what you did or will do at each of the following times:

1. Last week	**2.** 2 years ago	**3.** 2 weeks from now	**4.** 5 years from now

B Develop an ASL narrative that uses the past, present, and future tenses. Suggested topic: Something you did as a child, something you do now, and something you want to do in the future. Your narrative must have a minimum of six ASL sentences.

C Write assignments A or B in ASL gloss.

Journal Activities

1 What factors do you think contributed to the establishment of the Deaflympics? What motivates people to join together for recreation? Why do people who share a similar background seek to come together? Does this make people not want to socialize with people who are different?

2 Why is ASL literature prized within the Deaf community? In what types of cultures are storytelling and poetry highly regarded? Does your culture value literature? Compare your culture's esteem of literature to that of the Deaf community. What is similar or different, and what accounts for these differences?

3 In Unit 6 you learned about several Deaf individuals who play or have played sports at the professional level. Do you feel the motto "Equal Through Sports" to be valid? Why or why not? What obstacles, if any, must be overcome by hearing or Deaf individuals in order to be equal? How can this be done?

4 Develop an original ASL poem or ABC story that reflects your interests and creativity. Experiment with the language and have fun!

http://Search Search the web for more information:

What are each of these individuals known for?

- Don Bangs
- Bill Ennis
- Patrick Graybill
- Debbie Rennie

- Kitty O'Neill
- Curtis Pride
- Luther H. Taylor
- LeRoy Colombo

- William Schyman
- Eugene Hairston

Unit 6 Review

A

Comprehension I. Watch Kris' narrative titled *"The Storytelling Competition"* on your Student DVD. Respond to the questions below.

1. *What kinds of stories will Kris perform?*
2. *How many people will attend the competition?*
3. *In addition to the stories, what else can people watch?*
4. *What question does Kris ask?*
5. *What does Kris use the Listing and Ordering Technique for?*

Comprehension II. Practice signing Kris' narrative. Focus on clarity instead of speed, and include non-manual signals when necessary.

B A friend has asked what you did last month. Create an explanation based on the pictures below.

1

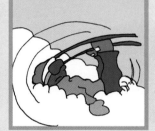

2

C Select a tense marker that best indicates the general time frame for each illustration.

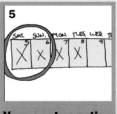

| The dinosaur age | Woman president | 1996 | 2019 | Your next vacation |

Unit 6 Review

D What are they doing? Develop a plot and fully explain the activity in each illustration sequence using classifiers and other ASL skills. Apply ASL Rule #11.

E Create complete sentences using the tense markers and prompts.

Tense Markers		Prompts
Yesterday	Will	Take off
Last year	Past	Homework due
Next Wednesday	All year	Soccer game
Two hours ago	Very recently	Graduate high school / college
Six months ago	In a few days	Watch water polo
Three days from now	Finish	Summer vacation
Last month	Next year	Won't
Last night	2 years from now	Can't
In ten minutes	Used to	To be late
Recently	Distant future	To win
Four minutes ago	Long ago	Live
Next weekend	3 weeks ago	To bungee jump

Units 4 – 6 Review

Review Exercise A

1   *ASL parameters.* What are the parameter errors in each sign? Explain the parameter error and provide the correct sign.

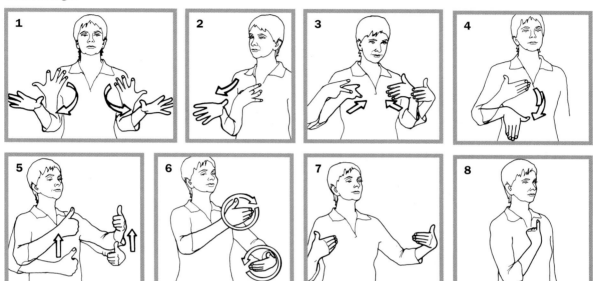

2   *Shades of meaning.* Many signs have minor parameter differences that affect meaning. Make complete sentences using each sign pair found below. What other signs can you think of that are similar?

1. *Enjoy / Happy*
2. *Old / How old*
3. *Address / Live*
4. *Male cousin / female cousin*

5. *School / Paper*
6. *Recently / Very recently*
7. *?*
8. *?*

A S L   T I P S

- A particular parameter error ASL students make involves a sign's location. Many signs are formed on the torso, yet students tend to place their hands away from their body, as seen in the examples below. When in doubt, remember that in most cases signs originate from, are located at, or come into direct contact with the torso.

 versus  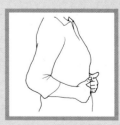 versus

- While signing, don't switch your dominant and non-dominant hands. Doing so is distracting for both you and the person to whom you're signing!

Review Exercise B

Profiles. Use the information provided to sign a profile about each individual.

This is Susan. She's unhappy today because she and her boyfriend recently broke up. They met two years ago and have been dating ever since. Susan enjoys skiing and going to the movies, and she loves to cook with friends during the weekend. Some day she wants to go to cooking school and cook in a restaurant in New York City.

Sam and his friends are studying for a science test tomorrow morning. Sam hasn't done well this semester in science and wants to get an A on the test. Last week he asked his friends to help him study and today they've been studying since

4:00. Sam needs a good grade on the test because next year he will take physics, and he doesn't want to go to summer school.

This is the Montez family. Pedro and Gloria have been married for 14 years and have three children, Maria, age 8, Mary, 6, and Marta, 4. Gloria is a teacher and Pedro manages a store near their home. Maria and Mary walk to school in the morning at 8:15 a.m.

Bryan is a sophomore at a school for the Deaf in California. His favorite classes are English and

world history. He doesn't really like math but he's very good at it. He and his good friends Scott and Derek are on the swim team, and in the fall he acted in the school play "Romeo and Juliet."

Review Exercise C

What time is it? Sign a complete sentence including the time shown. Topics are provided below.

1. *school's out*
2. *movie starts*
3. *school starts*
4. *watch TV*
5. *studies/does homework*
6. *go to work*
7. *plane lands*
8. *sleeps*
9. *practice begins*
10. *eats*

Review Exercise D

1 *Working with concepts.* Use classifiers to explain each illustration in ASL.

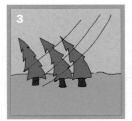

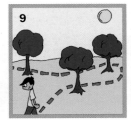

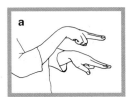

2 *More visual concepts.* Select the classifier that best matches each illustration. Explain the name of the classifier and its uses in a complete ASL sentence.

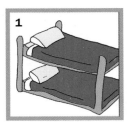

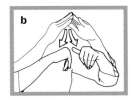
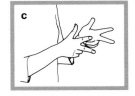
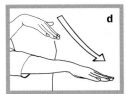

Review Exercise E

Have you ... Can you ask and answer the following questions? If you work with a partner, switch roles and repeat the exercise.

Finish

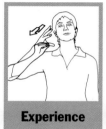
Experience

Not yet

1. *taken biology & chemistry (not yet / next year)*
2. *know how to ride a bike (yes / long time ago)*
3. *visited Mexico (yes / two months ago)*
4. *asked him / her out on a date (not yet / soon)*
5. *bungee jumped (yes / last summer)*
6. *studied for the test (yes / yesterday)*

7. *know how to surf (not yet / will)*
8. *rode a horse (yes / during spring vacation)*
9. *know how to cook (not yet / will learn)*
10. *sky dived (yes / very recently)*
11. *scuba dived (not yet / don't want to)*
12. *taken drama (yes / enjoy acting)*

Review Exercise F

Using the Rule of 9. Complete each sentence with signs from Column B.

Column A

1. *The movie starts / started ...*
2. *My birthday is / was in ...*
3. *I graduate / graduated ...*
4. *I will / won't be married ...*
5. *We must leave in ...*
6. *School's over ...*
7. *I will look for a job ...*
8. *The weekend begins ...*
9. *I go to class _____ days a week ...*
10. *I want to sleep for ...*
11. *Summer / fall / winter / spring begins in ...*
12. *I was born ...*

Column B

in 5 minutes

3 months ago

last year

7 days

12 hours

4 weeks

10 minutes ago

in 4 months

12 days

9 months ago

3 years from now

2 hours

2 days ago

6 weeks ago

in 4 weeks

1 minute

15 months

?

Review Exercise G

Yesterday & Tomorrow. Change the tense of each sentence, choosing from the past, present, or future tenses.

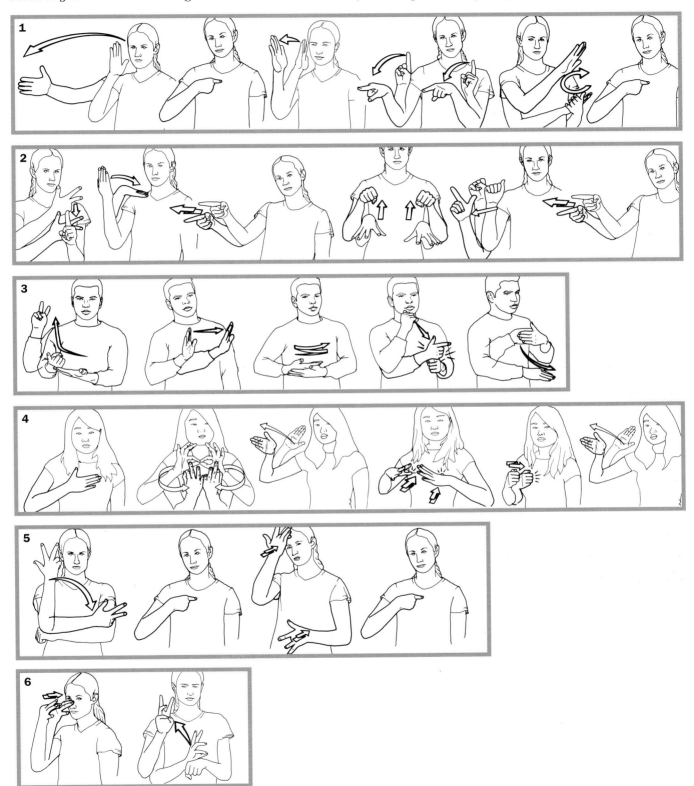

Review Exercise H

The right face. What is the function of each non-manual signal in ASL? Sign an example sentence using each NMS.

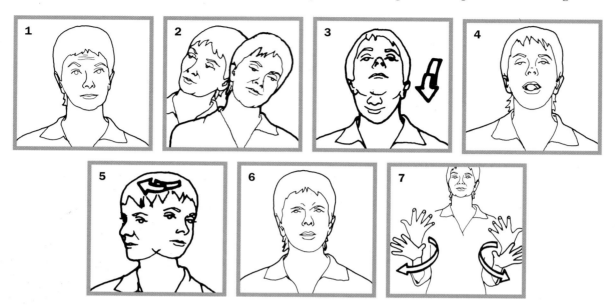

Review Exercise I

Grammar & structure review. In Units 1-6 you have learned 13 important rules governing ASL structure and grammar. Create a complete ASL sentence for each prompt, or explain in ASL how the rule is used.

Eyes on ASL

1. *Eye contact ...* **(page 8)**
2. *Closing signals ...* **(page 9)**
3. *One-word answers ...* **(page 10)**
4. *Non-manual signals with YES and NO ...* **(page 30)**
5. *"When" signs come first ...* **(page 59)**
6. *WH-signs come at the end of sentences ...* **(page 64)**
7. *Numbers 1 - 5 always ... except when ...* **(page 99)**
8. *Contrastive structure means ...* **(page 131)**
9. *The Age Spot ...* **(page 134)**
10. *Number and subject agree for ASL pronouns ...* **(page 153)**
11. *Classifiers must be identified first ...* **(page 194)**
12. *Time signs are also when signs...* **(page 199)**
13. *Tense markers are generally located ...* **(page 231)**

My Daily Routine

Unit Seven Objectives

- To sign about daily routines and activities

- To identify and understand noun-verb pairs in ASL

- To describe clothing

- To learn and use spatial organization

- To apply turn-taking strategies in conversations

- To understand the sign language continuum

Unit Seven Vocabulary

Key Phrases

What's your routine?

Hi, what's up? What do you do every day? My schedule varies each week. For example, after school on Mondays and Wednesdays I work, but on Tuesdays and Thursdays I have gymnastics from 3 until 5. When practice is over I take off and go home. I eat dinner, study, then go to bed at 11:00. I'm always running around!

What's your routine? Watch Kelly sign in full motion on your student DVD.

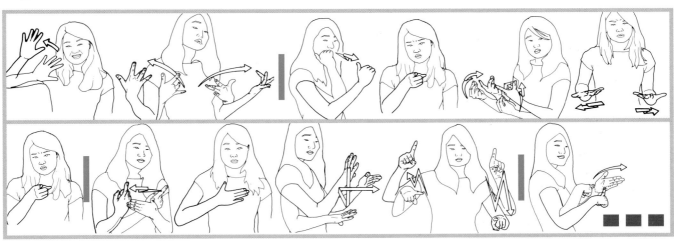

Vocabulary   What's your routine?

Other new vocabulary seen in the narrative is presented throughout Unit 7.

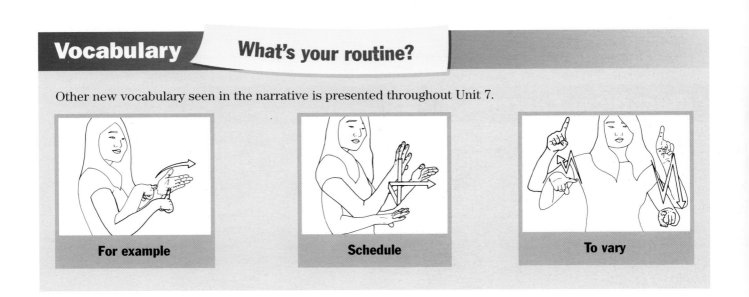

| For example | Schedule | To vary |

Daily Routines & Activities

Describing what you do every day is an important language skill. In this section you will learn how to explain recurring activities and routines. Look closely at the way ASL handles phrases like "on Sundays" and "every afternoon". Can you see a relationship between the parameters of the signs and a calendar? What is it? In the *Where are you going?* dialogue below, see how recurring events are signed.

Dialogue Translation

Kelly: *Where are you two going?*

Sean: *Every afternoon we have karate practice. What do you do?*

Kelly: *Oh, cool. I work every day and work out in the evenings*

Sean: *Oh, ok. Yikes! Look at the time! We need to take off!*

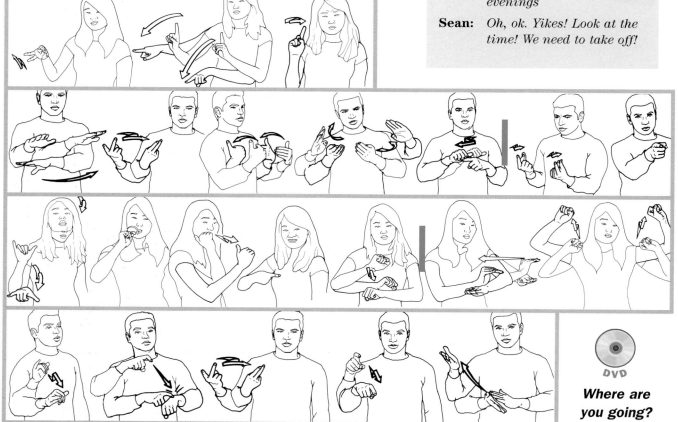

Where are you going?

Classroom Exercise A

 Dialogue. Sign the *Where are you going?* dialogue with a partner.

 Language analysis. Watch the *Where are you going?* dialogue with a partner and discuss the following items:

1. Which ASL pronouns are used?
2. Which recurring days are mentioned?
3. What non-manual signal is interpreted as yikes! *in the dialogue translation?*

Vocabulary — Signing *Every*

Every afternoon	Every morning	Every night	Every week	Every year

Classroom Exercise

1 *Schedules.* What can you say about Sean and Kelly's weekly schedules?

1. *Sean's schedule*

2. *Kelly's schedule*

2 *Discussion.* Answer the following questions in complete sentences.

1. When does Sean work? **2.** When does Kelly study? **3.** What do they do on the weekends?

Vocabulary — *Every* Days

Every Monday

Every signs are part of the *when* group of signs, so they come first in sentences. See Eyes on ASL #5 to review *when* signs. *Every* signs can be interpreted as "every" or as "on" interchangeably, but don't use the sign *during* with them. *Every* signs are made using the hand shape for the day of the week, moving it down as if through each week on a calendar.

Accent Steps

Sign *every weekend* like this!

Classroom Exercise C

1 *What time?* Ask a partner what time he or she does the following activities. When done, switch roles and repeat. An example is provided.

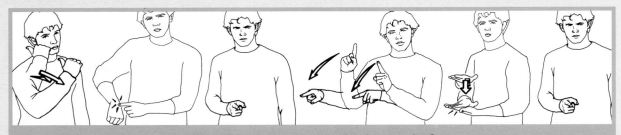

What time do you go to school every day?

I go to school at 7:15 every day.

1. *What time do you wake up every day?* (?)
2. *What time do you eat breakfast every morning?* (?)
3. *When do you go to ASL class?* (?)
4. *When do you work?* (?)
5. *What time do you get ready every morning?* (?)
6. *What time do you want to get up every day?* (?)

2 *My morning routine.* What is your morning routine? Explain what you do in a typical morning in complete sentences.

Classroom Exercise (continued)

3 *Comparisons.* Do you take a bath instead of a shower? Get up at 7:00 instead of 5:10? Not use makeup? For each scene shown, state in a complete sentence what you do differently.

Vocabulary — Morning Routines

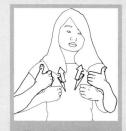
To take a bath

To eat breakfast

To brush one's hair

To brush one's teeth

To comb one's hair

To get dressed

To get ready

To get ready (2)

To get up

To put on makeup

To oversleep

To shave

To shave (2)

To shower

To wake up

See the Accent Step on Page 269 for more about *to shave.*

Classroom Exercise D

1. *What time?* Use *around* or *between* to complete the sentences below.

 1. *I wake up...* **(around 7:30)**
 2. *I get up...* **(between 8:00-8:15)**
 3. *On Saturdays I get up...* **(around 10:00)**
 4. *My alarm rings...* **(around 6:45)**
 5. *On the weekends I get up...* **(between 11:00 and 12:00)**

2. *Every morning....* What do people do every morning? Complete each sentence with vocabulary from the list.

 1. *Every day, people should...*
 2. *Every morning, I ...*
 3. *Every day I'm late because I ...*
 4. *I ___ in the mornings.*
 5. *People ___ every morning.*

Homework Exercise 1

A. What is your morning routine? Describe what you do every morning in a minimum of six complete sentences.

B. Do you ever oversleep? Describe how oversleeping for an hour would affect your morning routine. What would happen? Which activities of your morning routine would you do or not do? Why? Explain what would happen in a minimum of six complete sentences.

C. Write Assignments A or B in ASL gloss.

Accent Steps

Use *between* only when signing about time, as in "I get up between 7:30 and 8:00" or "I have to see the nurse at 10 or 11."

 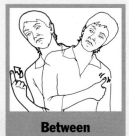

Around   **Between**

Classroom Exercise

1   *Routines.* Based on the illustrations shown, explain what the Lees do every day. Use Shoulder-Shifting where needed.

2   *What do you do?* Ask a partner what time he or she does the following activities. When done, switch roles and repeat.

1. *What time do you go to bed?*
2. *When do you eat lunch?*
3. *What time do you set your clock for?*
4. *Do you do chores every day? When?*
5. *What time do you tend to fall asleep?*
6. *What time do you cook dinner?*

Vocabulary   Evening Routines

To change (clothes)

To do chores, duties

To eat dinner/supper

Early

To fall asleep

To go to bed

To eat lunch

To rest, relax

To set a clock/alarm

ASL Up Close

Spatial Organization

The English word "then" is often used to describe a series of events, as in this sentence: "I woke up at nine, then I went to class, then I went to work, and then I went home." American Sign Language

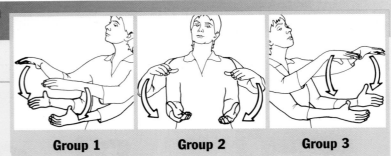

Group 1   **Group 2**   **Group 3**

has a visual way of organizing information into groups of related thoughts, actions, or details. This grouping is called **spatial organization**. Spatial organization uses Shoulder-Shifting and the *group* sign to separate details into related groups. Add a new group and shoulder-shift for each additional series of details. Use spatial organization when signing about several details. Look at the example below to understand how spatial organization is used to sign this sentence: Every morning I get up and brush my teeth. Then in the afternoons I have class and work. At night, I hang out with friends.

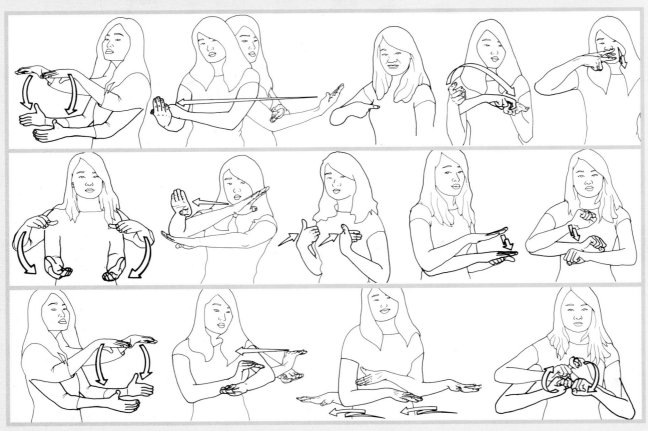

Eyes on ASL #14

Use spatial organization to group related information together.

Along with spatial organization, you may also need to incorporate the Listing and Ordering Technique.

Classroom Exercise F

Events. Use spatial organization to organize the following information into *morning, afternoon,* and *evening* categories.

1.

Morning	**Afternoon**	**Evening**
Wake up	*Go to school*	*Eat dinner*
Get up	*Go to work*	*Brush teeth*
Eat breakfast	*Relax*	*Get in bed*

2.

Morning	**Afternoon**	**Evening**
Alarm rings	*Go to school*	*Read*
Wake up	*Eat lunch*	*Cook dinner*
Get up	*Watch TV*	*Go to bed early*

3.

Morning	**Afternoon**	**Evening**
Go to ASL	*Exercise*	*Study*
Brush teeth	*Do chores*	*Set clock*
Shower	*Do homework*	*Fall asleep*

4.

Morning	**Afternoon**	**Evening**
Wake up early	*Shower*	*Visit friends*
Exercise	*Change clothes*	*Study*
Work	*Go to class*	*Brush teeth*

Classroom Exercise G

Activities. Use spatial organization to describe each person's daily activities.

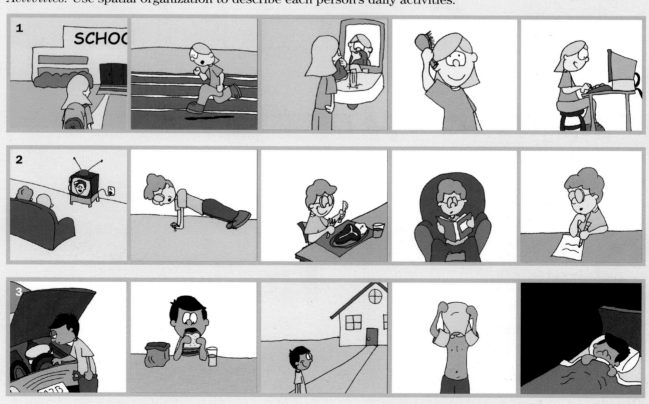

Classroom Exercise G (continued)

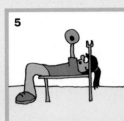    

Classroom Exercise H

1. *Dialogue.* Work with a partner to create a dialogue that includes the following:

   1. *a greeting*
   2. *comparing daily routines or activities*
   3. *making plans to meet again*
   4. *a farewell*

2. *Comparing routines.* Explain your daily routine to a partner. What similarities and differences do you have? Prepare to share this information with your classmates.

   1. *What time is each activity done?*
   2. *What are three similarities and three differences?*
   3. *What are two activities you like and dislike?*

Deaf Culture Minute

Earlier you learned that Deaf people use visual or vibrating devices for alarms, doorbells, and other alerts. This includes alarm clocks! Just as hearing people wake to a sound, Deaf people wake to a flashing light or vibration.

Classroom Exercise

1 *Working with concepts.* Complete each sentence prompt.

1

2

3

4

5

2 *More working.* Which of the following phrases fits the concept of the sign *errands*? Sign each phrase in ASL.

1. *I've been running around.*
2. *I have a lot of things to do today.*
3. *I have a lot going on.*
4. *He's very busy.*
5. *I will do some errands today.*

3 *Using errands.* Sign a complete sentence using the *errands* sign.

Errands

EXPRESSION CORNER

The *errands* sign is a common expression to say you have a lot to do. Use *errands* to sign about being busy in general or when describing specific errands.

Activities

Activities. Watch Kris sign in full motion on your student DVD.

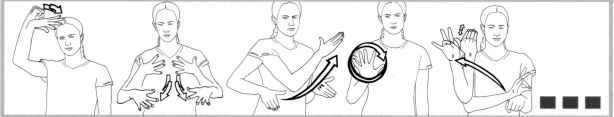

Classroom Exercise J

1 *Comprehension.* Based on Kris' *Activities* narrative, answer each question in complete sentences.

    1. *What is Kris' morning routine?*
    2. *What does Kris do on Monday and Wednesday afternoons?*
    3. *Where and when does Kris work? How long does she work?*
    4. *What does Kris do every night?*
    5. *What time does Kris go to bed? What time does she wake up?*

2 *Discussion.* Compare your routine with Kris'. Use Shoulder-Shifting when making each comparison.

    1. *Kris wakes up at 6:00. I wake up at ...*
    2. *Kris finishes school at 2:33. I finish school at ...*
    3. *On Monday and Wednesday afternoons, Kris is involved with drama. I ...*
    4. *Kris works on Tuesdays and Thursdays. I work on ...*
    5. *Every night Kris helps cook dinner. Every night I ...*

3 *Routines.* What is your fantasy daily routine? Describe the ideal routine to a partner. When done, switch roles and repeat.

Homework Exercise 2

A Generally, what do you do every day? Every week? Every month? Every year? Describe your routine in detail, including brief explanations of what you do every week, month, and year. Prepare to sign your extended routine to your classmates.

B Translate Kris' *Activities* narrative into English. Describe at least three translation challenges in ASL and English. What are these challenges, and how are they overcome?

C Write Assignments A or B in ASL gloss.

Personal Hygiene & Care

Many signs for common hygiene products use classifiers to depict their action or purpose. For example, what do you think is the sign for *shampoo*? If you can think of *shampoo*, then you already know how to sign *wash my hair*! Follow the clues provided to determine how each sign is made for the products below.

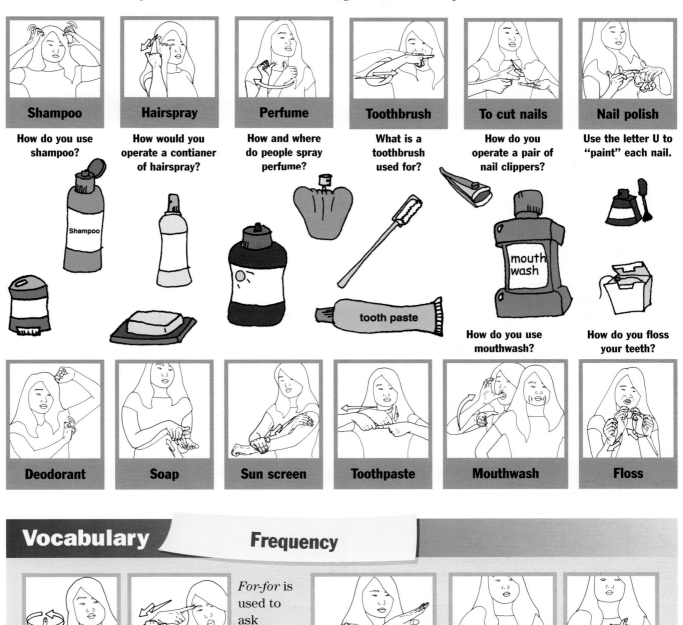

Shampoo	Hairspray	Perfume	Toothbrush	To cut nails	Nail polish
How do you use shampoo?	How would you operate a contianer of hairspray?	How and where do people spray perfume?	What is a toothbrush used for?	How do you operate a pair of nail clippers?	Use the letter U to "paint" each nail.

How do you use mouthwash?

How do you floss your teeth?

Deodorant	Soap	Sun screen	Toothpaste	Mouthwash	Floss

Vocabulary — Frequency

For-for is used to ask "What for?" and "Why did you do that?"

Always	For-for		Never	Sometimes	To use

Classroom Exercise K

1 *What's wrong?* Advise a friend what he or she should do to do to correct the problem shown in the illustration.

 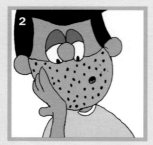  

2 *For-for?* Follow the example below to ask a partner why certain things are being done. Use your imagination to explain the reason in a complete sentence. When done, switch roles and repeat.

What's she getting into bed for?

She's tired.

3 *How often?* Ask a partner how often he or she does each activity. When done, switch roles and repeat.

Do you use deodorant? **Every day!**

1. Uses sun screen
2. Washes his / her hair
3. Uses perfume
4. Shaves his / her head
5. Brushes his / her teeth
6. Cuts his / her nails
7. Flosses
8. Shaves
9. Paints his / her nails
10. Uses mouthwash

Did you know?

It takes more than selecting the "captions" button on your television set for closed captioning to work. Each word and sound is keyed into a program that is then attached to the original material. If material has not been captioned already, then closed captioning will not work.

For many years the National Association of the Deaf (NAD) has lobbied to have captioning offered on television, movie screens, and other locations accessible to the public. Captioning does not only benefit the Deaf, but hard of hearing and hearing people as well. Since the passage of the Americans with Disabilities Act (ADA) in 1990, captioning has become increasingly available and is now common on music videos, news broadcasts, commercials, and home videos and DVDs.

To learn more, visit:
http://www.nad.org
http://www.ncicap.org

These logos indicate captioning is available.

Accent Steps

Change the location of the *to shave* sign to modify its meaning. The *x* form of *to shave* is not used on the head.

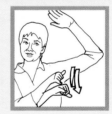

Homework Exercise 3

A Describe what is being done in each series of illustrations. Use your imagination to create a story explaining what they are doing and why. Each description should have at least six complete sentences.

B How would you mime the following activities? Be as detailed and thorough as you can.
1. *Brushing one's teeth*
2. *Washing one's hair*

C Write Assignment A or B in ASL gloss.

Household Activities

Like signs for personal hygiene and products, signs for household activities incorporate different classifiers for specific actions. In the dialogue between Sean and Kelly below, can you identify any signs that are also classifiers?

Dialogue Translation

Kelly: *What do you do when you get home?*

Sean: *Every day I walk the dog. Sometimes I do some cleaning. Every night I exercise and relax. On the weekends I do laundry and do yard work. What about you?*

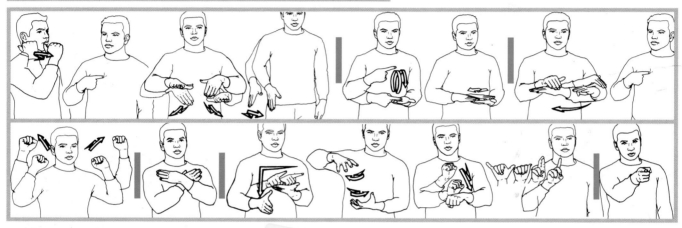

Classroom Exercise L

1. *Dialogue I.* Sign Sean and Kelly's dialogue with a partner. Add the following:
   1. *A greeting*
   2. *At least four activities Kelly does when she gets home*
   3. *Make plans to meet again*
   4. *A farewell*

2. *Dialogue II.* Explain to a partner what you tend to do when you arrive home. Include relevant times as needed. Switch roles when done.

Classroom Exercise M

1. *Non-manual signals.* Make each facial expression shown.

2. *Using non-manual signals.* What meaning is conveyed by each facial expression to the right? Sign a sentence whose meaning matches the facial expression.

Classroom Exercise

1   *What are you doing today?* Describe the activity in each illustration in a complete sentence.

2   *Do you?* Ask a partner the following questions. When done, switch roles and repeat.

     1. *Do you make the bed every day?*
     2. *When do you clean your house?*
     3. *Do you do the dishes after eating?*
     4. *When do you take out the garbage?*

Vocabulary   **Household Activities**

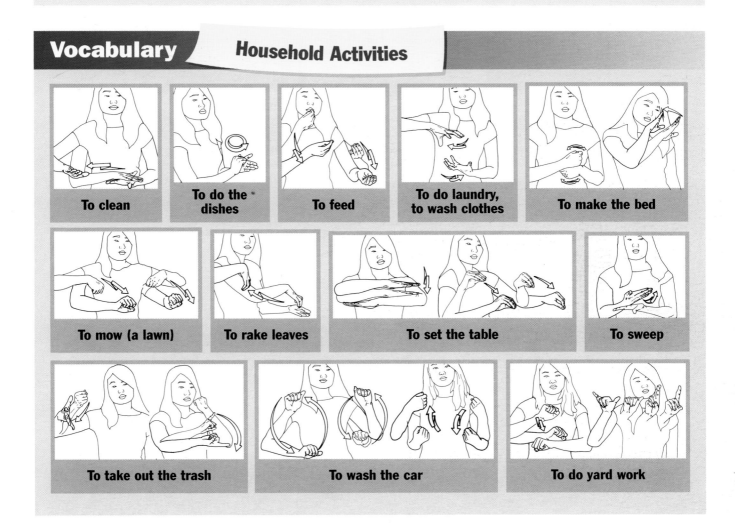

To clean	To do the dishes	To feed	To do laundry, to wash clothes	To make the bed
To mow (a lawn)	To rake leaves	To set the table		To sweep
To take out the trash	To wash the car	To do yard work		

Classroom Exercise

1 *How often?* Sign a complete sentence using the provided prompts and a sign from Column A.

I never do yard work because I don't have a yard.

Column A

Sometimes	*Every weekend*
Every day	*Always*
Every week	*Every month*
Every Friday	*Every Tuesday*
Every Saturday	*Never*
Every Monday	*Every Thursday*

 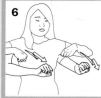  

2 *How often II.* Complete each phrase using Household Activities vocabulary.

3 *Activities.* Sign each sentence in ASL. Remember to place *when* signs in their correct location.

1. *I don't like raking leaves in the fall.*
2. *I wash the car every Saturday.*
3. *I never make my bed in the morning.*
4. *I don't mind mowing the lawn.*
5. *Every night I help cook, and then I do the dishes.*
6. *I do laundry on Wednesdays.*
7. *I feed my cat and dog every night.*
8. *Once in a while I clean my room.*
9. *I take out the garbage after dinner.*
10. *I always set the table.*

ASL Up Close

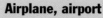

Noun-verb pairs in American Sign Language

What similarities do you see in these two sentences? Look closely and think of how each would be signed:

1. *I go to fly. Chair. Fly.*
2. *I go to the airport, sit down, and the plane departs.*

Airplane, airport   **To fly to**

Each sentence is signed exactly the same way except for one parameter difference: Movement. The movement parameter changes **nouns** into **verbs**, or sentences like the first one into the second. Many ASL nouns and verbs share every parameter except movement. These signs are called **noun-verb pairs**. Confusing nouns and verbs can be tricky, so keep an eye on the movement differences for each:

- Nouns: Typically have a double back-and-forth movement
- Verbs: Typically have one solid movement, or a wider back-and-forth movement than nouns.

Another way to understand noun-verb pairs is to think of what the signs show or do. See below for an example using the noun-verb pair scissors and to cut.

Example Non-Verb Pair: *Scissors & To cut*

Scissors

The sign *scissors* demonstrates the back-and-forth movement of the blades, but not the action of cutting.

To cut

By showing scissors doing *something*, an action is made and the noun changes to the verb *to cut*.

Common noun-verb pairs. Some verbs may also be directional.

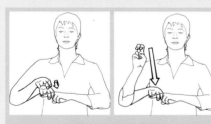

Chair vs. To sit

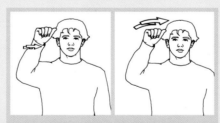

Eraser vs. To erase

The sign *to erase* implies a surface such as a whiteboard or chalkboard.

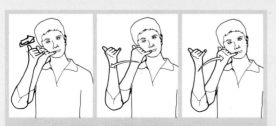

Telephone vs. To call vs. To be called

Car, auto vs. To drive to vs. To drive here

Classroom Exercise

1   *Noun-verb pairs.* Sign each noun-verb pair using the correct movement parameter.

1. Chair / to sit	**5.** Scissors / to cut	**9.** Telephone / you call me
2. Door / to open a door	**6.** Boat / to cruise	**10.** Eraser / to erase
3. Telephone / I call you	**7.** Pencil / to write	**11.** Car / to drive here
4. Car / to drive to	**8.** Window / to open a window	**12.** Airplane / to fly to

2   *More noun-verb pairs.* Provide the missing sign for each noun-verb pair.

3   *Dialogue.* Work with a partner to create a complete dialogue based on one of the following:

1. The signs "I call you" and "you call me"
2. The signs "to drive to" and "to drive here"
3. The signs "chair" and "to sit"

Noun	Verb	Noun	Verb
1 ?		**6**	?
2	?	**7** ?	
3	?	**8**	?
4	?	**9** ?	
5	?	**10** ?	

Homework Exercise   4

A   What duties do you have at your place of residence? What are you expected to do, and when? Prepare to share the information with your classmates in a minimum of six complete sentences.

B   Create a chart showing all the noun-verb pairs you know and prepare to sign a sample sentence for each.

C   Write Assignments A or B in ASL gloss.

Signing About Clothing

In this section you will learn vocabulary for clothing. In the dialogue between Kelly and Kris, how many clothing signs do you see?

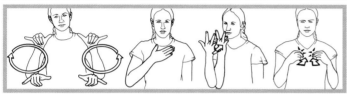

Dialogue Translation

Kris: *What will you wear next Friday?*

Kelly: *It might be cool, so I'll wear a blouse, skirt, and jacket. What about you?*

Kris: *The same old — my favorite overalls!*

Kelly: *You need to do laundry!*

Classroom Exercise Q

1. *Weather choices.* In the dialogue above, Kelly chooses clothing based on the weather. What else could Kelly wear if the weather was different? Explain her options in a complete sentence.
   1. *Cold weather*   2. *Hot weather*   3. *Snowing*   4. *Raining*

2. *Dialogue.* Sign the dialogue between Kelly and Kris with a partner.

Accent Steps

Use the sign *clothes* to sign "wear" and the sign *use* when signing about non-clothing items like glasses and shoes.

Vocabulary   The right clothes?

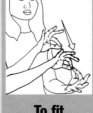

Clothes

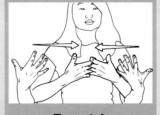

To fit

To match

Clothes

To use

Focus: The Sign Language

American Sign Language (ASL)

A visual language as unique as French or German, ASL exists independent of English and has its own complex grammar and syntax. Like other languages, ASL cannot be matched or translated sign-for-sign into another signed or spoken language. For example, the English word "run" refers to many different concepts, but ASL has separate signs for each concept. Only the first instance of "run" in the list below would use the ASL sign *to run*. Can you think of any others to add?

1. *She likes to run.*
2. *The elevator isn't running.*
3. *The water is running.*
4. *The children are running after the dog.*
5. *She is running for president.*
6. *He ran over my foot.*
7. *The car ran over a nail.*
8. *They run a business.*
9. *We ran overtime.*
10. *I need to run some errands.*
11. *They are front-runners to win.*
12. *I ran into her.*
13. *The river ran dry.*
14. *She ran out of money.*
15. *The children are running amok.*
16. *I don't know how to run the software.*
17. *She runs a tight ship.*
18. *The producer runs the show.*

Pidgin Signed English (PSE)

Many hearing individuals who know "sign language" actually use ASL signs in English word order. Those who mouth English words matched to every sign are using PSE. Some signers are "very English" while others are "very ASL." A PSE signer might not know or use each of the various signs needed for the different meanings of "run."

English Codes

These codes aim to show every word, prefix, and suffix in spoken English using signs borrowed from ASL or by creating new ones. These are not languages and cannot exist separate from English. Most codes use one sign for one word, regardless of the meaning or concept of the English word and the sign. For example, the sign below could be used for each concept of "run" since it is the sound of the word rather than its meaning, that is important. Here are some codes to be aware of:

1. *Seeing Essential English (1970s)*
2. *Linguistics of Visual English (1970s)*
3. *Signing Exact English (1980s – still in use)*

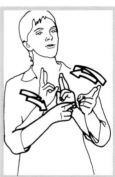

SEE sign, "run" (double Rs)

ASL & Pidgin Signed English:

A pidgin develops when two separate, unrelated languages are mixed together. The person speaking or signing a pidgen is never considered fluent in either language. The key difference between ASL and **Pidgin Signed English (PSE)** is the degree of interference or borrowing from English.

ASL & English Codes:

A code is an artificial way of conveying information, like Morse Code or Braille. It is a system that must be memorized. **Signing Exact English (SEE)** is one code that represents each word in spoken or written English, including prefixes and suffixes. For one word in spoken or written English there is only one SEE sign to represent it, regardless of the concept underlying the word. A well-known example is the word "butterfly." One code breaks the concept into two terms: Butter and to fly. The term **Manually Coded English** refers to any code representing the English language.

Continuum

How do ASL, PSE, and SEE differ from each other? Using the sample sentence "I am going to the store," differences are easy to spot.

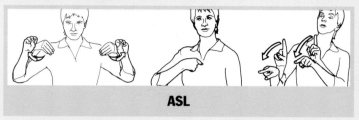

ASL

The topic-comment structure of ASL quickly establishes meaning and a visual concept.

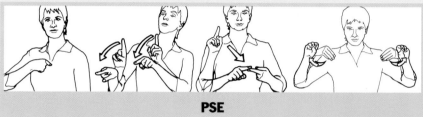

PSE

While using ASL signs in English word order, PSE is neither good English nor ASL. The signer overlooks the preposition already included in *to go to* and signs "I go to to store."

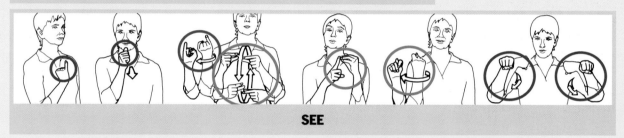

SEE

Most SEE signs use the first letter of the printed English word, indicated by the blue circles. Endings such as -ing, -s, -ed, are also included, seen in the red circle, and ASL signs are modified or supplanted by new, artificial signs, shown in green. In many ways, watching SEE is like "reading" English on the hands.

Why have PSE or English codes in the first place?

All manually coded English systems were created to help Deaf people learn English, and each has its benefits and drawbacks. A common criticism is that codes attempt to teach a language via a system that is itself not a language. For many hearing signers, PSE is a convenient middle-ground between ASL and English since ASL's complicated grammar is ignored in favor of English structure. Unfortunately, this means Deaf people must constantly "interpret" what the hearing signer says and means. Beginning in the 1990s, schools across the country now use ASL to teach English as a foreign language to Deaf students. This approach is called the **bilingual-bicultural** model because it emphasizes ASL and English as distinct — and equally important — languages and cultures.

So what does the sign language continuum mean?

The sign language continuum means there is a wide variety of signing among people. Some use only ASL, some use PSE when signing with hearing people, and others use SEE or a combination of it all, depending on the circumstances. As an ASL student, it is important to remember you are learning a foreign or second language and not simply a way to code English. If you become fluent in ASL, you will be able to move along the continuum from ASL to SEE and back again, and have a valuable skill. Those who learn PSE tend to struggle to understand or sign ASL, though Deaf people who learn SEE first tend to pick up ASL quickly.

Classroom Exercise

1 *Clothing.* How are your classmates dressed? Describe what the following people are wearing:

1. *Your ASL teacher*
2. *Yourself*
3. *A classmate*

Vocabulary — Clothing

Blouse	**Boots**	**Bra**	**Dress**	**Glasses**
Hat, cap	**Jacket, coat**	**Overalls**	**Overcoat**	**Panties**
Pants (1)	**Pants (2)**	**Sandals**	**Shirt**	**Shoes**	**Shorts, boxers**
Skirt	**Socks**	**Sweater**	**Sweatshirt**	
Tank top	**Tie**	**Turtleneck**	**Underwear**	**Watch**

Fingerspelled Terms
Jeans
Pajamas (PJ)
Suit
Sun (with glasses)

Classroom Exercise

1 *Fashion assistance.* A friend of yours needs some clothing advice. What feedback can you give to your partner? When done, switch roles and repeat.

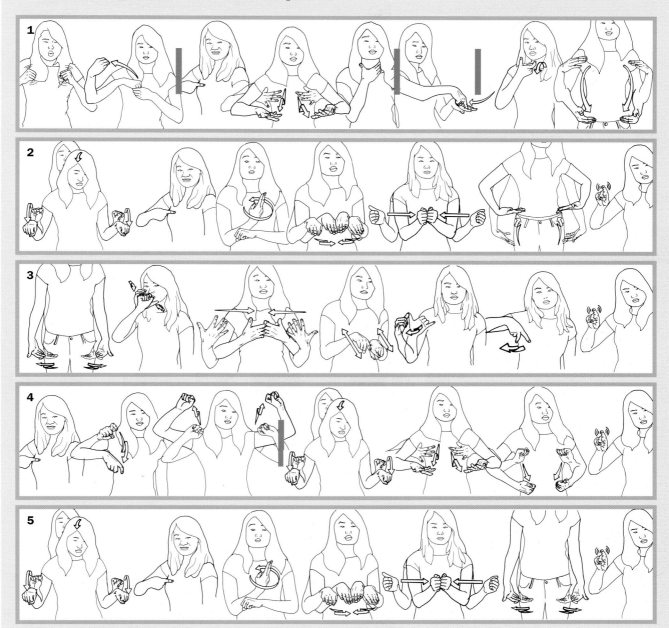

2 *Wear vs. use.* Select between *wear* and *use* for the following sentences. Sign each in ASL.

1. *I'm wearing sandals.*
2. *He has a sweatshirt on.*
3. *She's wearing boots with jeans.*
4. *I like wearing flip-flops.*

5. *She's wearing a blue blouse and jacket.*
6. *He's wearing brown shoes.*
7. *People wear shoes every day.*
8. *I'm wearing tennis shoes / sneakers today.*

ASL Up Close

Describing Clothing

Use topic-comment structure when describing clothing. Topic-comment structure means the topic — what is being described — comes first, with additional comments following.

The Ball Gown

That person is wearing a black jacket and a bright blue shirt.

Classroom Exercise T

1   *I saw . . .* Describe what you noticed people wearing on your way to class. Be as detailed as you can.

2   *Do you have a pair?* Ask a classmate whether he or she has the following items of clothing. Switch roles when done.

Classroom Exercise

Local weather. What is the weather like in your area? Work with a partner to select the items of clothing needed to dress for each type of weather.

CLOTHES FOR WARM WEATHER	CLOTHES FOR COLD WEATHER

Deaf Culture NOTE

DVD

Turn-taking & Exchanging Information

Inexperienced signers find maintaining a conversation awkward or difficult, especially if both signers begin signing at the same time or wait for the other to sign something. If you watch fluent signers interact, you may have noted how fast the conversation flows, with very few awkward pauses or stops. This is because Deaf people are familiar with a code of ASL **turn-taking strategies.**

In spoken languages, turn-taking strategies include raising one's voice and "talking over" another (though this is considered rude), making various sounds like "ahem" or waiting for a natural pause to interject a comment. Similar strategies apply to signed conversations. Watch for closing signals at the end of statements or questions to be ready to respond naturally, and keep an eye on facial expressions and non-manual signals to know when it is your turn to sign.

ASL Turn-Taking Strategies Include:

- closing signals
- Question-Maker & WH-Face
- using the *hold on* sign to ask someone to pause or wait
- moving up your hands to signal to the person signing that you wish to communicate
- using the *go on* sign to ask someone to continue signing after an interruption or when both signers begin signing at the same time

Go on, continue

I Want to Know . . .

Why do some signs have more than one meaning?

A better question for students to ask is, "Why are there so many words in English that mean the same thing?" Wondering why signs have more than one meaning most likely results from matching one English word to just one ASL sign. Rather than thinking this way, try to understand the meaning of a concept, whether it is an ASL sign or an English word. As you learned in Unit 5, the meaning of some signs is influenced by the literal or abstract definition of a word. Some signs have very subtle differences that many hearing signers overlook, like noun-verb pairs, while other nuances that affect meaning are conveyed by non-manual signals. Yet some signs are the same and have different meanings — how does that work? How does one know the difference? The answer is the two C's: **Concept** and **Context**.

What is the concept?

Clothing, dress, and *to wear* all share the same concept: *Something covering one's body.*

The English language lacks words for some ASL concepts, such as the influence of gender on cousin.

What is the context?

When the meaning of a single sign or word changes depending on how it is used in a sentence, then that sign's meaning depends on **context**. For example, the ASL sign pictured on the left means both *shirt* and *to volunteer*. Neither meaning shares a concept so why do they share the same sign? The answer is a matter of opinion. The role of context becomes clear with this example: If someone is signing about clothing and uses this sign, then the meaning is clear: *Shirt*. However, if signing about a project or activity, then the context means *volunteer*. Paying attention to context is essential. The more you practice, the more you'll "just know" differences between signs that have more than one meaning.

Homework Exercise ◀ 5

A   You are going out of town for the weekend and it's time to pack. What clothes will you bring? You need to dress appropriately for each situation: Going to the beach, going camping, and going to a fancy restaurant. Describe what you pack in a minimum of six complete sentences.

B   Describe the clothing in the illustrations and use your imagination to make a story about each scene. Your stories should have at least six complete sentences each.

C   Write Assignment A or B in ASL gloss.

Describing Clothing

Describing clothing in detail is an important way to develop your classifier skills. In the ASL Up Close section on page 280 you watched Kelly describe a dress that conveyed a strong visual impression. The goal is to create a clear visual image of the object being described. See how details are added in the description below.

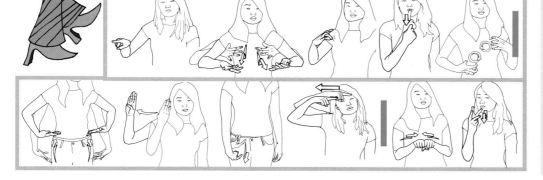

Dialogue Translation

Marc: *What is that woman wearing?*

Kelly: *She's wearing a red, patterned shirt, bright blue pants with black stripes, and pink shoes.*

Classroom Exercise V

Dialogue. Create a dialogue similar to the one between Marc and Kelly with a partner. Take turns describing the clothing of at least two people in as much detail as you can.

Accent Steps

Modify the *striped* sign to show horizontal, vertical, or wavy stripes.

Vocabulary — Describing Clothing

Buttons · Long sleeve · Patterned · Plaid · Polka dot · Scooped neck

Short sleeve · Striped · Striped (wide) · Too big · Too small · V-neck

Classroom Exercise

1   *Material swatches.* Describe the following illustrations.

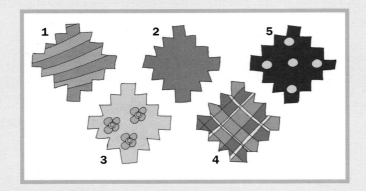

2   *Descriptions.* Describe each article of clothing in complete detail.

 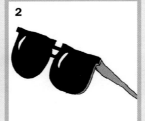  

3   *What's wrong?* You and a Deaf friend are going clothes shopping. Explain what's wrong with each item in a complete sentence.

Classroom Exercise X

Describing people. Your friend is trying to remember what people wore to a party. Refer to the illustration to correct the errors in each sentence. When done, switch roles and repeat.

Homework Exercise 7

A Find a photograph from a magazine or other source that can be described using vocabulary from this section. Prepare to describe the item in detail to your classmates in a minimum of six complete sentences.

B Find a photograph from a magazine or other source that shows at least two complete outfits. Create a story and explain who each person is, what each is wearing, and what they're doing. Your story should have at least six complete sentences.

C Write Assignment A or B in ASL gloss.

Classifiers

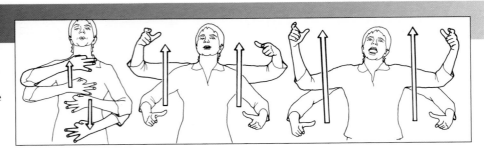

In this section you will learn how ASL uses classifiers as prepositions instead of separate signs for *in*, *on*, *under*, *over*, *behind*, *next to*, or *in front of*.

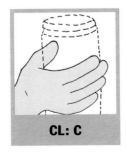

CL: C

CL: C   Cylindrical, hand-held objects

The CL: C classifier is used with cylindrical objects that fit into the handshape, as shown in the illustration.

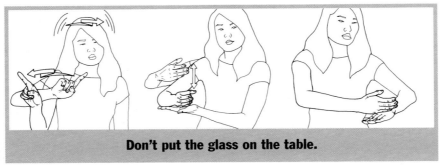

Don't put the glass on the table.

The concept of table, or any flat surface, is provided by CL: B. As you can see, there is no need for a separate sign for *on* since the two classifiers convey the meaning automatically. Because many signs and classifiers function as visual prepositions, ASL does not have many signs dedicated to that purpose.

Vocabulary   Classifiers

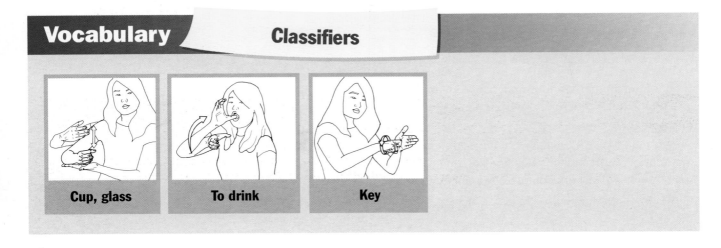

| Cup, glass | To drink | Key |

Classroom Exercise

1 *Descriptions.* Create a complete ASL sentence for each illustration. Remember to explain what is represented by the classifier before using it.

  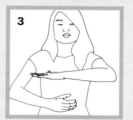

2 *Using classifiers.* Use CL: C and the handshape shown to describe where the keys and jar are in relation to each other. An example is provided.

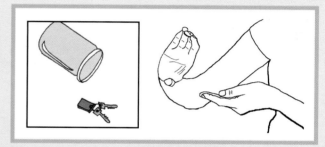

Homework Exercise 8

A Find a photo of one or more objects that use CL: C as a preposition. If you can't find a photo of CL: C, find one of another classifier. Prepare to describe the photo in detail in complete sentences.

B Write Assignment A in ASL gloss.

Journal Activities

1. Many people are unaware that American Sign Language and English are separate languages, despite constant correction. Why do you think it's difficult for hearing people to realize, and accept, that ASL has no relationship to English? Why is it easier to accept a spoken language as "real" but not a signed language?

2. Why do you think many people tend to use Pidgin Sign English (PSE) instead of ASL? Some suggest those who use PSE expect deaf people to "do all the work" to understand what is signed. What attitudes and assumptions does this imply about Deaf people, hearing people, and ASL? Can these attitudes and assumptions be changed? How?

3. Who benefits from captioning on television and movies? In your opinion, what are the benefits and drawbacks of captioning? Why do some places, such as airports, resist installing captioning systems? Write a business letter presenting your thoughts on captioning access.

4. Reflect on the mixed-media work titled *Deaf Pride* by Deaf artist Ann Silver. What is her point? Why did she choose to express herself this way? How does combining a national icon with her social commentary affect those who see it? What do you think Ann Silver wanted people to think about when looking at *Deaf Pride?* Why?

— *Deaf Pride (1999),* Ann Silver.
Reproduced by permission of artist

http://Search

Search the internet to learn more about these topics.

- Closed captioning
- Open captioning
- Subtitles
- Real time captioning

- Computer assisted real time captioning
- Americans with Disabilities Act, 1990
- Pidgin languages
- Creoles

Unit 7 Review

A *Comprehension.* Watch Kelly's narrative titled *What's your routine?* on your Student DVD. Respond to the questions below.

1. *Is Kelly's schedule the same every day? Why not?*
2. *What does Kelly do after school? Does she do this every day?*
3. *What time does Kelly have practice? What sport does she practice?*
4. *What does Kelly do every night?*
5. *What is Kelly always doing?*

 Expressive Skills. Practice signing Kelly's narrative. Focus on clarity instead of speed, and include non-manual signals when necessary.

B It's time for spring cleaning and the residents of this apartment building are catching up on chores. Describe each scene and explain what is being done.

C Describe your typical week, including times, activities, and routines. Then describe your ideal routine, and explain what you would do differently. Use the following prompts to enhance your description.

exercise	*school*	*dream vacations*
chores / duties	*morning routines*	*ASL class*
work	*weekend plans*	*wake up times*

Unit 7 Review

D   *Describe the Pick family routine.*
Arrange each activity into morning,
afternoon, and evening periods using
spatial organization.

E   Discuss Marc's montly schedule.
What does he do every week?

F   Describe each individual's
attire in complete detail.

Describing People

Unit Eight Objectives

- To describe people's physical appearances

- To describe personality traits and characteristics

- To improve ASL narrative skills

- To learn about Deaf-Blind communication

- To discuss health issues

- To describe the natural world and environment

Unit Eight Vocabulary

Key Phrases

My Grandfather

I look just like my grandfather, a Sioux Indian. I'm half Native American, half white. My grandfather is funny, quiet, and humble. What does he look like? He's short and thin, and used to have a spare tire but he exercised and got into shape. He's bald with some brown hair on the sides, and his eyes are light brown. He's always smiling! What do you look like?

DVD

My grandfather. Watch Sean sign in full motion on your student DVD.

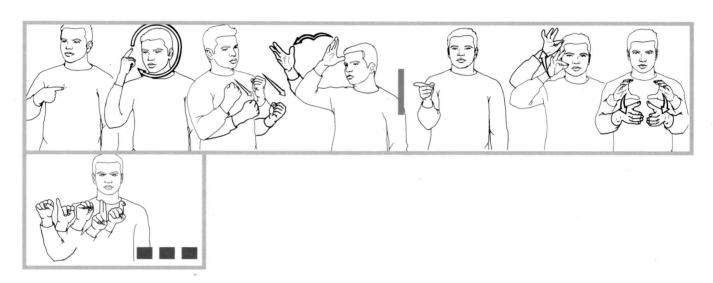

Vocabulary — My Grandfather

Other new vocabulary is presented throughout Unit 8.

To be humble

To be quiet

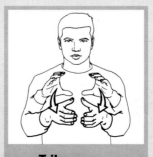
Tribe, group

Fingerspell the specific tribe name after making the sign. Do you see any relationship between the signs *tribe* and *class*? What does this mean?

Describing People

Descriptions of people and objects come naturally to a visual language such as ASL. Descriptions are expected to be highly detailed and specific in order to create a clear visual image of the person or object. When describing people, keep in mind that Deaf culture and hearing culture have two very different perspectives on what is considered polite and impolite. An example of a polite description is seen below in the *Looking for a friend* dialogue between Kris and Sean.

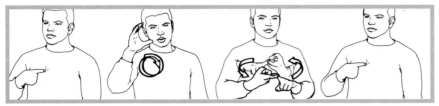

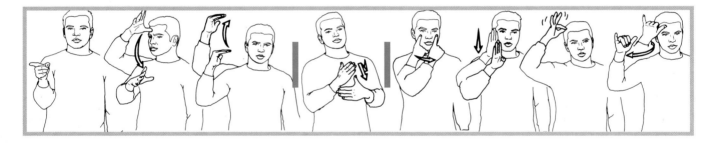

Dialogue Translation

Kris: *What are you doing?*

Sean: *I'm looking for a friend.*

Kris: *What does he look like?*

Sean: *He's a tall guy in decent shape, with brown eyes and blond hair.*

Classroom Exercise A

1. *Dialogue.* Sign the *Looking for a friend* dialogue with a partner.

2. *Basic descriptions.* Take turns describing each illustration to a partner, following the sequence described in Eyes on ASL #15.

Eyes on ASL #15

Follow this sequence to describe physical characteristics:

1. *Gender*

2. *Ethnicity / background (optional)*

3. *Height*

4. *Body type*

5. *Eyes, hair, and other details such as clothing*

Classroom Exercise B

1 *Details. Follow Eyes on ASL #15 to describe each illustration.*

2 *Concepts. Match the words and phrases with the sign that best matches the concept.*

1. *Shed a few pounds*
2. *Skinny*
3. *Pot belly*
4. *Overweight*
5. *Acne*
6. *Obese*
7. *Has a bald spot*
8. *Get in shape*
9. *She's expecting*
10. *Plump*
11. *Muscular*
12. *Spare tire*

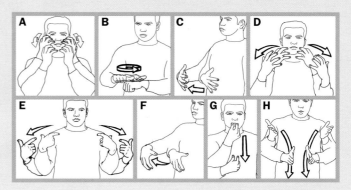

Vocabulary — Describing the Body

To be bald

To be chubby, fat

Face

Freckles

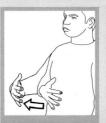
Gut, belly

Hair

To be in good shape

To look like

To lose weight

To be pregnant

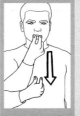
To be thin

To be well built

Classroom Exercise C

1 *Physical descriptions.* Use the information provided to sign a detailed description of each individual.

1. *woman named Madeline*
   • *short, in good shape*
   • *blue eyes*

2. *young woman named Sarah*
   • *age 25*
   • *tall, a little plump*
   • *pregnant*
   • *blonde hair*

3. *little boy named Deion*
   • *8 years old*
   • *brown eyes, brown hair*

4. *man named Craig*
   • *tall, in good shape*
   • *brown hair, mostly bald*
   • *blue eyes*

2 *What do you look like?* How would you describe yourself? Do you look like anybody else in your family? A celebrity? Who? Use *look strong* to explain who you best resemble.

3 *Resemblances.* Use the signs *look like* and *look strong* to describe each pair to the right. Describe in a complete sentence how similar or dissimilar each appears.

Accent Steps

Things to know when describing people:
• point towards these body parts: *eyes, ears, nose*
• *short* and *tall* share the same signs as *child* and *adult*
• fingerspell *DA* for *disabled* and *HC* for *handicapped*
• first sign *hair*, then add the color

EXPRESSION CORNER

Look strong

Use *look strong* to compare physical similarities between people.

I Want to Know . . .

Isn't it rude to be so descriptive?

Many people, accustomed to a society where often the prevailing sense of being polite means thinking one thing but saying another, are uncomfortable being matter of fact with descriptive signs. For Deaf people, describing a person's appearance is neutral, a simple explanation of what the eyes see. However, descriptive signs become rude when paired with unflattering facial expressions or are deliberately exaggerated.

Signing Ethnicity

Be sensitive when describing ethnicity, so avoid unflattering facial expressions or exaggerated signs. Drawing attention to physical characteristics may be uncomfortable for some people, so be respectful. Alternative signs for ethnicity are explained in this section's ASL Up Close. Keep in mind that one sign may carry several concepts, as in *Hispanic*: Depending on the signer, it may mean *Latino/a* or *Mexican*. Similarly, *Black* may mean *African American*, *White* may mean *Caucasian*, and *Native American* may mean *Indian*. Look at the examples to see how to use ethnicity signs.

Classroom Exercise

Ethnicity. What ethnicity are you? What is your background? Ask your ASL teacher for signs not provided here.

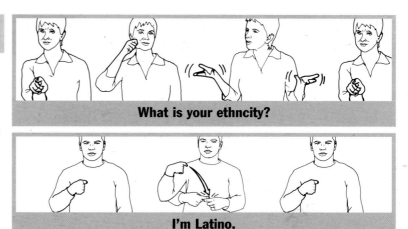

What is your ethncity?

I'm Latino.

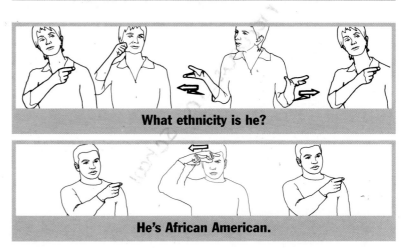

What ethnicity is he?

He's African American.

Vocabulary — Ethnicity

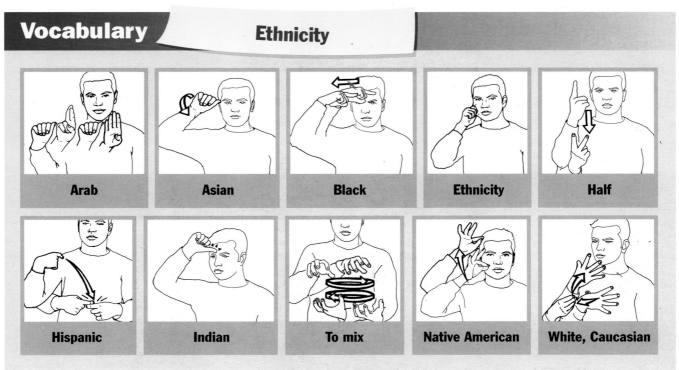

| Arab | Asian | Black | Ethnicity | Half |
| Hispanic | Indian | To mix | Native American | White, Caucasian |

Classroom Exercise E

1 *Background information.* Look at the illustrations below to explain each person's background and ethnicity in a complete sentence.

2 *Describing family.* You and some Deaf friends are exchanging pictures to help describe each person's family. Present in ASL the information learned to another friend who wasn't there.

Shawn has one sister and a seven-month-old nephew named Ryan. His family lives in Louisiana, but Shawn goes to college in New York City.

Michelle has a big family. Her Deaf grandparents live with her family in California. They enjoy getting together to chat and play games.

Luis is half Black and half Latino and lives in Texas. He has a big family with three sisters and one brother. Luis and his brother are Deaf.

Linda Yee recently moved here with her husband Daniel and daughters, Rachel and Amy. Linda and her husband are Deaf, but Amy is not. She is very good at American Sign Language and English. Linda teaches ASL at a college.

3 *Interview & dialogue.* Create a dialogue with a partner comparing and contrasting your backgrounds and ethnicities. How do you identify yourself? Where is your family from? Your dialogue should include the following:

1. *Greetings*
2. *Discussion of ethnicity / background*
3. *Plans to meet again*
4. *A farewell*

ASL Up Close

Please sign African American.

Common Alternatives

Africa

Asia

Alternative Ethnicity Signs in ASL

Some Deaf and hearing signers prefer to use alternative signs for ethnicity or background. Most often, these alternative signs follow the English "hyphening" convention in which two words are paired together. As you attend Deaf functions and gain more exposure to ASL, you will notice some of the alternative signs in use. Being familiar with them is always helpful, and remember both are acceptable.

Classroom Exercise F

Ethnicity II. Sign each sentence in ASL.

1. *I am African American.*
2. *They are from Asia.*
3. *We are Asian Americans.*
4. *She is Mexican American.*
5. *I am Native American and Black.*
6. *He is half White, half Arab.*

Deaf Culture NOTE

❝ The Great Spirit . . . gave us the power to talk with our hands and arms ... and when we meet with Indians who have a different spoken language from ours, we can talk to them in signs. ❞ —*Chief Iron Hawk, Sioux Nation*

Deaf Native Americans

When large groups of Deaf people assemble at events like Deaf Way or the Deaflympics, you can see that deafness is present in every ethnicity, race, and nationality. The Deaf World is uniquely diverse! However, few Deaf individuals have as unique a sign language background as Deaf Native Americans. For hundreds of years Native Americans, particularly the Plains Indians, have used sign language to communicate. It is certain that American Sign Language borrowed signs from this sign language, similar to the way English speakers borrow words from other languages. The Deaf Native American community is proud of their rich legacy of sign languages. The Intertribal Deaf Council works hard on behalf of Deaf Native Americans to preserve their unique heritage and promote awareness of their valuable contributions to the Deaf World. To learn more visit http://www.deafnative.com.

Classroom Exercise G

1   *More descriptions.* Describe what each person looks like in a complete sentence using the information provided. Follow the order shown in Eyes on ASL #15.

     1. *Sharon*
     2. *Daryl*
     3. *Martha*
     4. *Ryan*
     5. *Hannah*

2   *Who is it?* In the scenes below, each person is thinking of someone he or she knows. Explain who this person might be and describe what he or she looks like in complete sentences.

3   *What do they look like?* Take turns describing the following people to a partner.

     1. *Your significant other*
     2. *A grandparent or other relative*
     3. *A friend or coworker*
     4. *A family member*
     5. *A former girlfriend / boyfriend / significant other*
     6. *Your ASL teacher*

Homework Exercise 1

A   How would you describe yourself to somebody who can't see you? What details would be important to share? Practice describing yourself in complete sentences. Follow Eyes on ASL #15 as a guide.

B   Locate a photo of an admired celebrity such as a movie or sports star. Practice describing the person, in complete ASL sentences using as much detail as possible.

C   Write Assignment A or B in ASL gloss.

Describing Hairstyles

A variety of classifiers describe hairstyles to enhance the visual image of a description. As you practice describing hairstyles, think about the relationship between a sign and its concept, and what characteristics are shown by particular classifiers. Notice the three different signs for *short hair* in the vocabulary section below. Can you visualize the different hairstyles and understand why there is more than one sign for *short hair*? Look at the example below to see how hairstyles are signed.

I have short, curly red hair, and no sideburns.

Classroom Exercise

1   *Describing hairstyles.* Describe each person's hairstyle in a complete sentence. Follow the example above.

1. *Yourself*	**3.** *The student closest to you*
2. *Your ASL teacher*	**4.** *A student far from you*

   5. *A female student*
   6. *A male student*

2   *Dialogue.* Create a dialogue with a partner that includes descriptions of at least two different hairstyles. Include the following:

1. *A greeting*
2. *A description of a friend*
3. *A description of the friend's hairstyle*
4. *Making plans*
5. *A farewell*

FYI

Blonde = hair + yellow
Redhead = hair + red
Brunette = hair + brown

Vocabulary   **Hairstyles**

		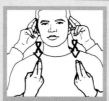	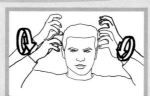		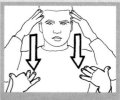
Bangs	**Beard**	**Braids**	**Curly hair**	**Goatee**	**Long hair**
		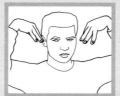			
Mustache	**Pony tail**	**Short hair**	**Short hair (2)**	**Short hair (3)**	**Sideburns**

Classroom Exercise

1. *Details.* Select a classifier from the list provided that best describes the illustration. Use the classifier to describe the hairstyle in a complete sentence.

Classifiers

  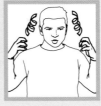  

   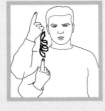

2. *Visualizing classifiers.* Below is a list of classifiers, some which you've already learned, and others that you have not. Which classifier best matches each concept? Using the classifier, how would you sign the concept? How do you know?

Concepts		**Classifiers**
1. *a line of people*	5. *pigtails*	*CL: 1*
2. *rope*	6. *a little bit of water*	*CL: R*
3. *a crew / buzz cut*	7. *a stray hair*	*CL: G*
4. *cornrows*	8. *a soul patch*	*CL: 4*
		CL: S

3. *Before and after.* Describe each person's before-and-after hairstyle in a complete sentence. An example is provided.

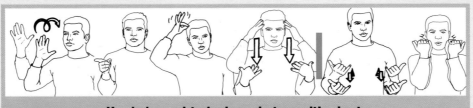

Her hair used to be long, but now it's short.

A good hair day?

A good hair day? Watch Kelly sign in full motion on your student DVD.

Classroom Exercise J

1. Comprehension. Answer the following questions based on *A good hair day?*

   1. *What do you think these three signs mean? How do you know?*

   A B C

   2. *Why does Kelly think working there could be fun?*

   3. *What does Kelly think she can do while working?*

   4. *What are some reasons you think would change Kelly's mind?*

   5. *What do you think about Kelly's idea?*

2. *What I look like.* Watch the *What I look like* description on your Student DVD. When done, complete the following questions.

   1. *What is Kelly's ethnicity?*

   2. *Is Kelly tall or short?*

   3. *Is she wearing sandals?*

   4. *How does Kelly wear her hair?*

   5. *What three words does Kelly fingerspell?*

Accent Steps

Compare *to braid* with *braid*. What differences are there? Are they a noun-verb pair? Why or why not?

To braid

Focus: Sometimes Normal, Sometimes

Do you consider Deaf people to be disabled or handicapped? What is the difference between each label? What do you think Deaf people consider themselves? Recall the two conflicting perspectives of the medical (pathological) and cultural models you learned about in Unit 2. Do the definitions of disabled or handicapped serve the perspectives of the medical or cultural model?

Both disabled and handicapped are applied to groups of people considered different in some way from the majority, regardless of how the person described feels about the label. The negative connotations of disabled and handicapped are clear:

- Disadvantaged
- Deficient
- Physically or mentally impaired

- Unable to function normally
- Helpless
- Unable, unfit, or unqualified

The medical model emphasizes "What can't be done?" while the cultural model asks, "What can I do despite the disability?" If being "normal" means succeeding in a career or school, starting and raising a family, and actively participating in one's community, then what does it mean when a Deaf person achieves those goals? This is the position many Deaf people find themselves in: Considered handicapped or disabled by others, but not by themselves.

dis·a·bil·i·ty

n. pl.   **dis·a·bil·i·ties**
1. a. The condition of being disabled; incapacity.
   b. The period of such a condition: never received a penny during her disability.

2. A disadvantage or deficiency, especially a physical or mental impairment that interferes with or prevents normal achievement in a particular area.

3. Something that hinders or incapacitates.

hand·i·capped

adj.   Physically or mentally disabled: *a pool equipped for handicapped swimmers.*

n. (used with a pl. verb)
   People who have a physical or mental disability considered as a group. Often used with *the.*

Usage Note: Although handicapped is widely used in both law and everyday speech to refer to people having physical or mental disabilities, those described by the word tend to prefer the expressions *disabled* or *people with disabilities. Handicapped*, a somewhat euphemistic term, may imply a helplessness that is not suggested by the more forthright *disabled.* It is also felt that some stigma may attach to the word *handicapped* because of its origin in the phrase *hand in cap*, actually derived from a game of chance but sometimes mistakenly believed to involve the image of a beggar. The word *handicapped* is best reserved to describe a disabled person who is unable to function owing to some property of the environment. Thus people with a physical disability requiring a wheelchair may or may not be *handicapped*, depending on whether wheelchair ramps are made available to them.

Disabled, Sometimes Handicapped?

Regardless of the disability, the term *handicapped* is insensitive and outdated when referring to a group of people. The term reflects a medical perspective that someone can't lead a fulfilling life while disabled, a point disproven by millions of disabled individuals. A cultural view favors *disabled* over *handicapped*, but the emphasis is on the whole person, not simply the part considered "broken" or not normal.

The medical perspective on deafness, in which it is a deficiency that must be corrected to make deaf people like everyone else, strongly affects the Deaf community. From an early age many Deaf people are fitted with **hearing aids** to increase the level of sound available through the ear.

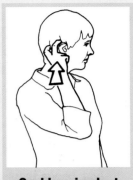

Hearing aid   **Cochlear implant**

Some people use hearing aids daily and others don't, depending on personal preference. In recent years the number of people with **cochlear implants** has grown, especially among hearing parents who have deaf children. While similar in concept to a hearing aid, cochlear implants bypass the ear itself to deliver sound converted into electrical impulses through a noticeable device attached to the skull.

Deaf-Blindness

To be blind

Within the Deaf community there are people who have additional physical or mental disabilities. Proportionately the numbers of people with multiple disabilities is the same within the Deaf and hearing communities. One of the most well-known disabilities within the Deaf World is Deaf-Blindness. Modern-day people who are Deaf-Blind encounter the same challenges in gaining access to education and services, especially in employment, that Helen Keller faced over 100 years ago.

Deaf-Blind individuals access the world of communication via Braille and / or tactile sign language. Tactile sign language involves the Deaf-Blind person placing his or her hands on top of another signer's hands to "read" the ASL being signed. Look at the illustration to understand how tactile sign language works. Tactile sign language is proof that any communication barrier can be overcome!

Classroom Exercise

1 *Lost & found.* You've lost sight of your friend and need help locating him or her. The officer will ask you for important information for the Missing Person Report. Describe the lost individual thoroughly. Work with a partner and alternate roles.

Missing Person Report

Name _____

Age _____

Height ☐ Tall ☐ Short ☐ Medium

Body type _____

Ethnicity _____

Hair _____

Eyes _____

Clothing _____

Hometown _____

1
Andy, 24 years old
Very tall, average weight, muscular
Black hair, brown eyes
African-American, from Portland

2
Lara, 19
medium height
Long brown hair, maybe in braids, blue eyes
Thin

4
Kevin, 22, Sarah, 20
Kevin's tall, White
Sarah's short, Asian
Kevin's overweight
From Ohio

3
Tracie, 12
short
Medium-length black hair, brown eyes
Thin
Deaf

5
Breanda, 27, hard of hearing
not tall
Half Black, half White
A little chubby
Light brown hair, brown eyes
From New York

Homework Exercise 2

A Select one of the following situations to sign about in a minimum of six complete sentences.

 1. *The worst haircut you've had. What did it look like?*
 2. *A hairstyle you would like / not like to have. Why or why not?*

B Practice signing *A good hair day?* Prepare to sign the narrative to your classmates.

C Sign your own response to Kelly's question at the end of *A good hair day?* Your response should include a minimum of six complete sentences.

D Write Assignment A, B, or C in ASL gloss.

Describing Characteristics

In this section you will learn how to describe personality traits and other characteristics using *tend to* and the ASL expression *Deaf tend theirs*. Don't overlook appropriate non-manual signals when commenting on personality traits and characteristics.

Classroom Exercise L

1. *Signing about people.* Use each sign in a complete sentence. An example is provided. Include a facial expression that best matches the concept.

S/he tends to be polite.

1. *Shy*	3. *Nosy*	5. *Embarrassed*	7. *Nervous*	9. *Broken-hearted*
2. *Emotional*	4. *Worry*	6. *Frustrated*	8. *Rude*	10. *Motormouth*

Vocabulary — Characteristics

To be afraid

Broken-hearted

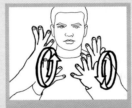
To be embarrassed

To be emotional

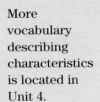

More vocabulary describing characteristics is located in Unit 4.

To be frustrated

Motormouth

To be nervous

To be nosy

Personality

To be polite

To be rude

To be strong

To be weak

To worry

Classroom Exercise

1 *Traits.* Complete the following sentences using the suggested vocabulary.

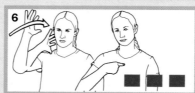

Suggested Vocabulary

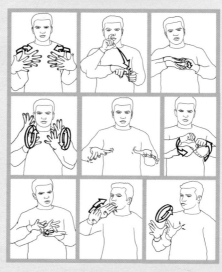

2 *Tend to?* Use *Deaf tend theirs* and *Hearing tend theirs* to explain which community exhibits the following traits.

1. No eye contact is rude
2. It takes a long time to say good-bye
3. Don't like facial expressions
4. Love to get together and chat
5. Love music
6. Stop to chat when someone says "How are you?"
7. Often hug and shake hands when saying hello or good-bye
8. Believe nosiness is bad
9. Believe nosiness is good
10. Always stop to say "Hello" and "How are you?"

3 *Tend to what?* Work with a partner to think of three different traits or characteristics that can be described as *Deaf tend theirs* and *Hearing tend theirs*.

a. _____   b. _____   c. _____

a. _____   b. _____   c. _____

EXPRESSION CORNER

Deaf tend theirs

Deaf tend theirs commonly refers to specific attitudes, beliefs, habits or other characteristics found within Deaf culture as a whole. In other words, *Deaf tend theirs* is a way to say "something Deaf people do." The phrase *tend theirs* can be applied to an individual or a group of people.

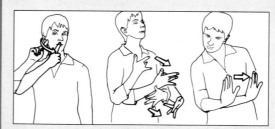

Classroom Exercise N

1   *Interview.* What kind of personality does your partner have? Find out the following information from a partner. When done, switch roles and repeat.

1. *Get along with people?*
2. *Shy or outgoing?*
3. *Quiet or a motormouth?*
4. *Polite or rude?*
5. *Nervous or laid back?*
6. *Funny or boring?*

2   *Personality insight.* Give the Personality Quiz to a classmate. Do you share any characteristics? Switch roles and repeat when done.

PERSONALITY QUIZ

A. *Go for a run*
B. *Watch TV, study*
C. *Sleep*

A. *Busy*
B. *Kick back*
C. *Lazy*

A. *Outgoing*
B. *Friendly*
C. *Shy*

A. *Angry, mad*
B. *So-so*
C. *Happy*

A. *Restaurant*
B. *Play*
C. *Movies*

A. *Stress out*
B. *Run*
C. *Take it easy*

A. *Nervous*
B. *Smile*
C. *Friendly*

A. *Sad*
B. *Emotional*
C. *Laugh*

A. *Work*
B. *School*
C. *Sleep*

A. *Money*
B. *Happiness*
C. *Friends*

Scoring

Count up how many A, B, C answers your partner has. If there are . . .

more A answers: This person is the very motivated type
more B answers: This person is the very cool and steady type
more C answers: This person is the easygoing type

My Friend Tara

My Friend Tara. Watch Sean sign in full motion on your student DVD.

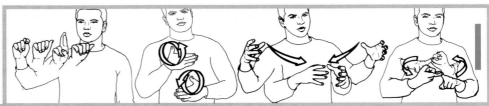

Classroom Exercise O

EXPRESSION CORNER

Use *big head* to describe somebody who is arrogant, a know it all, overconfident, or is self-absorbed.

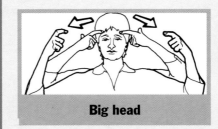

Big head

1. *Comprehension.* Respond to the following in complete sentences.

 1. *List three of Tara's personality characteristics:*
    a.
    b.
    c.
 2. *What is one of Tara's pet peeves?*
 3. *What does Tara enjoy doing?*
 4. *Which sports does Tara play?*
 5. *Sean and Tara are good friends despite what?*

2. *Good & bad traits.* Make a list with a partner outlining personality traits you like and dislike in a friend. Then describe your ideal friend in complete ASL sentences.

Positive Traits	Negative Traits
. . . .	. . . .
. . . .	. . . .
. . . .	. . . .
. . . .	. . . .
. . . .	. . . .

Classroom Exercise P

Lips and cheeks. Focus on the lips and cheeks as you make each facial expression.

Classroom Exercise

1   *Opposites*. Match opposite signs from each column. Then sign a complete sentence using one or both signs.

Column A   Column B

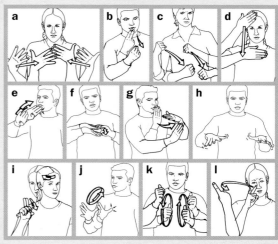

2   *Observations*. Use your imagination to explain what's happening in each illustration. An example is provided.

      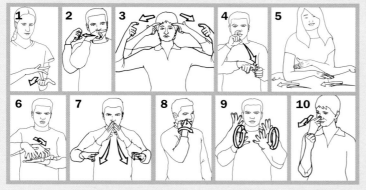

Homework Exercise   3

A   Describe a good friend of yours. What does he or she look like? What are some characteristics of his or her personality? Your description should include a minimum of six complete sentences.

B   Select six different signs used to describe personality. For each sign, explain whether the meaning applies or doesn't apply to your own personality. Give an example for each sign.

C   Write Assignment A or B in ASL gloss.

Signing About Health

Making inquiries about health is an important part of conversational skills. In this section you will learn to use *pow* in addition to *have* when signing about health issues. Notice how *pow* is used in the dialogue below.

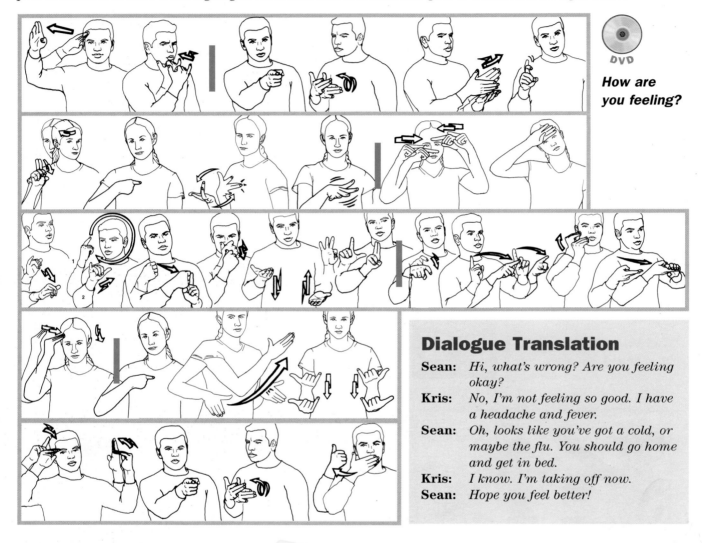

How are you feeling?

Dialogue Translation

Sean: *Hi, what's wrong? Are you feeling okay?*

Kris: *No, I'm not feeling so good. I have a headache and fever.*

Sean: *Oh, looks like you've got a cold, or maybe the flu. You should go home and get in bed.*

Kris: *I know. I'm taking off now.*

Sean: *Hope you feel better!*

Classroom Exercise

1. *Dialogue I.* Create a dialogue with a partner about an illness. Use vocabulary from this section as needed. Include the following:

   1. *A greeting*
   2. *Ask how he or she is feeling*
   3. *Mention an illness*
   4. *A suggestion or advice about what should be done*
   5. *A farewell*

   FYI Don't repeat yourself by following *to feel* with *to feel nauseous!*

2. *Dialogue II.* Practice signing the *How are you feeling?* dialogue with a partner.

Classroom Exercise S

1. *Using pow.* Use the sign *pow* for the phrases in bold. Sign each sentence in ASL.

   1. I **got** sick.
   2. **Out of the blue** I didn't feel so good.
   3. My allergies **started acting up** yesterday.
   4. He **has** the chicken pox.
   5. I **just started** coughing.

2. *How do you feel?* Ask a partner how he or she feels. Your partner will respond based on the illustrations. Switch roles and repeat when done.

EXPRESSION CORNER

Pow

Use *pow* in these situations:
- Catching an illness (instead of *to have* or *get*)
- Signing about something unexpected happening

Vocabulary — Health

Fingerspell these terms: *Flu, sunburn*

All right, okay	**Allergies, to be allergic**	**To be better**	**Chicken pox**	**Cold (health)**

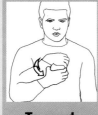	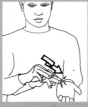				
To cough	**Doctor**	**To feel**	**Fever**	**To heal, get better**	**Medicine**

		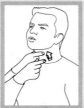			
To feel nauseous	**To sneeze**	**Sore throat**	**To sprain**	**Tonsils (to remove)**	**To vomit**

Classroom Exercise

1 *What's wrong?* Ask a partner what's wrong. Your partner will respond by explaining what happened, based on the illustration. Switch roles and repeat when done. An example is provided.

The mother has a headache because the baby isn't quiet.

 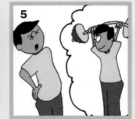 

2 *How long?* In a complete sentence, explain how long it takes to heal from each illness.

1. *Sunburn* (**4 days**)
2. *Flu* (**5-6 days**)
3. *Chicken pox* (**2 weeks**)
4. *Cold* (**2–3 days**)
5. *Nosebleed* (**10 minutes**)
6. *Sprained ankle* (**1 day**)

I Want to Know . . .

What's the sign for *gesundheit*?

There is no specific sign for *gesundheit*. Some Deaf people use a variety of signs in response to a sneeze, two of which are shown here.

Gesundheit   **Gesundheit**

Did you know?

There are approximately 50 – 60 deaf medical doctors in the United States. As more deaf doctors graduate medical school, assumptions about deafness are fading. Armed with special equipment like visual stethoscopes, interpreters, and a can-do attitude, deaf doctors are breaking stereotypes and perceptions about what being deaf means.

ASL Up Close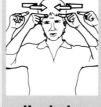

Location Changes: *Hurt* & CL: 4

Earlier you learned that parameter changes affect the meaning of a sign. This feature of ASL is often used with the signs *hurt* and CL: 4. Location changes affect the meaning of *to hurt* into *earache*, *stomachache*, or *headache*. Similarly, CL: 4 can mean *running water*, *nosebleed*, or *blood*.

| **To hurt** | **Headache** | **CL: 4** | **Nosebleed** |

Classroom Exercise

At the clinic. What's wrong? State the problem and decide whether each person needs to see a doctor, a nurse, stay home and rest, or take medicine.

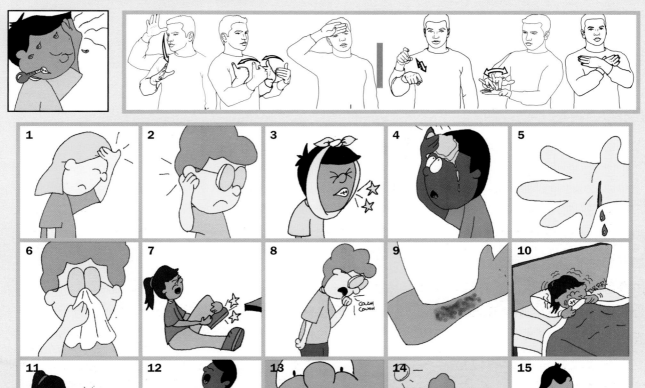

Homework Exercise 4

A   Select one of the following topics and practice signing a short narrative. Your narrative should have a minimum of six complete sentences.

     1. The last time I went to the beach ...   **2.** How I hurt my ...   **3.** All of a sudden ...

B   When was the last time you were ill? What type of illness was it? How long were you sick? What was the cause? Describe what happened in a minimum of six complete sentences.

C   Write Assignment A or B in ASL gloss.

Describing the Natural World

Describing natural objects involves a broad mix of iconic, abstract, and classifier signs create a strong visual image. Notice how this English sentence is signed: "Recently I was hiking in the mountains and spotted a lake at the bottom of a valley. The many trees were covered in red and gold. It was beautiful!" The sign *California* also means *gold*.

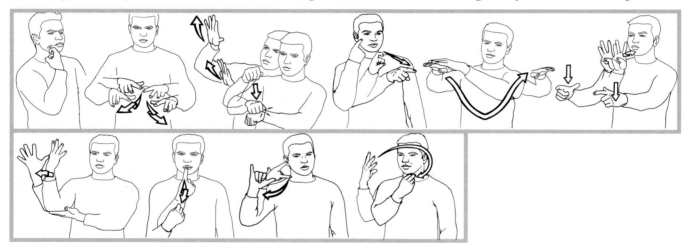

Classroom Exercise V

1   *Language.* Respond to the following questions based on the sentence above.

     1. *What is the relationship between* hill *and* valley? *What kind of sign is this?*
     2. *How does additional movement change* tree *into* forest *or* many trees? *How would you sign* big forest?
     3. *Why do* gold *and* California *share the same sign?*

2   *Dialogue.* Create a dialogue with a partner comparing two different dream destinations. Include the following:

     1. *What does each location look like?*
     2. *Why do you want to go there?*
     3. *What can you do there?*

FYI   Fingerspell the full name of a lake or body of water when signing about a specific location. Otherwise, use *lake* when not mentioning its name.

Classroom Exercise

1 *Descriptions.* Describe each scene in as much detail as you can.

FYI

Describing natural objects follows a similar pattern to describing people: Start with basic information (is it a mountain? Lake?) and then add details (trees, flowers).

2 *More descriptions.* What do the following places look like? Describe each in as much detail as you can.

1. *The area you live in*
2. *Your home state or province*
3. *A favorite vacation location*

4. *Natural objects near you:*
   a. *Ocean / river / bay*
   b. *Mountains / hills / valleys*
   c. *Islands or deserts*

5. *What types of vegetation do you have in your area?*

Vocabulary   Natural World

Earth and *geography* share the same sign

   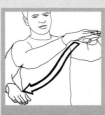 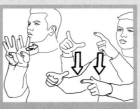 

Desert   **Flower**   **Hill**   **Island**   **Lake**   **Moon**

Mountain   **Plant**   **River**   **Star**   **Sun**   **Tree**

Classroom Exercise

1 *Topography.* Based on the description, what is being described?

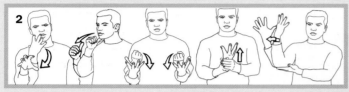

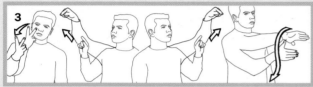

Accent Steps

What are the parameter differences between the signs *ocean* and *river*?

Ocean

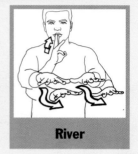

River

2 *Nearby places?* Match the name of each natural object in Column A with a sign that best describes the natural formation in Column B.

Column A

1. *Atlantic*
2. *Puerto Rico*
3. *Waikiki*
4. *Mojave*
5. *Niagara*
6. *Sierra Nevadas*
7. *Michigan*
8. *Mississippi*
9. *Aleutian*
10. *Great Salt*
11. *Appalachians*
12. *Miami*

Column B

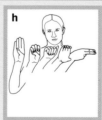

Homework Exercise 5

A Describe a famous natural landmark you've visited or would like to visit. What does it look like? Where is it? Why do you want to go there? Your description should have a minimum of six complete sentences.

B Practice signing the *Describing the Natural World* sentence at the beginning of this section. Add at least three new sentences that provide more details about the environment around the mountain lake.

C Write Assignment A or B in ASL gloss.

Journal Activities

1   Deafness is often called the invisible disability. What does this mean? Do you agree or disagree with this opinion?

2   "Political correctness" affects American Sign Language as much as it does English. What does this suggest to you about the relationship between ASL and English? If you speak a language other than English, have you noticed "political correctness" in that language?

3   Are you surprised to know that there are deaf doctors in the United States? Why or why not? Would you feel comfortable having a deaf doctor tend to your medical needs? What reactions do you think hearing patients have upon meeting a deaf doctor for the first time? If you were a deaf doctor, what would you do to make a hearing patient feel comfortable? What would you want a deaf doctor to do to make you feel more comfortable?

4   In what ways do the definitions of handicapped and disabled apply to Deaf people? In what ways do the definitions not apply? Write a letter supporting your perspective on the topic of "Are Deaf people handicapped or disabled?"

http://Search   Search the web for more information:

- National Black Deaf Advocates

- Storystones.com

- Deaf Native American Reading List

- Cochlear implant controversy

- Hearing aids

- Intertribal Deaf Council

- Deaf Latino

- Indian Sign Language Conference & Memorial

- Asian Deaf Congress

- Association of Medical Professionals with Hearing Loss

Unit 8 Review

A *Comprehension.* Watch Sean's narrative titled *My Grandfather* on your Student DVD. Respond to the questions below.

1. *What tribe does Sean's grandfather belong to?*
2. *What is Sean's ethnic background?*
3. *What does Sean's grandfather look like?*
4. *How did he lose weight?*
5. *What are three characteristics of Sean's grandfather's personality?*
6. *What is his grandfather always doing?*

 Expressive Skills. Practice signing Sean's narrative. Focus on clarity rather than speed, and include non-manual signals when necessary.

B Describe the friends you met at a Deaf/ASL Weekend recently. What are their names and where do they live? Describe each person in detail.

C Describe each person and hairstyle in detail.

Unit 8 Review

D

Receptive & Expressive Skills. Watch Marc's narrative titled *What I Look Like*. Respond to the following:

1. *How well do you understand Marc's narrative on a scale of 1-10?*
2. *Does Marc sign too fast for you to understand? When do you realize you're missing details?*
3. *How does Marc describe himself differently than the way you describe yourself? Do you:*
   a. *Sign slower?*
   b. *Start general and become specific, or vice versa?*
4. *After watching Marc's narrative, describe yourself in detail.*

E You work at a busy clinic. Explain to a friend some of the patients you saw today, describing their problems and how they happened in complete sentences.

F Describe each scene in as much detail as possible.

Units 7 – 8 Review

1 *Describing people* Describe what each person looks like and explain what you think each is doing.

2 *Comprehension.* Use the illustration in Exercise A to answer the following questions.

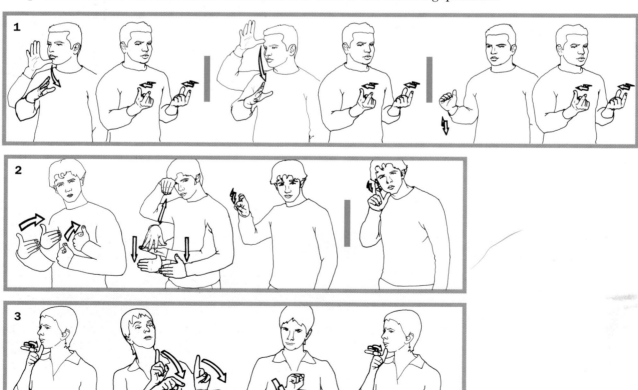

Review Exercise B

1 *Using eye gaze.* For each sentence below you will play two roles: The person asking the question and the one who answers. Using eye gaze is one technique for a signer to show more than one character. Ask and answer each question following the example, changing eye gaze to show each character.

 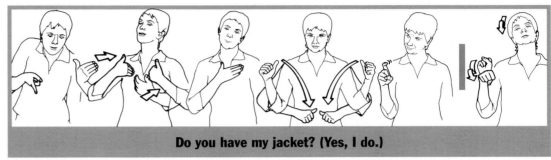

Do you have my jacket? (Yes, I do.)

1. *Did you go camping last weekend? No, I didn't.*
2. *Are you feeling okay? No, I'm feeling nauseous.*

3. *Did you drive there from New York? Yes, I did.*
4. *Are those two going with us? Yes, they are.*

2 *Shoulder-Shifting.* Describe each pair using Shoulder-Shifting. Create a complete sentence comparing both illustrations.

A S L   T I P S

- When using Shoulder-Shifting to describe two perspectives, you don't need to sign "he said" or "she said" each time you change. Shoulder-Shifting is very clear, especially when accompanied by eye gaze and facial expressions or other non-manual signals. Remember: If one person is shorter or taller than the other, alter eye gaze and pointing to show both perspectives, or use different facial expressions for each. Remember not to confuse them!

- If you're in a conversation and get lost, don't panic! Instead, try to piece together the topic and the "bigger picture" from context rather than becoming flustered and fixating on an unknown sign.

- When using the Shoulder-Shifting technique, don't move your feet or "hop" from one side to another.

Review Exercise C

1 *Repeated events.* What can you say about Sean's activities? Answer the following questions in a complete sentence. Refer to the calendar below.

2 *The calendar.* What does Sean's week look like? Describe his schedule and activities in complete sentences.

Review Exercise D

Going shopping. Sign the narrative about Bill's trip to the clothing store, using your imagination to fill in the missing pieces.

Bill went to a clothing store yesterday, looking for a new jacket. He looked at the jackets and saw three he liked. He tried on the blue jacket, but it was too small. **1.**_____ *The third jacket was brown with gold buttons and wasn't too big or too small.*

Bill looked at three pairs of pants. The first was brown and **2.**_____. *The second was* **3.**_____ *and* **4.**_____. *The third pair looked like* **5.**_____. *Bill liked the* **6.**_____ *pair of pants.*

Bill **7.**_____ *home. The next day Bill got ready to go to* **8.**_____. *Bill opened the box and saw the pants and jacket were* _____! *Bill's wife asked,* **10.** "_____?" *and Bill said, "The jacket is the wrong color! It's supposed to be* **11.**_____, *not* **12.**_____, *and the pants are* **13.**_____!"

What should Bill do? **14.**_____.

Review Exercise E

I Spy. Describe what you see in complete sentences.

Review Exercise F

Now & Then. At class reunions, many people are often unrecognizable at first because they have changed dramatically. Describe how each person used to look, and how they appear now.

Review Exercise G

Photo album. You and a friend are looking through a photo album. Describe in complete sentences what each person looks like and is wearing. What else can you say about each person?

Close friends from college. Every year we get together for a vacation. This year we're going to an island!

Aunt Lisa and Uncle Ryan. They're very funny and always busy. My aunt is a famous writer and my uncle loves football. They've been married for 23 years.

Boss, Gary. He's nice but sometimes rude. He's nosy! What do you think he's doing in this picture?

Cousin Louise, from California. She's an actor. She's famous for being emotional.

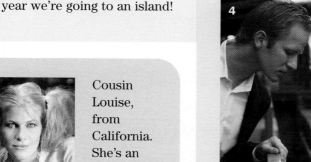

Best friend Shannah. She's a motormouth and we're never bored! Last winter we went skiing in the mountains and enjoyed ourselves.

Review Exercise H

1   *Working with time.* Sign each sentence in ASL. Use *between* and *around* where needed in each sentence.

    1.   *I tend to wake up between 7:00 and 8:00 during the week.*
    2.   *I get up around 10:00 on the weekends.*
    3.   *Every day I eat lunch at 11:30.*
    4.   *The movie starts around 7:00.*
    5.   *I go to bed around 11:00 every night.*

2   *Spatial organization.* Use spatial organization to sign each morning, afternoon, and evening routine.

Morning	Afternoon	Evening
Wake up	*Take break at 10:30*	*Do laundry*
Get up	*Go to a restaurant for lunch*	*Cook dinner*
Brush teeth	*Finish work at 5:00*	*Watch TV, read book*
Shower	*Go to gym and exercise*	*Read email*
Get dressed		
Eat breakfast		
Go to work		

Review Exercise I

Grammar & structure review. In Units 1 – 8 you have learned 15 important rules governing ASL structure and grammar. Create a complete ASL sentence for each Eyes on ASL.

Eyes on ASL # . . .

    1.   *Eye contact ...* **(page 8)**
    2.   *Closing signals ...* **(page 9)**
    3.   *One-word answers ...* **(page 10)**
    4.   *Non-manual signals with* yes *and* no *...* **(page 30)**
    5.   *When signs come first ...* **(page 59)**
    6.   *WH-signs come at the end of sentences ...* **(page 64)**
    7.   *Numbers 1-5 always ... except when ...* **(page 99)**
    8.   *Contrastive structure means ...* **(page 131)**
    9.   *The Age Spot ...* **(page 134)**
    10.   *Number and subject agree for ASL pronouns ...* **(page 153)**
    11.   *Classifiers must be identified first ...* **(page 194)**
    12.   *Time signs are also* when *signs ...* **(page 199)**
    13.   *Tense markers are generally located ...* **(page 231)**
    14.   *Use spatial organization to ...* **(page 262)**
    15.   *The sequence used to describe somebody is ...* **(page 294)**

My Home & Community

Unit Nine Objectives

- To describe your home and community
- To sign money using the Money Spot and Dollar Twist
- To describe objects using spatialization techniques
- To understand and give street directions
- To understand how social changes affect the Deaf World
- To learn and apply non-manual signals

Unit Nine Vocabulary

Key Phrases

What's your hometown like?

Hi, how are you? What's your hometown like? I live in a very large city on the East coast that has at least a million people. Traffic is lousy, it's crowded, and sometimes there's smog, but I love it. Why? Because there is a lot to do. You can go out dancing, to the zoo, there's lots of different restaurants, and there are professional sports teams. Do you like where you live?

What's your hometown like? Watch Marc sign in full motion on your student DVD.

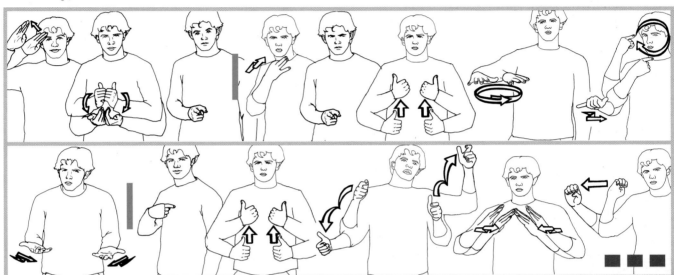

Vocabulary — What's your hometown like?

Other new vocabulary seen in the narrative is presented throughout Unit 9.

Also

Curious

Different (plural)

East

Lousy

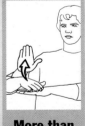

More than

Curious is used to introduce a question or ask for an opinion. Use this sign the same way you say *I was wondering* in English.

Different uses a NMS: Use your lips to mouth diff-diff-diff.

North, south, east, and *west* are initialized signs. The direction of each sign depends on its compass point.

Where Do You Live?

In this section you will learn how to ask and answer questions about your home. In the dialogue below see how the sign *what kind?* is used to inquire into a person's living arrangement.

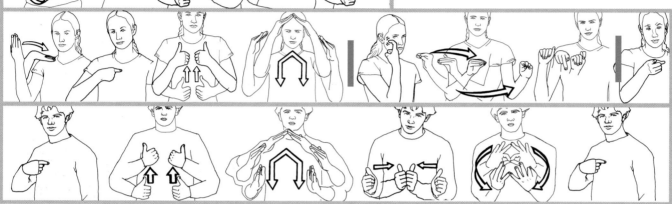

Classroom Exercise A

1. *Where do you live?* What kind of home do you have? In complete sentences explain the following:

1. *The type of home you live in now*
2. *The type of home you lived in as a child*
3. *The type of home you want in the future*

2. *Dialogue.* Create a dialogue with a partner that includes the following:

1. *A greeting*
2. *Asking at least two questions about housing*
3. *Exchange information about a past or future move*
4. *A conclusion and farewell*

Vocabulary — Types of Housing

Fingerspell: *apt* (apartment), *cabin, condo* (condominium), *duplex, studio, th* (townhouse)

Dormitory

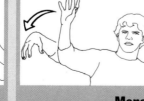

House

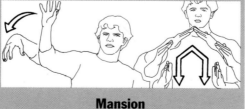

Mansion

Mobile home

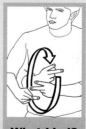

What kind?

Classroom Exercise B

1 *Housing.* Describe the type of housing in each illustration. What can you say about each? An example is provided.

It's a dorm at the university.

  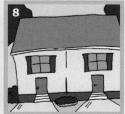  

2 *I think ...* What are the pros and cons of living in each type of housing? Think of two reasons you would like to live in the following places and two more reasons why you wouldn't. Use the Listing and Ordering Technique.

1. *beach house*
2. *apartment*
3. *dormitory*
4. *mansion*
5. *condo*
6. *mobile home*
7. *small house*
8. *mountain cabin*
9. *duplex*
10. *nursing home*
11. *studio*
12. *living with parents*

NMS Alert

Mouth the word *cha* while signing *big* or *mansion* to emphasize an object's size.

ASL Up Close

To have

Using Have

The sign *to have* can be used for possession ("I have a sister") as well as to show that something *exists* ("Is there a bathroom?"). In English you say "Is there?", and in ASL you sign *have*. Use the Question-Maker NMS when using *have* to ask a question.

**Is there an elevator? /
Do you know if there is an elevator?**

Classroom Exercise C

1 *Using have.* You are looking for a home with certain features. Use *have* to ask a partner the following questions, who will respond using the given information. An example is provided. Switch roles when done.

1. *Is there a basement?* **(No, there isn't.)**
2. *Is there an elevator?* **(Yes, there is.)**
3. *Is there a pool?* **(Yes, there is.)**
4. *Is there a garage?* **(No, there isn't.)**
5. *Is there an office?* **(Yes, there is.)**
6. *Is there one bathroom?* **(No, there are two.)**
7. *Is there a big kitchen?* **(Yes, there is.)**
8. *Does it have A.C.?* **(Yes, it does.)**
9. *Does it have a yard?* **(No, it doesn't.)**
10. *Is there a restaurant nearby?* **(Yes, there is.)**

Is there a washing machine?

Yes, there is.

2 *Apartment hunting.* Use *have* or *how many* to ask a partner questions about the apartment. An example is provided. Switch roles when done.

How many bathrooms are there?

There are three bathrooms.

3 *Dialogue.* You and a friend are house-hunting for a place to live next year. Create a dialogue that includes the following:

1. *Discussion of the type of housing needed or wanted and why*
2. *Comparing two alternative housing options, including two pros and cons for each*
3. *Discussion of three must-have features and three features you do not want*
4. *A conclusion*

Vocabulary — Places Around the House

Basement

Bedroom (1)

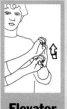
Dining room

Elevator

Entrance, to enter

Floor, level (1)

Garage

Kitchen (1)

Living room (1)

Variation Alert! Add the *room* sign where indicated.

Floor, level (2)

Kitchen (2)

Kitchen (3) (cook+room)

Bedroom (2) (bed+room)

Living Room (2) (formal + room)

Accent Steps

Many signs for rooms around the house reflect the activity generally associated with that room. One *cooks* in the *kitchen*, *sleeps* in the *bedroom*, and *eats* in the *dining room*. In addition to concepts like these, several place signs use classifiers. Can you identify at least two signs that use classifiers? What do they show?

Classroom Exercise D

Characteristics. What rooms or amenities do the following places tend to have? In complete sentences, use the Listing and Ordering Technique to list a minimum of three different features for each.

1. *Apartment*	5. *Mansion*	9. *Restaurant*
2. *School*	6. *Townhouse*	10. *Condominium*
3. *Houseboat*	7. *Dormitory*	11. *Doghouse*
4. *Workplace*	8. *Cabin*	12. *Large house*

Homework Exercise 1

A Compare and contrast the home you live in now and your ideal home. What differences do you want? Why? Use Shoulder-Shifting and the Listing & Ordering Technique in a minimum of six complete sentences.

B Few people ever stay in one place from birth to death. In a minimum of seven complete sentences describe where a person might live at the following ages.

1. *10-18 years old*	3. *23-30 years old*	5. *51-70 years old*	7. *81-? years old*
2. *18-22 years old*	4. *31-50 years old*	6. *71-80 years old*	

C Write Assignment A or B in ASL gloss.

ASL Up Close

Spatial Visualization: Virtual Reality in ASL

Spatial visualization is the ability to describe spatial relationships both receptively and expressively. Spatial visualization describes the surroundings of a house or other structure, describes where an object is located in relationship to other objects, and creates strong three-dimensional images. These skills are essential to sign complex thoughts and descriptions, to understand ASL literature, and to give and follow directions.

Look at the illustration of a house. The goal of spatial visualization is to provide enough detail for someone to create a mental image of what the signer sees, as if going on a virtual reality tour. The key is to remember that your descriptions reflect your own perspective, as if you were walking through the structure.

All spatial descriptions start with the big picture or overall concept: *House, two story.* Then select a specific starting point, such as the front door, and describe what your eyes see as you move around, across, or through a room: *Stairs on left, couch in front of me, door to kitchen on right.* Convey distance by using the sign *over there* with non-manual signals and eye gaze. Describe what you see in your mind's eye!

Some tips:
- You are the reference point
- Start general and add secondary details
- Use eye gaze
- Use non-manual signals
- If you're watching something being described, look at things from the signer's perspective, not your own

View and practice *My House* on your student DVD.

DVD

Non-manual signals: Proximity

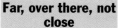

| Far, over there, not close | Lower, in front of me, on the ground | Right there, very close |

Classroom Exercise E

1 *Non-manual signals.* Practice signing each non-manual signal accurately.

   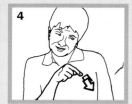 

2 *Using NMS.* How would you communicate the following only using your eyes, eyebrows, lips, and head?

1. *Something on your right shoulder*
2. *Something directly in front of your face, an inch from your nose*
3. *Something on the floor to your left*
4. *Something barely visible in the distance*
5. *Something on a shelf across from and higher than you*
6. *Two things at your immediate left and right*

Classroom Exercise

1 *Spatial visualization.* Describe each illustration based on the reference point marked X.

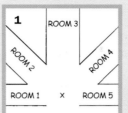

2 *Layouts.* Describe each illustration starting at the reference point marked X. An example is provided.

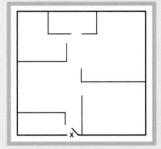

Open the door and at the far end of the hallway is the bathroom. The kitchen is right there on the left.

3 *Challenge.* Use spatial visualization techniques to sign each description. Use proximity NMS as needed.

1. *Open the door into the hall-way. Right in front of you are stairs that lead up to the living room and down to the family room.*

2. *In the living room there is a door on the immediate right. That area is the kitchen. Across from the stairs is a hallway that has two bedrooms on the left and one on the right.*

3. *Walk down the stairs to the family room. On the left across the room is the bath-room. On the far side is a door to the outside.*

Eyes on ASL #16

Visualize descriptions from the signer's perspective.

The signer's right does *not* become your left or vice versa! Visualize yourself in the signer's position for the correct perspective.

Classroom Exercise

1. *Using classifiers & NMS.* Match the classifiers and NMS below with objects in the illustration.

2. *Visualizing homes.* Use visual spatialization skills to describe what you think the interior of each home looks like.

3. *More layouts.* Use visual spatialization skills to describe each layout. Remember to change a bird's-eye perspective to your own.

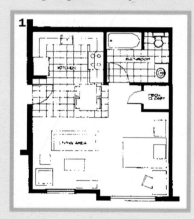 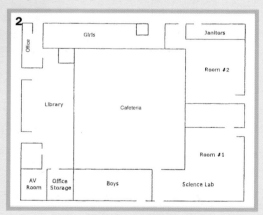 

Homework Exercise 2

A. What does the interior of your home look like? Describe its floorplan using visual spatialization techniques. Limit your description to a minimum of five complete sentences.

B. Locate a photo of a suggested scene to describe using visual spatialization. Your description should have a minimum of five complete sentences. Possible descriptions:

   1. *A picture of a nature scene*   **2.** *A picture of a sporting event*   **3.** *A picture of a model home*

C. Write Assignment A or B in ASL gloss.

Places Around Town

As you learn vocabulary for locations around your community, pay attention to those signs that can be paired with the Agent Marker. These secondary meanings are printed in blue. For example, adding the Agent Marker to *jail* creates the sign *prisoner*.

Dialogue Translation

Marc: *What are you two doing?*

Kris: *We're going to a movie. Want to go?*

Marc: *Sure! After I'm done at the bank I'll meet you there.*

Classroom Exercise H

1. *Dialogue I.* Practice signing Kris' and Marc's dialogue with a partner. Add the following:

   1. *A greeting*   **2.** *An introduction*   **3.** *A specific time to meet*

2. *Dialogue II.* Create a dialogue with a partner on a topic that includes at least two different community locations.

Vocabulary   Places Around Town

Clinic Clinician	**Convenience store / 7-11®**	**Fire station Firefighter**	**Gas station**	**Grocery store**	**Hospital (1)**
Hotel	**Jail Prisoner**	**Museum**	**Pharmacy, drug store**		**Police station, Officer, cop**

Fingerspell: *Bank, Cafe, Mall, Park, Post Office (PO), Zoo*

Classroom Exercise

1 *Where are you?* Explain the location and activity in each illustration in a complete sentence.

2 *What for?* Explain why people go to the following locations. An example is provided.

People go to a cafeteria because they're hungry.

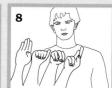

I Want to Know . . .

Why isn't there a sign for station?

Remember that English and American Sign Language don't correspond word-for-sign. In English, station refers to a location where a service or operation is performed. For several ASL signs, this meaning is already included in the sign. For example, people fill autos with gas at a gas station. Now make the sign *gas station*. What concept do you think it shows? Adding a separate sign for station would be redundant!

Classroom Exercise

1 · NMS Alert

1 *Information desk.* Ask your partner for the address of the following businesses in a complete sentence. Your partner will provide the address. Switch roles and repeat when done.

NMS Alert

Each time you sign *post office*, add this NMS: Use your lips to mouth "po."

323 PINE AVE.

12 MAIN ST.

MALL, UPSTAIRS

27 LARK ST.

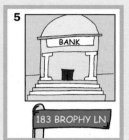

183 BROPHY LN

2 *People & Places.* Use the illustration and your imagination to sign a complete sentence.

This man enjoys cars. He works at a gas station.

1

2 POLICE

3

4

5

6 HOTEL CHECKOUT

7

8 BANK

Variation Alert!

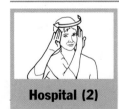

Hospital (2)

Police Station (2)
Officer, cop

Homework Exercise 3

A Locate the addresses of six places in your hometown. Sign the address and explain in complete sentences why people go to these places.

B Select five locations you go to often in your community. Use the Listing and Ordering Technique to explain what they are and what you do there. You should have a minimum of six complete sentences.

C Write Assignment A or B in ASL gloss.

Focus: The Deaf and

❝ Society regards the deaf as unfortunate. Is this general opinion not largely due to self-regard, which makes us pity them the more for being unable to understand what we are saying? **❞**
—*Nicholas Sebastian Roche de Chamfort*

Do you recall your first encounter with a deaf person or sign language? Did you watch Deaf individuals signing to each other? Were you offered a card with the ASL alphabet on it by a deaf peddler? Did you have a Deaf neighbor or relative? For many people today, initial exposure to the Deaf community and ASL comes from seeing Deaf characters and sign language on television, the movies, or the theatre. From television commercials to comedies, Deaf actors in particular continue to expose the American public to the unique culture and language of the Deaf World. From Marlee Matlin appearing on "Seinfeld" to the 2003 Broadway hit musical **Big River**, the Deaf World is no longer hidden from the hearing public.

This interaction between the Deaf and Hearing worlds was not always the case. For many centuries deafness was considered a curse or divine punishment, and deaf individuals were often institutionalized or kept hidden from non-deaf family members and the public. Even in modern times sign language has been mocked and deafness pitied as an overwhelming communication barrier.

Deaf West Theatre, Inc., was founded in 1991 to enrich the cultural lives of the 1.2 million deaf and hard-of-hearing individuals who live in the Los Angeles area, and to expose the hearing world to deaf theatre. It provides exposure and access to professional theatre for deaf artists and audiences. All productions are presented in American Sign Language with simultaneous interpretation in English, providing an enhanced theatrical experience for deaf and hearing audiences.

Hearing Worlds

This Bayer commercial is one of the first television commercials to feature a Deaf person using sign language. This breakthrough opened the doors for Deaf people to appear in more commercials for popular products.

Photo courtesy of BBDO

As the hearing and Deaf worlds come closer together in mutually beneficial ways — such as the arts, theater, and film — the Deaf community has gained much exposure, understanding, and appreciation by the hearing world. One of the most important aspects of this appreciation and acceptance is the visibility of American Sign Language. Not so long ago, many deaf people avoided signing in public because doing so drew stares, unflattering imitations, and condescension. Hearing people, whether well-meaning or not, expected and demanded deaf individuals fit into the larger hearing world, and thus differences were not embraced.

A Deaf time traveler from the past would be shocked to see how visible American Sign Language and Deaf people are in today's world. Much of this visibility comes from Deaf actors using sign language on television and the movies, a breakthrough that first occurred in 1968. Prior to that time, deaf characters were portrayed by hearing actors, with little thought of opening the door to deaf actors themselves. Audrey Norton was the first Deaf actor to appear on television, and almost overnight other Deaf actors began appearing in numerous roles on television, commercials, movies, and theatre productions. Now, American Sign Language is less of a novelty and simply a language used by millions of Deaf Americans, proudly visible in every part of the country. Both the Deaf and Hearing Worlds have realized each has much to learn from the other in language, culture, and respect for differences, and now both are able to freely exchange ideas and communicate on a level playing field. The Deaf time traveler from the past would be astounded to realize that hearing people who watch Deaf people sign are more likely to be ASL students than people making fun of the language!

The visibility of American Sign Language on television shows, commercials, movies, and the theater has evolved over the years due to the determination of Deaf actors proving they are as equally talented as their hearing counterparts. In the words of the first Deaf president of Gallaudet University, Dr. I. King Jordan, *Deaf people can do anything but hear.*

Survivor, **a popular reality television show, featured Christy Smith, a Deaf graduate of Gallaudet University. Christy showed that she could interact with hearing people and compete on an equal footing. She was extremely popular with viewers.**

ASL Up Close

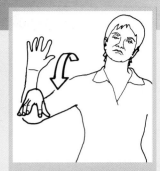

CL: Claw 5

Using CL: Claw with spatialization

Convey distance between two places by using CL: Claw 5. This classifier is a spatial placeholder for one or more places. Concepts like *nearby, not too far, next to, across from,* and more can be shown by varying the space between two hands forming the CL: Claw 5 handshape. CL: Claw 5 is often used to describe the location of buildings or other structures in relation to each other. In the example below notice how space is used with CL: Claw 5 to show distance between *bank* and *salon,* and then the empty space is identified as *clinic.*

The clinic is between the bank and salon.

Classroom Exercise K

1. *Using CL: Claw 5.* Sign the following directions, using *CL: Claw 5* for the italicized terms.

   1. My house *is across from* the school.
   2. The store *is right next* to the post office.
   3. The museum *is behind* the hotel.
   4. The cafe *is on the other side of* the book store.
   5. My office is *between* a restaurant and flower shop.
   6. His house is *right around the corner from* mine.

2. *More CL: Claw 5.* Refer to the illustration to fill in the blanks with the correct location.

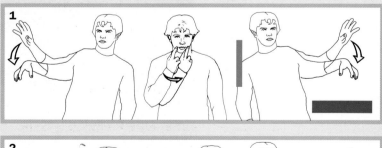

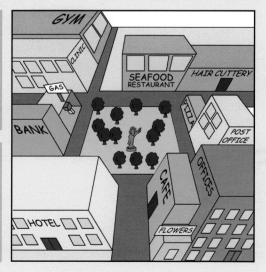

Classroom Exercise K (continued)

Many mass

EXPRESSION

CORNER

Use *many mass* to describe a bird's eye view of many buildings or crowds of people.

Many Mass

Classroom Exercise L

1 *Dialogue I.* Use the illustration in Exercise K to describe where the following places are located.

1. *Seafood restaurant*
2. *Bank*
3. *Gym*
4. *Hair salon*
5. *Post office*

6. *Hotel*
7. *Flower shop*
8. *Park*
9. *Gas station*
10. *Pizza shop*

2 *Dialogue II.* Create a dialogue with a partner about making plans to meet at a specific location. Your dialogue should include the following:

1. *Selecting a date and time to meet*
2. *Selecting a place to meet*
3. *An explanation of where the destination is located*
4. *A minimum of two uses of CL: Claw 5*
5. *One use of many mass*
6. *A farewell*

Deaf Culture NOTE

Collective values

The dominant cultural value in the United States and Canada is called **individualism**. Individualism is a social pattern or expectation that the individual is loosely connected to his or her community. If personal goals conflict with group beliefs, individualists prioritize their personal preferences. The dominant cultural value among the Deaf is called **collectivism**. Collectivists consider themselves interdependent and closely linked together, so a high value is placed on group harmony, solidarity, and cooperation. When an individual behaves in a way that conflicts with Deaf culture's group expectations or norms, then the individual may be seen as yielding to the more dominant values of hearing society.

Behaviors considered rude in collectivist societies include the following: Bragging about one's wealth or accomplishments, acting in a manner that causes the larger society to view the smaller group negatively, and avoiding social activities with other members of the community. Because the Deaf World is so small, differences in income, education, employment, and other status symbols are de-emphasized, traits that conflict with the larger hearing society's values. Similar to the experience of other minority groups, the Deaf community encounters criticism of its cultural values by hearing people who insist the Deaf must "live in a hearing world."

Classroom Exercise M

Using finish. Use *finish* to explain the different places you plan to go to today in complete sentences. Use your imagination to explain what you'll do in each place. An example is provided.

After school I work. I work right by school.

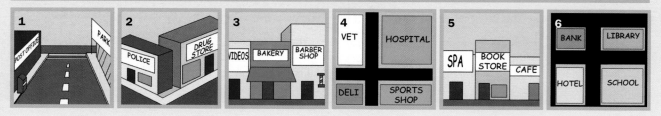

1. POST OFFICE, PARK
2. POLICE, DRUG STORE
3. VIDEOS, BAKERY, BARBER SHOP
4. VET, HOSPITAL, DELI, SPORTS SHOP
5. SPA, BOOK STORE, CAFE
6. BANK, LIBRARY, HOTEL, SCHOOL

Homework Exercise 4

A Describe your neighborhood. What types of stores or other places are nearby? Use *CL: Claw 5* to help describe where you live in a minimum of six complete sentences.

B Use *finish* to explain the errands you might do on a weekend. Where will you go, and in what order? Where is each place located? Sign the information in a minimum of six complete sentences.

C Write Assignment A or B in ASL gloss.

Signing About Money

ASL money signs distinguish between amounts involving cents only, dollars only, or mixed sums. Each type of amount is signed differently. In this section you will learn to use the **Money Spot**, the **Dollar Twist**, and how to combine dollars and cents. See the dialogue to the left for examples of how money signs are used in conversation.

Dialogue Translation

Marc: *How much is it?*

Kelly: *Around $40.00.*

Marc: *Oh, OK. I'll give you eleven dollars and leave six bucks for a tip.*

Kelly: *Where do you want to eat tomorrow?*

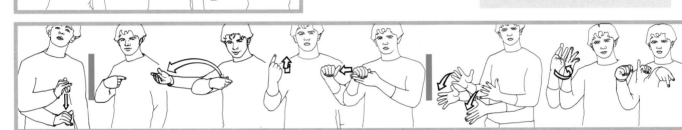

Classroom Exercise

1. *Dialogue.* Complete Marc and Kelly's dialogue with a partner. How does it end?

2. *Concepts.* What is the difference between *10 dollars* and *5 dollars / bucks?* What do you think this means?

Did you know?

The Deaf World has its own telephone book! Featuring Deaf-owned businesses, ads for deafness-related agencies and organizations, TTY access for emergency police and fire services, and telephone / videophone numbers of thousands of Deaf people all over the world, contact information is always close at hand. Called the "Blue Book" for its distinctive blue cover, TDI has long been an appreciated part of Deaf culture. The Blue Book provides access to Deaf products and services, strengthening relationships in the close-knit Deaf community. Whether you need a videophone number, a pager address, or a local Deaf repairman, the Blue Book is the Deaf World's directory assistance. To learn more about TDI, visit: http://www.tdi-online.org

Vocabulary — Money Signs

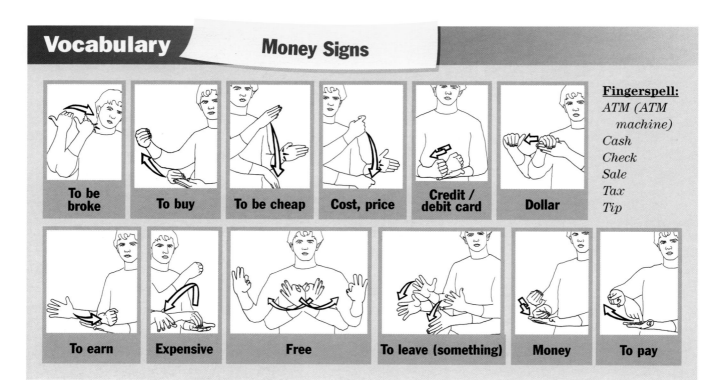

To be broke	To buy	To be cheap	Cost, price	Credit / debit card	Dollar
To earn	Expensive	Free	To leave (something)	Money	To pay

Fingerspell:
ATM (ATM machine)
Cash
Check
Sale
Tax
Tip

ASL Up Close

Money Spot   Dollar Twist

Money Signs

There are four forms money signs may take, depending on the concept being signed. Practice signing the example for each form:

1. <u>Only signing about cents</u>: Touch the Money Spot before making a number sign. You may also touch a number sign directly to the Money Spot as well.
2. <u>Only signing about dollar amounts up to $9.00</u>: Twist the wrist forming a number sign, up to 9. This is called the Dollar Twist.
3. <u>Signing dollar amounts higher than $9.00</u>: Follow a number with the *dollar* sign.
4. <u>Signing about mixed amounts of dollars and cents</u>: Use the Dollar Twist if necessary, but do not touch the Money Spot for the cents amount. The numbers following the dollar amount are understood as cents.

1. $.01 / 1¢   2. $6.00   3. $64.00   4. $6.34

Eyes on ASL #17

Use the Dollar Twist for amounts $1.00 – $9.00. Larger amounts use the *dollar* sign.

Eyes on ASL #18

Cent signs originate or touch the Money Spot unless signed with a dollar sign.

Classroom Exercise

1 *Money signs.* Form the correct dollar and cent signs for each number shown below. An example is provided.

One **One cent** **One dollar**

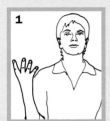    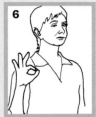 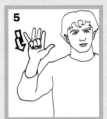

1 **2** **3** **4** **5** **6**

 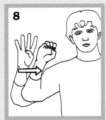 

7 **8** **9**

Accent Steps

Use number signs for *cent, penny, nickel, dime,* and *quarter.*

2 *Money signs II.* Ask a partner how much each item costs. Your partner will respond with the price and explain whether the cost is *expensive, cheap, medium,* or *free.* An example is provided. Switch roles and repeat when done.

How much does it cost? **It's cheap. It costs a dollar.**

   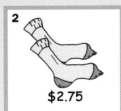 

1 $163.00 **2** $2.75 **3** $42.33 **4** $19.99 **5** $48.30

6 $15.50 **7** $5.75 **8** $67.00 **9** $10.00

Classroom Exercise

1 *Options.* Explain in a complete sentence what you could buy with each amount of money. Raise your eyebrows for the sign *have*. Follow the example below.

If I have a dollar, I can buy a soda / pop.

1. $150.00	**4.** $1,000,000	**7.** *five dollars*	**10.** $35,000	**13.** $50.50
2. $80.00	**5.** $0.75	**8.** $20.00	**11.** $250,000	**14.** $10.00
3. *3 bucks*	**6.** $15.00	**9.** $0.99	**12.** *50 cents*	**15.** $8.50

2 *Local prices.* How much do these items cost in your area? What is the price you might pay for each? Respond in a complete sentence.

1. *A house*	**3.** *Gasoline*	**5.** *New shoes*	**7.** *Movie admission*	**9.** *A DVD*
2. *Lunch*	**4.** *A date*	**6.** *An old car*	**8.** *Birthday gift*	**10.** *Rent*

3 *Dialogue.* Work with a partner to create a dialogue that includes the following:

1. *A greeting*
2. *At least three money signs*
3. *These signs: "To be broke", "blow air," "cost", "to earn," and "to pay"*
4. *Plan to meet again, including when and where*
5. *A farewell*

Lost & Found?

DVD

Lost & Found?
Watch Kelly sign in full motion on your Student DVD.

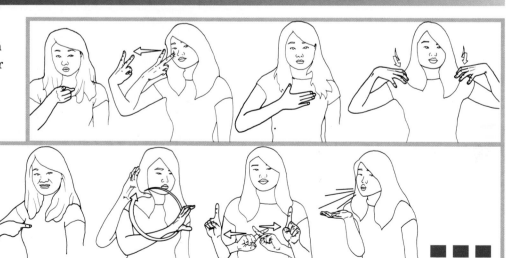

Classroom Exercise **Q**

1 *Comprehension.* Answer the following questions in complete sentences.

1. *What do the signs on the right mean? How do you know?*
2. *Why is Kelly worried?*
3. *How much money does Kelly have? Is it cash?*
4. *What is inside Kelly's backpack?*
5. *Do you think Kelly will find her backpack? Why or why not?*

2 *Comparisons.* Do you have anything in common with Kelly? In a complete sentence explain whether you do or have the same things as Kelly.

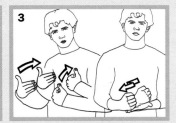

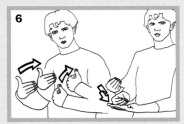

Homework Exercise ◆ **5**

A If money were no object, what three things would you buy? Explain each purchase, its price, and why you want it in a minimum of six complete sentences.

B Practice signing the *Lost & Found?* narrative. Add a conclusion to Kelly's backpack situation. Does she find it? What happens? Your conclusion should have a minimum of five complete sentences.

C Write Assignment A or B in ASL gloss.

EXPRESSION CORNER

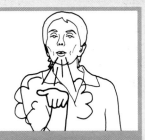

Blow air

Use *blow air* for phrases like:

I have no money	*zip*
I have nothing	*nada*
not a dime	*zilch*

Getting Around Town

In this section you will learn how to sign about transportation options and to give driving directions. The classifier Bent V plays an important role in describing transportation. Look at the dialogue below to see the different ways CL: Bent V is used in conversation.

Dialogue Translation

Marc: *How do you get to school?*

Kris: *I usually drive. Sometimes I take the bus. What about you?*

Marc: *I ride the subway for a while and then walk here.*

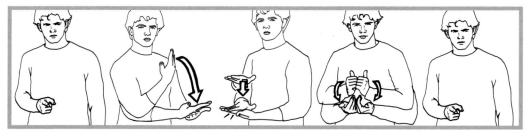

How do you get here?

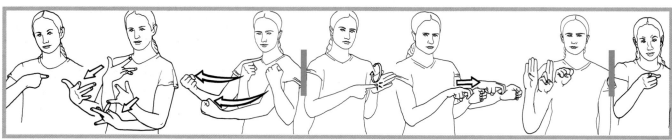

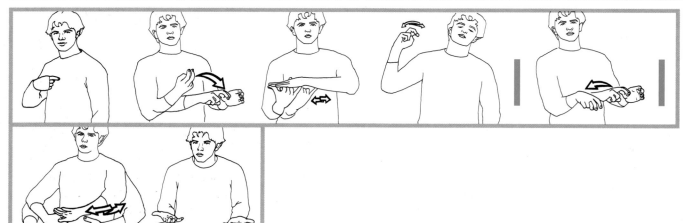

Classroom Exercise R

1. *Dialogue I.* Create a dialogue with a partner to explain how each gets to school or work.

2. *Dialogue II.* Practice signing the *How do you get here?* dialogue. Add material to explain why Kris and Marc are talking about how they get to school.

Vocabulary — Getting Around Town

Fingerspell: *Block, Bus, Hybrid, Mile, Minivan, SUV, Taxi, Truck, Van*

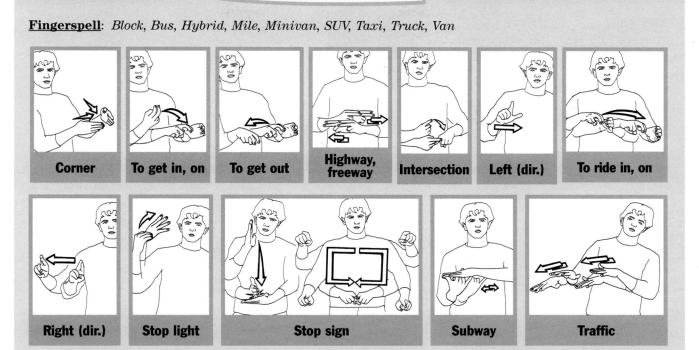

Corner	To get in, on	To get out	Highway, freeway	Intersection	Left (dir.)	To ride in, on

Right (dir.)	Stop light	Stop sign	Subway	Traffic

ASL Up Close

Using CL: Bent V

To ride for a while

To switch, transfer

As you learned in Unit 6, CL: Bent V describes people in a seated position. This classifier forms many signs related to the concept of taking or riding transportation: *To get out of, to get in / on, to ride in / on,* and *to switch.* When signing about going from one mode of transportation to another, *to switch* becomes a transition, similar to the word "then" in English.

Another related concept using CL: Bent V is the sign *to ride for a while,* which suggests a general length of time during which a person is moving in a vehicle. You may use a combination of CL: Bent V and CL: 3 to describe transportation, but keep in mind that the focus of CL: Bent V is on the person inside the vehicle rather than the vehicle itself, represented by CL: 3. See below for an example of how to use CL: Bent V.

We boarded the train and after a long ride, arrived at 10:00.

Classroom Exercise S

1 *Transportation.* Explain how each person arrives at work, school, or home in a complete sentence. An example is provided.

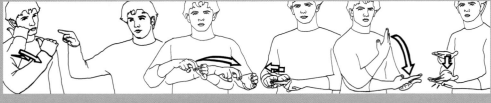

He takes the train to school every day.

8

YOURSELF?

2 *How far?* Explain how long it takes to get to each place from where you are now.

Work is about a half-hour ride away.

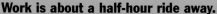

3 *Transportation II.* Sign a complete sentence using each prompt below.

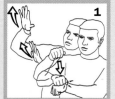   

     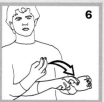

Accent Steps

Be careful not to use the sign *to take* rather than *to ride in* or *to use* when signing about transportation.

To take up

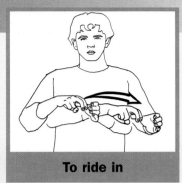

To ride in

My Commute

DVD

My Commute. Watch Kris sign in full motion on your Student DVD.

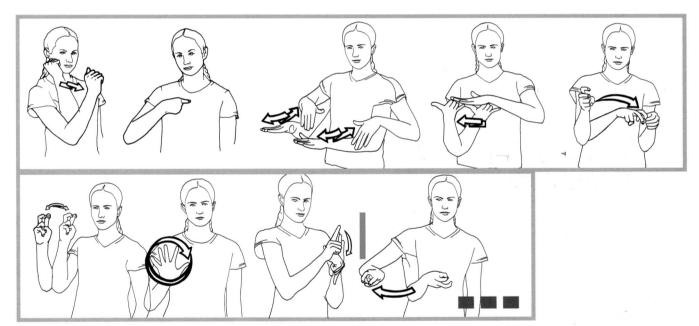

Classroom Exercise

1   *Comprehension.* Answer the following questions from *My Commute* in complete ASL sentences.

1.   *How does Kris get to school?*
2.   *Why doesn't Kris take a taxi to school?*
3.   *How long does Kris ride the subway?*
4.   *How does she get home in the afternoons?*
5.   *How long does Kris ride the bus?*
6.   *When will Kris take a taxi?*

Classroom Exercise

1. *Intersections.* Explain in a complete sentence what is located at each intersection using the illustration below.

   1. *Pine / Main Street*   **3.** *Maple / Main*
   2. *Main Street / Davis*   **4.** *Highway / Main Street*

2. *City streets.* Use the map below to explain how to reach the following locations. An example of giving directions is below.

Keep going down Martin Luther King. At the intersection turn right and go down three blocks. The house is on the left.

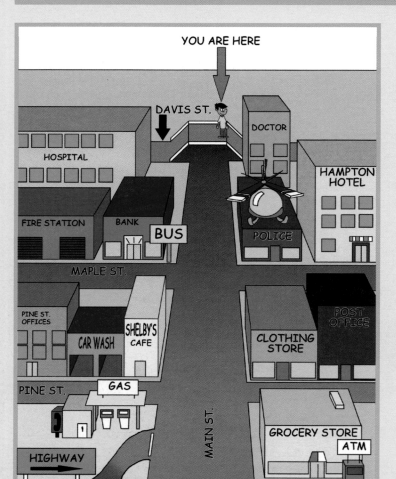

1. *Clothing store*
2. *Hampton Hotel*
3. *Post office*
4. *Shelby's Cafe*
5. *Gas station*
6. *Doctor's office*
7. *Grocery store*
8. *Fire station*
9. *Bank*
10. *Hospital*
11. *Car wash*
12. *Pine Street office building*
13. *Police station*
14. *Highway*

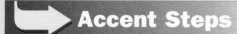 **Accent Steps**

Turning left or right depends on how the turn is made: On foot or in a vehicle. Do not add separate signs for *left* or *right* when using CL: 1 or CL: 3 . Simply maneuver the hand-shape to show a left or right turn.

Classroom Exercise

1   *Keep going.* Sign the directions below. Use CL: 3 and *keep going* for the underlined terms.

     1. *Drive down* Blake Street and *make a left onto* King.
     2. *Keep going on* Olivera Ave. At the intersection of Olivera and Park, *make a right*.
     3. *Get on* the freeway. *Go for* about an hour, *then exit at* Laney Road.
     4. *Drive on* San Carlos until you see Polk. *Go right* at the stoplight.
     5. On weekends, I *go for long drives* near the ocean.

2   *Your community.* Sign complete directions from your home to the following locations in your area.

  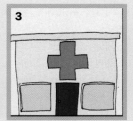  

3   *Dialogue.* Create a dialogue with a partner that includes the following:

     1. *A greeting*
     2. *Making plans to see each other again*
     3. *Two examples of signing directions*

     4. *A conclusion*
     5. *A farewell*

Homework Exercise   6

A   If you do not or could not drive, how would you go to a favorite destination? Describe the destination, why you like it, and explain how you would get there in a minimum of six complete sentences.

B   Compare and contrast the ways you and Kris each arrive at school. How long is your commute? What kind of transportation do you use? Explain three similarities or differences between the two commutes in a minimum of five complete sentences.

C   Write Assignment A or B in ASL gloss.

EXPRESSION CORNER

Rather than extending your arm straight to show a long distance covered by vehicle, use the sign *keep going*. The expression conveys continuous travel in a vehicle, similar to phrases like *keep driving*, *to drive for a while*, and *a long drive*.

Keep going

Journal Activities

1 Some Deaf people are ashamed of peddlers while others consider peddling as a legitimate way of making a living in an oppressive hearing society. Have you had an encounter with a deaf peddler? What was your reaction and impression of deaf people in light of that experience? How do you think the average hearing individual reacts to a deaf peddler? What effect do you think peddlers have on the Deaf community? What are the pros and cons of peddling?

2 Is there such a thing as a Deaf or Hearing world? What do you think of the phrase "Deaf people must learn to live in a hearing world"? What does the sentence mean and what type of perspective or attitude towards Deaf people does it reflect? Can a person belong to and identify with more than one culture or world? Can hearing people live in a Deaf world?

3 At a world conference of teachers of the deaf held in 1880, a proposal was made to prohibit the teaching and use of sign languages in schools around the world. Only the American delegation voted against the proposal, which passed with overwhelming support. While attitudes regarding sign language for both Deaf and hearing people have changed dramatically since then, there are many who view sign language negatively. The painting *Milan, Italy, 1880* is Deaf artist Mary J. Thornley's interpretation of the 1880 conference and its goals. What is Thornley communicating? Is ASL still under fire today? Why or why not?

— *Milan, Italy, 1880.* Mary J. Thornley. Reprinted by permission of Gallaudet University Archives

Unit 9 Review

A *Comprehension.* Watch Marc's narrative titled *What's Your Hometown Like?* on your Student DVD. Respond to the following in complete sentences.

1. *Describe where Marc is from. What are three characteristics of his hometown?*
2. *Where is Marc's hometown located? Is it a large or small city?*
3. *What are some activities people can do in Marc's hometown?*
4. *What are two problems people encounter in this city?*
5. *Why does Marc enjoy living there?*

B How much does each item cost?

1  $47.63	**2** 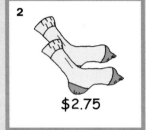 $2.75	**3**  $32.89	**4**  $89.57
5  $22.22	**6**  $48.30	**7**  $15.96	**8** 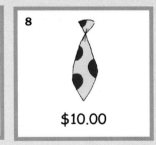 $10.00

C Create a brief story based on each scene.

Unit 9 Review

D Explain where each object is located.

1. ATM machine
2. Post office
3. Clinic
4. Police station
5. Clothing store
6. Barber / salon
7. Theater
8. 7-11, convenience store
9. Hotel
10. Zoo
11. Museum
12. Jail
13. Pharmacy
14. Bank
15. Gas station
16. Train station

E Describe the city scene below. What do you see?

Conversation

Unit Ten Objectives

- To converse about occupations and fields of study

- To use *become* and *to be* in conversation

- To discuss food

- To describe animals and a trip to the zoo

- To expand visualization and description skills using classifiers

Unit Ten Vocabulary

Making Plans

This is going to be a busy week for me! First, I'm looking for a new job. Then, I have to go to the grocery store because I'm having a party. Third, visit the zoo with my nephew and niece for their birthday. After that, go out to eat with my boyfriend's family. Then I'm taking my emergency training course. If I have time, I'll drop off my car at the mechanic. After I've bought a computer then finally my week will be over! Do you have plans?

Making Plans. Watch Kris sign in full motion on your student DVD.

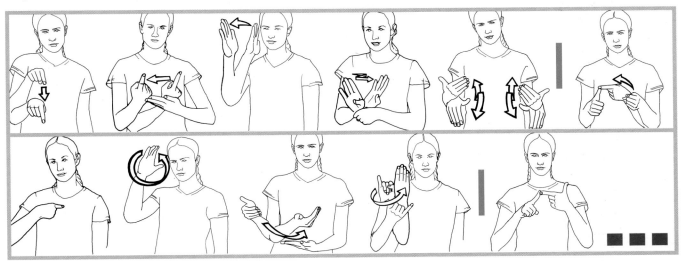

Vocabulary   **Making Plans**

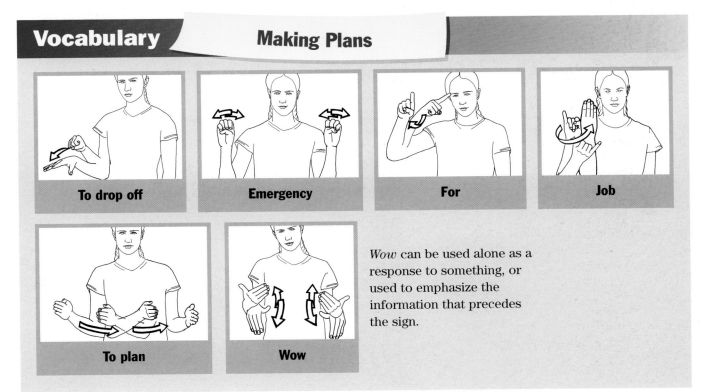

To drop off

Emergency

For

Job

To plan

Wow

Wow can be used alone as a response to something, or used to emphasize the information that precedes the sign.

Signing About Work & Study

Adding the Agent Marker distinguishes most occupation signs from signs for fields of study. Note that several signs do not use the Agent Marker, such as *police officer*. Observe how the Agent Marker is used in conversation in the dialogue below.

Do you have a job?

Dialogue Translation

Kris: *Do you have a job? What do you do?*

Sean: *I'm a computer programmer. I used to work at a bike shop. What about you?*

Kris: *I just applied for a job in web design. I need to get hired!*

Sean: *Good luck!*

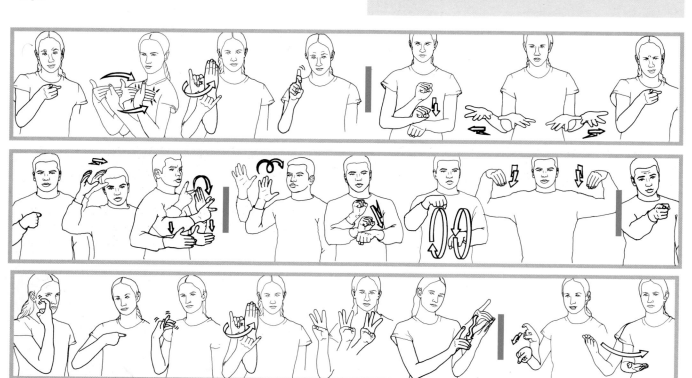

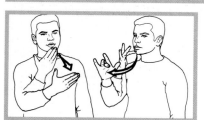

Classroom Exercise A

1 *Dialogue.* Practice signing *Do you have a job?* with a partner. Include the following:

1. *A greeting*   **2.** *A farewell*

2 Ask a partner the following questions. When done, switch roles and repeat.

1. *Do you have a job? What do you do?*
2. *What kind of work do you want to do?*
3. *Do you like your job? Why or why not?*

Accent Steps

You already know these signs! Add the Agent Marker (AM) to the base meaning.

Actor (*act* + AM)
Athlete (*sports* + AM)
Biologist (*biology* + AM)
Chef (*cook* + AM)
Chemist (*chemistry* + AM)
Counselor (*advice* + AM)
Doctor (does not need AM)
Economist (*economics* + AM)
Entrepreneur / business owner
    (*business* + AM)
Fisherman (*fishing* + AM)

Florist (*flower* + AM)
Interpreter (*interpret* + AM)
Janitor (*clean* + AM)
Journalist (*newspaper* + AM)
Manager (*manage* + AM)
Mathematician (*math* + AM)
Nurse (does not need AM)
Pharmacist (*medicine* + AM)
Photographer (*camera* + AM)
Physicist (*physics* + AM)
Physiologist (*physiology* + AM)

Pilot (*plane* + AM)
Police officer (does not need AM)
Principal (does not need AM)
Psychologist (*psychology* + AM)
Sales person (*store* + AM)
Scientist (*science* + AM)
Teacher (*teach* + AM)
Technician (*tech* + AM)
Trainer (*practice* + AM)
Waiter (*serve* + AM)

Classroom Exercise **B**

1 *Do-do?* Ask a partner to describe each occupation. Your partner will explain the occupation and give an example of where the work is performed. An example is provided. Switch roles and repeat when done.

What do accountants do?

They work at a business, with the money.

1. *Plumber*
2. *Clothing designer*
3. *Day care provider*
4. *Mechanic*

5. *Computer programmer*
6. *Teacher*
7. *Scientist*
8. *Veterinarian*

9. *Optometrist*
10. *Nurse*
11. *Engineer*
12. *Lawyer*

2 *What should I study?* You and a friend are discussing career options. Based on the information given, recommend two occupations or fields of study that match the interest. Switch roles and repeat when done.

1. *wants to work at a jail or business*
2. *likes to learn languages*
3. *wants to work in a clinic*
4. *enjoys working on cars and planes*
5. *wants to work with children*

6. *likes math and the outdoors*
7. *wants to be the boss*
8. *enjoys giving people advice*
9. *likes working with many people every day*
10. *doesn't like doing the same thing every day*

Vocabulary — Work & Study

Add the Agent Marker to each sign to make the secondary meanings printed in blue.

**To advertise,
advertising**

**To apply
Applicant**

**Cash register
Cashier**

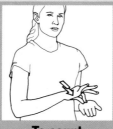
**To count
Accountant**

**To design
Designer**

**To hire,
be hired**

**Law
Lawyer**

**To measure
Engineer**

**Military
Soldier**

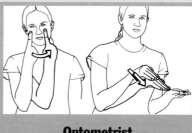
Optometrist

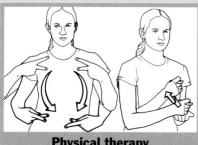
**Physical therapy
Physical therapist**

**Program
Programmer**

Teeth, dentist

**Therapy
Therapist**

**Wrench
Mechanic,
Plumber**

Fingerspell: *architect, day care, TV news (newscaster), Vet (veterinarian)*

Did you know?

Having good ASL skills can make the difference between being hired and not getting the job you want! Many employers across the country recognize the value of second language skills, which can be a valuable addition to your resume. People fluent in ASL are not limited to interpreting or teaching but rather can be found in many fields ranging from big business to retail to public service. The demand is especially high for skilled ASL interpreters. But be careful — you can be held responsible for any miscommunication that arises from inadequate ASL skills.

ASL Up Close

Using *To Be*: Topic & Transition

American Sign Language does not use deixis for the **abstract** form of the verb *to be*. You use the abstract form in English sentences like "They will be late" or "She wants to be a physicist." Signing the abstract form in ASL depends on the topic being signed and whether the concept involves a transition or change. Think about what you really mean by *be* or *to be* and select a sign that matches the concept, as in Example 1. If the concept is a transition from one state to another, use the sign *become*, shown in Example 2.

To become

1   **Sentence: *I want to be a doctor.***   **Concept: I want to work as a doctor.**

2   **Sentence: *I will be 18 next week.***   **Concept: I am changing from 17 to 18 years of age.**

Classroom Exercise C

1.   *Topic or transition?* Read the English sentences below and identify whether the underlined terms would use the signs *arrive*, *work*, or *become*. Then sign each in a complete ASL sentence. Don't forget to modify ASL word order where necessary.

   1. *You need <u>to be</u> there by 5:00.*
   2. *They want <u>to be</u> actors.*
   3. *I will <u>be</u> 25 tomorrow.*
   4. *Don't <u>be</u> late.*
   5. *<u>Being</u> a police officer is hard work.*
   6. *The weather <u>is getting</u> warm.*

To arrive   **To work**   **To become**

2.   *Concept check.* Sign each of the following sentences in ASL.

   1. *She became Deaf when she was 3 years old.*
   2. *When I was little, I wanted to be a firefighter.*
   3. *They will be on vacation for 2 weeks.*
   4. *He wants to be a physical therapist.*
   5. *My brother will be 12.*
   6. *I want to be a lab technician.*
   7. *Be home by 11:00!*
   8. *I work in a cafe. I'm studying to become a doctor.*

Classroom Exercise D

1 *I'll be...* What does each person do now, and what does he or she want to be? Explain each goal in a complete sentence. An example is provided.

Right now he drives a taxi. He wants to be an engineer.

2 *Job tips.* Describe each occupation and suggest what skills or education are needed for each job. An example is shown.

This is an interpreter. Interpreters work with people. To be a sign language interpreter you need to major in ASL.

Classroom Exercise

1 *Pros & cons.* Would you enjoy working in these occupations? Why or why not? Use the Listing and Ordering Technique to describe three reasons you would or would not want the following jobs.

2 *What do you think?* Sign a complete sentence using the vocabulary provided. An example is below.

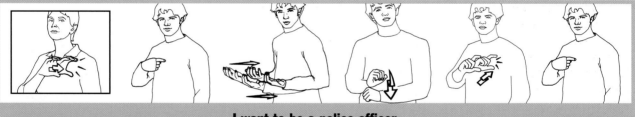

I want to be a police officer.

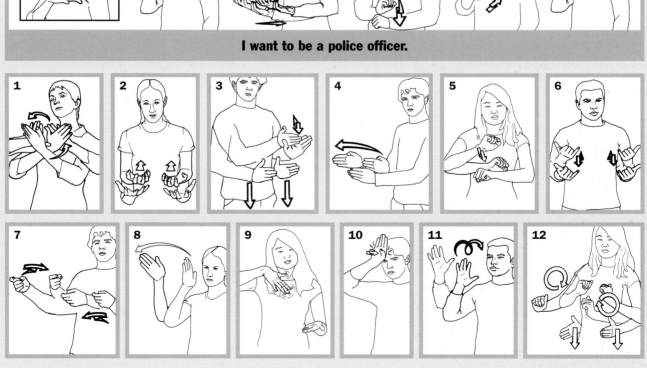

Classroom Exercise F

1   *Employees* What kinds of employees work at each location? Sign a complete sentence based on the illustration. An example is provided.

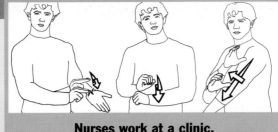

Nurses work at a clinic.

2   *Future plans.* Use the vocabulary below to ask a partner about his or her current or future plans in the following areas. An example is shown. Switch roles and repeat when done.

What do you plan to do in the future?

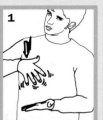

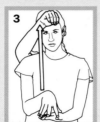

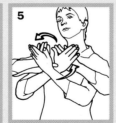

Homework Exercise 1

A   What do you consider to be the worst type of occupation? The best? Provide several examples in support of your opinion. Your explanation should have a minimum of six complete sentences.

B   What type of job do you have now? Explain what you do now and what you'd like to do in the future. If you don't have a job, what type would you like to do? How come? Your explanation should have a minimum of six complete signed sentences.

C   Write Assignment A or B in ASL gloss.

Going to the Grocery Store

Most food items are fingerspelled in American Sign Language. Foods similar in shape or size, such as cucumbers and zucchinis, are often signed using a classifier followed by the fingerspelled word. If you don't know a particular sign, describe the food in detail and you will likely be understood.

What food signs do you see in the dialogue between Kelly and Kris? Are these food signs abstract or iconic? How do you know?

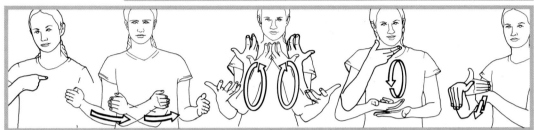

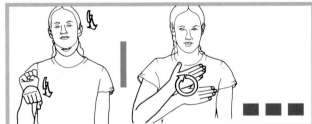

Dialogue Translation

Kelly: *What are we having tonight?*
Kris: *I'm planning on salad, soup, and bread.*
Kelly: *Do you want any help?*
Kris: *Yes, please ...*

Classroom Exercise

1. *Dialogue.* Continue the dialogue between Kelly and Kris with a partner. Include the following:

   1. *What does Kris ask Kelly to do?*
   2. *Describe what ingredients go into the salad.*
   3. *Exchange information about what Kris and Kelly did earlier in the day.*

2. *Interview.* Interview a partner to find the answers to these questions. Prepare to share the information with your classmates.

   1. *What is your favorite food?*
   2. *What are your three favorite fruits and vegetables?*
   3. *What are two foods you dislike the most?*
   4. *What do you eat every day?*

Classroom Exercise

1 *Fruit or vegetable?* Identify the illustration in a complete sentence. An example is provided.

It's a carrot. It is a vegetable.

1	2	3	4	5	6
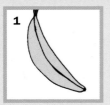		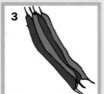			

2 *Descriptions.* How would you describe these foods without using fingerspelling? What classifiers could you use?

1. *cucumber* **2.** *string beans* **3.** *corn* **4.** *orange* **5.** *onion*

Vocabulary   Fruits & Vegetables

Apple	**Banana**	**Cherry**	**Fruit**	**Grapes**	**Melon**	**Peach**

Pineapple	**Potato**	**Salad**	**Strawberry**	**Tomato**	**Vegetable**	The same sign is used for the fruit orange and the color. (See Unit 3.)

Fingerspelled words:

apricot	bell pepper	carrot	cucumber	papaya	radish	string beans
artichoke	berry	cauliflower	garlic	pear	raisins	tangerine
asparagus	blackberry	celery	grapefruit	peas	raspberry	
avocado	broccoli	corn	mango	plum	spinach	

Classroom Exercise

1. *At the store.* What is in each basket? Use the Listing & Ordering Technique to describe the contents of each basket.

Basket #1

2 apples
3 peaches
berries
corn

Basket #2

carrots
peas
bananas

Basket #3

oranges
watermelon
plums

Basket #4

broccoli
tomatoes
green apples
cherries

Basket #5

5 potatoes
3 carrots
1 onion
fish

2. *Shopping list.* Follow the example to ask your partner for the price of each product. Switch roles and repeat when done.

How much does the soda cost?

$1.99 $0.59 $3.19 $2.29 $6.22 $4.15 $3.25 $6.00 $0.99 $3.00

Vocabulary — Meat and Dairy

Bacon

Butter

Cheese

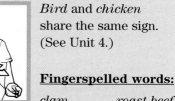
Egg

Bird and *chicken* share the same sign. (See Unit 4.)

Fingerspelled words:

clam   roast beef
crab   salami
ham   shrimp
lamb   sushi
lobster tofu
oyster yogurt
pastrami
pork   *Names of*
pork chops *fish &*
ribs   *cheeses*

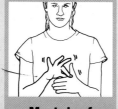
Hot dog, sausage

Meat, beef

Milk

Turkey

Vocabulary — Desserts & Sweets

Candy

Chocolate

Cookie

Dessert

Ice cream

Fingerspelled terms:
brownie
cake
chips
cupcake
pie
Flavors of ice cream &
types of dessert

Classroom Exercise J

1 *Food groups.* To which food groups do the following foods belong? Use Spatial Organization to sort items by *dairy (milk), fruit, vegetable, seafood (fish), poultry (chicken),* and *meat.* An example is provided.

Apples are in the fruit group. Cheese and butter are in the dairy group.

1. *blueberries, plums*
2. *mango, papaya, melon*
3. *tuna, salmon*
4. *yogurt, grapes, turkey*

5. *beef, ham, potatoes, oranges*
6. *eggs, milk, sushi, trout*
7. *Swiss cheese, avocado, ham*
8. *oysters, clams*

9. *turkey, chicken, strawberries, salami*
10. *lettuce, banana, corn, broccoli*
11. *ribs, lamb, tomatoes, string beans*
12. *Monterey Jack, butter*

2 *What is it?* Based on the clue provided, what kind of food do you think is being described? Select responses from Column A.

1. *torte*
2. *Rocky Road*
3. *sirloin*
4. *mozzarella*

5. *pumpkin spice*
6. *oatmeal*
7. *margarine*
8. *rhubarb*

9. *peanut butter*
10. *vanilla, chocolate*
11. *fudge*
12. *cheddar*

Column A

pie	dessert
cheese	butter
cookie	milk
ice cream	cake
meat	candy

Homework Exercise 2

A What are the ingredients to your favorite food or dish? Use the Listing and Ordering Technique or Spatial Organization to describe the different ingredients. Do you prepare the dish yourself? How long does it take? Your explanation should have a minimum of six complete sentences.

B Do you cook? When was the last time you made something to eat? What was it? Did you cook alone, or with somebody's help? Explain what you made and how it turned out in a minimum of five complete ASL sentences.

C Write Assignment A or B in ASL gloss.

Classroom Exercise

1   *Meals.* Ask a partner what he or she usually eats for breakfast, lunch, and dinner. Switch roles and repeat when done. An example is provided.

What do you usually eat every day?

2   *Daily specials.* You work as a server at a local restaurant. Ask your partner whether he or she is interested in breakfast, lunch, dinner, or dessert. Depending on the answer, explain what specials are available and ask for their order. Switch roles when done.

Daily Specials

Breakfast
Scrambled Eggs and Toast
Waffles with Strawberries
Pancakes and Bacon

Lunch
Green Salad
Vegetable Soup
Chicken Sandwich

Dinner
Hamburger and French Fries
Spaghetti
Turkey with Vegetables

Dessert
Chocolate Cake
Apple Pie
Ice Cream

Beverages   Coffee, Tea

Deaf Culture Minute

Many Deaf people can share stories of being handed Braille menus at restaurants. When Deaf individuals eat out, the most important preference is having enough lighting to see the conversation!

3   *Holiday foods.* What do people eat on the following occasions? Describe what each holiday is known for in a complete sentence.

Classroom Exercise

Matching. What's missing from each well-known food combination? Fill in the missing segment. An example is provided.

Bread and _____.

Bread and butter.

1

2

3

4

5

6

Vocabulary — Meals & Fast Food

Bread

Cereal (1)

French Fries

Hamburger

Pizza

Sandwich

Soup

Spaghetti

Toast

Variation Alert!

Cereal (2)

Fingerspelled words:

bagel	casserole	ketchup	mustard	pasta	taco
beans	grits	mayo	nachos	pepperoni	tortilla
burrito	juice	milkshake	pancake	rice	waffle

Classroom Exercise

1 *Suggested menu.* Use the chart below to plan a healthy 5-day lunch or dinner menu with a partner. You may expand on the food items if desired. Prepare to share the menu with your classmates.

Food Group	Children, women, older adults	Teen girls, active women, most men	Teen boys, active men
Grains	6 servings	✓ 9 servings 32·4	11 servings
Vegetables	3	✓ 4 ∤ ₃	5
Fruit	2	✓ 5 4 ∤	4
Dairy	2–3	✓ 2–3 ₃	2–3
Meat/beans	2	2 ₂	3

Source: USDA

Fruit	**Dairy**	**Vegetables**	**Meat/beans**	**Grains**
fruit salad (2)	1 cup milk (1)	big salad (3)	hamburger (5)	peanut butter/ jelly sandwich (3)
1/2 cup fruit juice (2)	cheese (3)	small salad (1)	steak (5)	pizza, cheese (3)
banana, apple, orange (1)	ice cream (5)	raw carrots (1/2)	pizza, pepperoni (4)	taco (2)
strawberries (2)	pudding (2)	tomato (1/2)	fish taco (2)	spaghetti (4)
fruit smoothie (4)	yogurt (1)	baked potato (1)	egg salad (2)	
			bean burrito (3)	

Monday	**Tuesday**	**Wednesday**	**Thursday**	**Friday**

2 *Dialogue.* Develop a dialogue with a partner. Include the following:

1. *A greeting and farewell*
2. *Make plans for a future get-together*
3. *What is the reason for the get-together?*
4. *Include at least five different food signs*
5. *When and where will the get-together be held?*

Homework Exercise **3**

A If you were planning a feast, what foods would you serve? Who would you invite? What would be the reason for celebration? Describe your feast in a minimum of six complete sentences.

B Does food play an important role in your family's traditions? Describe a holiday or special event when your family or friends gather together to share a meal. What is the occasion and what foods are eaten? Describe the event in a minimum of six complete sentences.

C Write Assignment A or B in ASL gloss.

A Trip to the Zoo

Many animal signs incorporate classifiers that describe prominent physical characteristics of the animal. In this section you will learn various animal signs and use classifiers to describe them. Notice the animal signs in the dialogue below. Do the signs *tiger*, *elephant*, and *lion* incorporate classifiers?

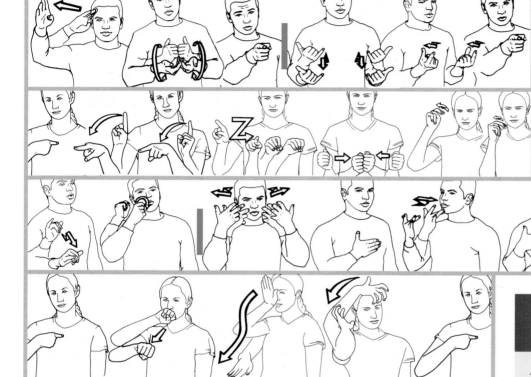

Classroom Exercise

1   *Dialogue.* Make plans to visit your local zoo with a friend. Include the following:

    1. *A meeting time, date, and place*
    2. *A reason for going to the zoo*
    3. *Who did you go with?*
    4. *What is your favorite animal? What does it look like?*

2   *Interview.* Ask a partner the following questions. Switch roles and repeat when done.

    1. *Do you like going to the zoo? Why or why not?*
    2. *When is the last time you went to a zoo?*
    3. *Who did you go with?*
    4. *What is your favorite animal? What does it look like?*

Dialogue Translation

Sean: *Hey, how are you? What are you doing today?*

Kris: *I'm going to the zoo with my nephew and niece.*

Sean : *Oh, cool. Tigers are my favorite animal. What about you?*

Kris : *I love the elephants and lions!*

Deaf Culture Minute

Are you familiar with the terms *seeing eye dog* and *hearing ear dog?* Often these animals are referred to as **guide dogs**. They are specially trained to provide assistance to handicapped or disabled individuals. The majority of people who use guide dogs are blind or Deaf-blind, though there are some Deaf individuals who use dogs to alert them to environmental noises like doorbells and alarms.

Classroom Exercise

1 *Giving explanations.* What do you know about each animal? Provide several details about each in a complete sentence. An example is shown.

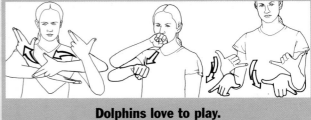

Dolphins love to play.

2 *Habitat.* Which animals would you find living in each habitat? Use the Listing and Ordering Technique as needed.

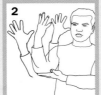

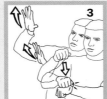

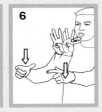

Vocabulary — Animals

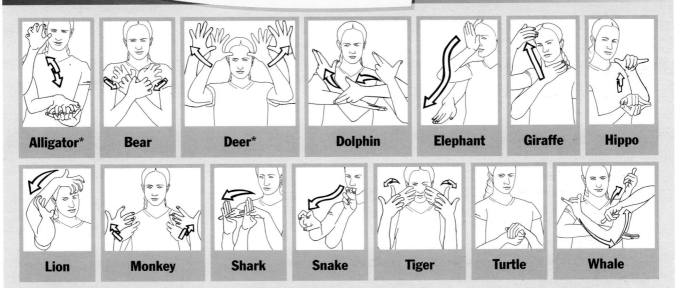

| Alligator* | Bear | Deer* | Dolphin | Elephant | Giraffe | Hippo |

| Lion | Monkey | Shark | Snake | Tiger | Turtle | Whale |

*The signs *alligator* and *deer* are classifiers. The same classifiers describe *crocodile*, *antelope*, and *elk*. When signing about a particular animal, use the classifier and then fingerspell the specific name.

Classroom Exercise P

1. *At the zoo.* Describe what Kris plans to do at the zoo in complete sentences.

2. *Feeding time.* It's feeding time at the zoo. Describe what each animal eats in a complete sentence.

3. *Favorites.* What can you say about each person's favorite animal? Use your imagination to give details about the illustrations in complete sentences.

I Want to Know . . .

How do I know which classifiers to use?

ASL students often find using classifiers difficult because they're uncertain where to begin or how to describe the object. As you develop "Deaf" eyes and become used to this visual emphasis, using classifiers will become easier. For starters, don't fingerspell what you want to show! Use your hands and signs you know to draw a visual picture. Don't worry about finding the "right" classifier but follow your instincts. Remember to work from general to specific details. Here is an example of how someone might describe an elephant.

CL: B for ears

CL: C for proboscis

CL: C for legs

CL: C for body mass

The San Diego Zoo

The San Diego Zoo. Watch Sean in full motion on your student DVD.

DVD

Classroom Exercise Q

1. *Comprehension I.* Answer the following questions based on Sean's story about the San Diego Zoo.

   1. *When did Sean go on vacation? Where did his family go?*
   2. *Why did Sean's family go there?*
   3. *Whose idea was it to visit the zoo?*
   4. *Which part of the zoo was Sean's favorite?*

   5. *What animals did Sean like best?*
   6. *Did Sean see the entire zoo? Why not?*
   7. *What four new animal signs does Sean mention? What are they?*

2. *Classifier descriptions.* How would you describe these animals without using fingerspelling or their signs? Describe each animal in detail.

Homework Exercise 4

A. Have you been to a zoo? Describe a trip you've made to a zoo, including when you went, with whom, and what you liked or disliked. If you haven't been to a zoo, what animals would you like to see at one? Why? Your description should be a minimum of six complete sentences.

B. Practice signing *The San Diego Zoo* to present to your classmates.

C. Write Assignment A or B in ASL gloss.

Journal Activities

1 Have you seen a guide dog at work? What was the situation, and what were your reactions? What functions do guide dogs serve for the blind and Deaf-blind? Should abled Deaf people use guide dogs? Why or why not?

2 In what kinds of occupations is it useful to know a second language? What about ASL? Are there jobs where fluency in ASL can be an advantage? Do you think ASL will ever be helpful to you? Why or why not?

3 The poem "Recipe for ASL" below conveys one Deaf person's feelings towards ASL. What is your opinion of the poem? Write a poem of your own that expresses your perspective on American Sign Language.

4 Practice signing "Recipe for ASL" to present to your classmates.

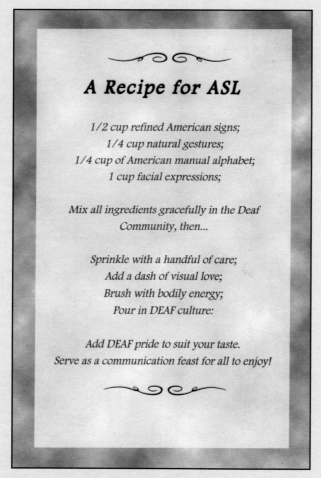

A Recipe for ASL

1/2 cup refined American signs;
1/4 cup natural gestures;
1/4 cup of American manual alphabet;
1 cup facial expressions;

Mix all ingredients gracefully in the Deaf
Community, then...

Sprinkle with a handful of care;
Add a dash of visual love;
Brush with bodily energy;
Pour in DEAF culture:

Add DEAF pride to suit your taste.
Serve as a communication feast for all to enjoy!

— Recipe for ASL, Gil Eastman. From: Just a DEAF
Person's Thoughts, published by Sign Media, Inc.

Unit 10 Review

A *Comprehension.* Watch Kris sign *Making Plans.* Respond to the following questions.

1. *List five activities Kris will do this week.*
2. *What plans does Kris have with her nephew, niece, and boyfriend?*
3. *Why will Kris go to the grocery store?*
4. *What kind of class will Kris take?*
5. *What will Kris do with her car?*

B *Signing about food.* The Food Pyramid is a well-known chart that provides suggestions about the different types of food people should eat. Explain the Food Pyramid in complete sentences, including the following:

1. *What are the different food groups?*
2. *What should people eat little of?*
3. *Suggest three foods people should eat from each food group.*
4. *Plan a healthy meal for breakfast, lunch, or dinner. What do you suggest people eat?*

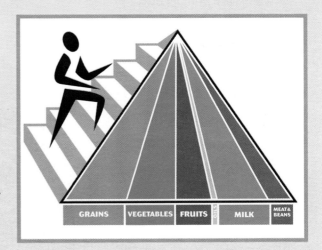

GRAINS · VEGETABLES · FRUITS · OILS · MILK · MEAT & BEANS

C *Work & Study.* If someone majors in the following fields, what kinds of occupations could they enter? Use the Listing and Ordering Technique to suggest at least three possible occupations in a complete sentence.

     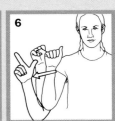

D *Transitions.* Use *become* in a complete sentence for each pair.

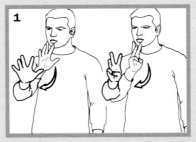 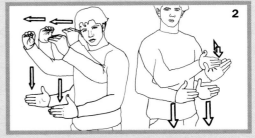

Unit 10 Review

E *Planning a trip to the zoo.* Use the map below to plan a trip to the zoo. Where will you begin and end? What are the animals and exhibits you will see?

F   *Comprehension.* Watch the dialogue *Why work?* between Kris and Sean. Answer the following questions:

1. *Where does Kris work?*
2. *How long has she worked there?*
3. *What does Kris want to do?*
4. *Will the new job help Kris do the things she wants to do?*

G *Signing narratives.* You work at a television station and are doing a human-interest story on some local people. What will you say about each person? Sign each narrative using correct ASL grammar and structure.

1. *Bill began working at the grocery store 8 years ago. He was looking for a job and spotted advertisement. He was hired and became a cashier. He worked hard and became the manager and now is vice president.*

2. *Shari is a medical student. She teaches children to swim on the weekends. She enjoys being a coach and helping people become good swimmers. She is very busy with school and is motivated to be a doctor. She wants to travel and help people become healthy.*

Units 9 – 10 Review

Review Exercise A

1 *Travel guides.* You work in the tourism department of your town and are gathering information for a travel guide. What information will you share with potential tourists? What attractions would you recommend? Describe your town's attractions in complete sentences.

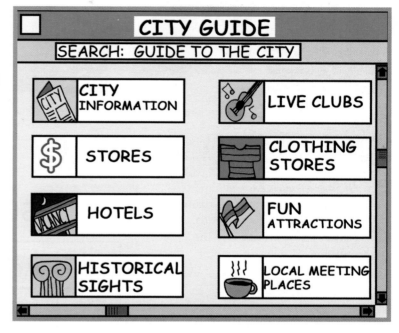

2 *At the tourism office.* A Deaf family has asked you for some sight-seeing tips in your community. Use this situation to create a dialogue with a partner.

Review Exercise B

Directions. Give directions to at least four different locations using the map below. The starting point is the hotel.

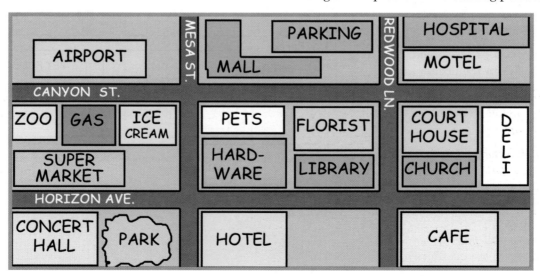

Review Exercise C

Classifier review. Describe each scene in a complete sentence using the appropriate classifier.

  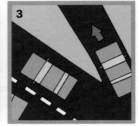 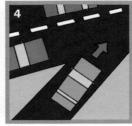 

Review Exercise D

1 *Giving directions.* Use spatialization skills to explain to a customer how to get to particular locations. Use the entrance as a starting point.

1. *frozen foods*
2. *seafood*
3. *florist*
4. *fruits and vegetables*
5. *dairy products*
6. *pet food*
7. *cakes and pastries*
8. *candy aisle*
9. *meats and poultry*
10. *?*

2 *Asking for assistance.* Answer a partner's questions using the given information.

1. *Where can I buy bread?* **(between ice cream and cakes)**
2. *Where can I find fruit?* **(near checkout number 3 and pet food)**
3. *Where can I get ice cream?* **(near deli and florist)**
4. *Where can I buy milk?* **(between meat and drinks)**
5. *Where do I pay?* **(have three cashiers)**

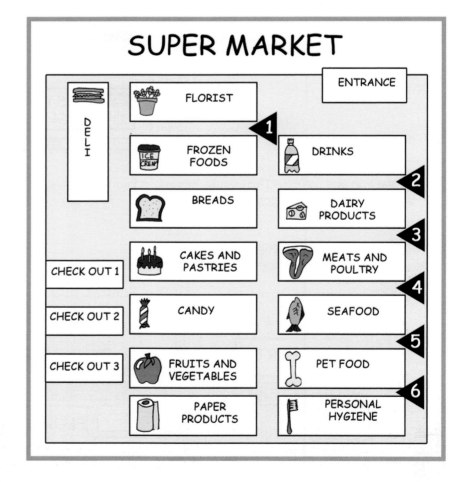

Review Exercise E

1 *Garage sale.* Your family is hosting a garage sale and people are asking you how much items cost. In complete sentences, provide the price. An example is provided.

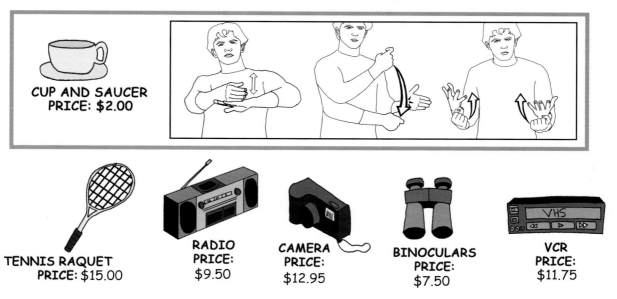

CUP AND SAUCER
PRICE: $2.00

TENNIS RAQUET
PRICE: $15.00

RADIO
PRICE:
$9.50

CAMERA
PRICE:
$12.95

BINOCULARS
PRICE:
$7.50

VCR
PRICE:
$11.75

2 *Bargains.* Ask a partner if the price for each item is expensive or cheap.

BIKE- $428

T.V.- $15.00

OLD FASHIONED
PHONE $1.10

C.D. PLAYER- $8.50

BASKET BALL- $6.25

A
S
L

T
I
P
S

• Take your time when giving directions. Visualize in your mind what you would see or pass to arrive at the destination. Give plenty of examples to narrow down the exact location. Picture yourself walking through the scene rather than maintaining a bird's eye perspective.

• It takes time and practice to learn how to use classifiers well. Don't worry about trying to find the exact sign to describe an object. Describe one detail at a time working from the larger details to the smaller ones. With practice, your confidence using classifiers will improve dramatically.

Review Exercise F

Sentence creation. Create a complete ASL sentence using each sign.

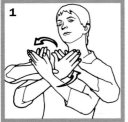

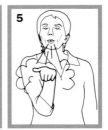

Review Exercise G

Descriptive classifiers. How would you describe the following creatures without using fingerspelling?

Review Exercise H

Occupations. Work with a partner to classify various occupations into the four divisions seen below. Come up with a list of at least four occupations per division, and explain what's involved in each job. What kind of work does each do?

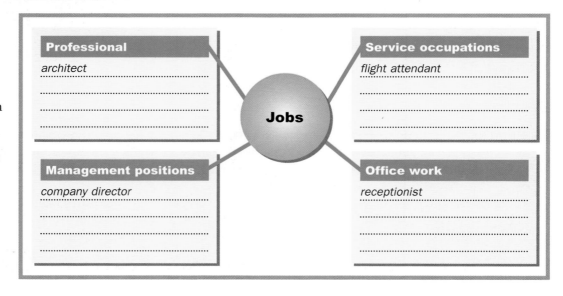

Professional

architect
....
....
....
....

Service occupations

flight attendant
....
....
....
....

Jobs

Management positions

company director
....
....
....
....

Office work

receptionist
....
....
....
....

Review Exercise I

1   *Using be.* Use the correct form of *to be* in each sentence.

    1.   *Some day, I want to be a lawyer.*
    2.   *She wants to be a mother and have many children.*
    3.   *We will be there at 7:30.*
    4.   *They must be here by 9:15. They can't be late.*
    5.   *I want to be a computer programmer or teacher.*

2   *To be & context.* Sign a complete sentence using the correct form of *to be* for the following illustrations.

Review Exercise J

Grammar & structure review. In Units 1-10 you have learned the basic concepts of ASL grammar and structure. Each of the signs below refer to one of the ASL rules you studied in MasterASL, Level One. Explain what each rule is and give an example of how to use the concept. Refer to the page numbers in parenthesis to review each concept.

(8)   **(9)**   **(10)**   **(30)**

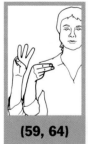    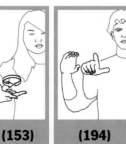  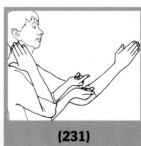

(59, 64)   **(99)**   **(131)**   **(134)**   **(153)**   **(194)**   **(199)**   **(231)**

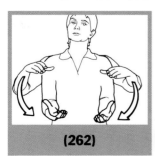    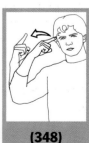

(262)   **(294)**   **(337)**   **(348)**   **(348)**

M

Q

R

Y

Z

H